CW01337771

The
Humanist Guide

Neoteric Humanism

THE
HUMANIST GUIDE

How to obtain ...
Peace, Health, Happiness and Prosperity!

A philosophy one can follow to acquire these four desirable outcomes, improve oneself as an individual and make our world a better place.

ROBERT POOR

PALMETTO
P U B L I S H I N G
Charleston, SC
www.PalmettoPublishing.com

Copyright © 2024 by Robert Poor

Hardcover ISBN: 979-8-8229-5248-5
Paperback ISBN: 979-8-8229-5249-2

I dedicate this guide to everyone!

May you all enjoy … Peace, Health, Happiness and Prosperity!

Bob Poor

TABLE OF CONTENTS

Please note that Neoteric Humanism does not attempt to supply any answers as to "Where, when or how, we as human beings, first originated in this world", or suggest "What happens to us after our death". It is organized to provide a positive model to live by in the "Here and Now" with the ultimate goal of improving oneself, one's family and community, advancing universal peace, enhancing health, providing greater joy, elevating individual prosperity, and cultivating the creation of a better world. It is the pursuit of protopia, making today better than yesterday, and tomorrow better than today. If the readers of this ideal follow through, apply its principles, and improve conditions where ever they can, therefore making life a little sunnier for others, then I will be content.

Please keep this in mind …there are many routes to the top of the mountain for the theology or ideology you are pursuing; I hope you will examine and then implement this one or include its values and principles on the path you eventually decide to follow.

Bob Poor

"Be always at war with your vices,

at peace with your neighbors,

and let each new year find you a better individual."

Benjamin Franklin

PREFACE

*G*reetings, welcome, and thank you for taking time to review and examine this philosophy. I trust you will find this alternative ideology enticing and that you will be encouraged to seriously contemplate its calling. It is my hope that it will eventually sway you to accept the ideals, mission, and the challenge it poses and that you will begin your own journey by living a life with peace, health, happiness, prosperity, genuine purpose and greater contentment. To do so, adhere to the methodology this philosophy will lay before you.

Begin your journey and assessment here. The fourfold purpose of Neoteric Humanism will aid a sincere adherent by:

- offering a guide and format to pursue the Neoteric Humanist way of living a complete, meaningful, serene, healthy, successful and happy life.
- providing a clear and well-defined ideal life model for one to emulate.
- submitting step by step practices and events to forge exceptional individuals, closer family, and relationship ties … and
- encouraging individuals to become actively involved in making our world a better place.

Neoteric Humanism provides numerous opportunities for personal growth, the building of robust family bonds, the formation of durable relationships, and the expectation of making a positive impact in the here and now.

Therefore, if your heart beats with the aspiration to improve the surroundings we live in for ourselves, our families, and our community, or if you have a strong desire to shed old behavior and develop yourself into a transformed and better individual, then read on.

Is it your desire to?

- *achieve greater joy, expertise, knowledge, success, and wisdom?*
- *form meaningful family, friendship, business, and community relationships?*
- *grow stronger, healthier, and more physically fit?*
- *have support, protection, and skills in times of need or hardship?*
- *become more culturally aware and involved in the lives of others?*
- *play a part in advancing art, nature, virtue, and kindness in our world?*
- *become more respected, joyful, and valued by those around you?*
- *improve the human condition in our world and join others with a similar mission?*

If your answer is yes, please continue. What follows in this book is a blueprint and guide that will aid you in reaching these goals. You will be encouraged to practice activities that are both healthy for the body and stimulating to the mind. Suggested events are planned and designed to be socially beneficial, provide ongoing education, help build solid family ties, and lifelong friendships. The result of this being the fulfillment of individual potential and an overall sense of personal satisfaction. This will, in turn, bring forth completeness, safety, contentment, and well-being because your life will have true meaning, value and genuine significance.

Before we commence, let me explain what I mean by "Neoteric" version of Humanism. I use the term Neoteric (nē'ə-těr'ĭk) Humanism to define this philosophy as markedly similar to traditional Humanist ideals … yet not necessarily "secular" in nature. It is designed to be a philosophy which is inclusive to both "religious" and "secular" individuals and either will find it useful, beneficial, and valuable to practice. The adherents who follow this guide must be open and receptive to other's viewpoints and be forward-thinking in Humanist ideals, principles, and methods. It was with this in mind, that "Neoteric" Humanism was conceived. A philosophy that provides a clear guide to abide by in pursuing worthy Humanist ideals while at the same time welcoming and supporting those who also abide by their spiritual beliefs and traditions.

Neoteric Humanism offers an organized process to realize both an individual's personal goals as well as a method to fulfill the desirable endeavors within this Philosophy. …

One question surely to be raised is … how this approach compares to other existing and past forms of Humanism? … As a broad philosophy and in the way it is advocated … the existing model of Humanism does promote many beneficial and positive goals. Among these are that:

- *we should strive to develop a higher standard of living for all people in the world.*
- *we should live by the highest standards of ethics and morality.*
- *human beings should pursue innocuous and communally beneficial occupations.*

- *reasoning, empathy, and foresight are the best guides for solving humanity's problems.*
- *all conclusions, theories, and opinions may be freely and openly challenged.*
- *the arts and nature's beauty should be incorporated into one's everyday life.*
- *society should provide an economic and health safety net for all individuals.*
- *democracy, freedom, justice, a bill of rights and civil liberties should exist for all.*

All of the above are worthy ideals and would profit humanity. Unfortunately, an enormous share of present-day "Secular" Humanist's effort is focused on one rigid and unbending position. That position is their absolute rejection of God, faith, or any belief system with a spiritual foundation. From a traditional "Secular" Humanist's standpoint ... God is dead and religion serves no purpose ... or, worse yet, is evil incarnate. So much time and energy are devoted to this one theme that very little passion is left to advance the many other positive aspirations that are professed. Neoteric Humanism, on the other hand, eliminates this draining and negative force from the equation. It embraces a new attitude of inclusiveness, that is unique, in that it neither rejects nor endorses religion. What it does do, is recognize the importance of tradition, faith, and the need for hope in our lives. It would be impossible for many people living today to lead a complete life if their religious beliefs were not part of that equation. Hence, this modified Humanist alternative, the methodology offered in this handbook, and the established ideology and mission that ensue can be utilized by almost anyone. Therefore, this philosophy is a good fit for nearly any individual, God-fearing, Atheist, or Agnostic, who is willing to become actively involved in improving themselves, doing what is right, and making a positive impact in our world.

Who is this new breed of Humanist? He or she is one who has been aroused out of their daily routines and casual diversions. One who wants to adopt a fresh approach centered on an idea of an enriched world community and the betterment of the individual. Neoteric Humanism and the approach offered here provide both a reference text and a guide that welcomes those people desiring to lead a valuable, rewarding, and gratifying life. A meaningful life that is filled with contentment, well-being, and satisfaction. ... To attain this sought-after state, adhere to the step-by-step process laid before you in this book and embrace the goals, principles, and objectives of this philosophy.

So, are you willing to investigate or accept this process of attaining a complete, meaningful, and happy life? Are you willing to study and become a positive force in making our world a better place? If the answer is yes, then open your mind ... and we shall begin!

Neoteric Humanism asserts ... we can be one united community!!

Welcome are...

- *Christians, Jews, Muslims, Hindus, Deists, Buddhists, other religions, Humanists, the non-religious, Agnostics, and Atheists.*
- *Republicans, Democrats, Progressives, Libertarians, Independents, other political factions, and the non-political.*
- *Straight, bi, gay, or somewhere in-between.*
- *All nationalities and colors ... Egyptians, Kenyans, Mexicans, Malaysians, Germans, Blacks, Whites, Reds, Yellows, Bi-Color, and No-Color.*

Everyone is encouraged to join in and participate, all religions, all nationalities, all races, and all political parties. All are welcome ... all who are willing to adhere to the step-by-step practices offered in this book and who agree to abide by its fundamental laws and will work towards the established standards, values, and purpose of this philosophy.

Neoteric Humanism strives to be as all-inclusive as possible in its character and concerns regarding its teachings, activities, and internal proceedings. It is structured to hopefully bring a large and diverse group of people together regardless of their background or particular spiritual belief. While individual religious practices, political parties, and their related customs and ideology are wholeheartedly accepted, they can cause disruptions and conflicts within mixed assemblies and therefore should be practiced at more appropriate venues. This association's gatherings, meetings, and functions will remain as neutral and non-participatory as possible in all matters of religion, politics, customs, and/or their related activities and functions.

Neoteric Humanism is focused on people and their common concerns that take place in the here and now. It is centered on the individual, the family, and the community. While there may be activities and dialogue regarding religion, politics, customs, and/or traditions and their various practices to gain knowledge, advocating or promotion of religious beliefs, political party goals or the agendas of various outside organizations will be avoided whenever possible.

It is important to state again, this philosophy is not anti-religion. Religion plays an important role in many lives by providing hope, optimism, and inspiration for the future. For countless individuals' religious beliefs, values, and principles bring greater bliss into their life. Religion can also impart a powerful source of strength and endurance when tragedy or disaster strikes at people's hearts. Religious tradition and rituals allow many in the community a focal point to mark key celebrations, announcements, and memorials that are important and necessary to us as a civilized society.

Neoteric Humanism is also not anti-political. Political rallies, demonstrations, and activism offer people a platform when change is called for or when rights are violated or threatened. It can be a source of great pride and enthusiasm. One that bonds together a home and or community with a sense of unity, cohesion, shared aims, and goals. One's culture, language and political persuasion should be embraced and respected. Nevertheless, except for acquiring knowledge and familiarity ... these traditions, rituals, rallies, and political meetings, as a general rule ... will not be practiced or promoted within our gatherings.

Neoteric Humanism does not refuse to recognize that people have their differences, it just respectfully declines to dwell on them. Within the workings of our association (including its teachings, its activities, and its pursuits) individuals will not act or be viewed as different sects, factions, or groups ... but rather ... as one united community... with a common cause, shared needs, and aspirations. All members are expected to participate and work together for the betterment of each individual, the enrichment of their families, and the improvement of society.

As you become familiar with this approach and its organized structure, you will quickly discover that Neoteric Humanism requires a significant amount of personal self-discipline. The practice of this self-discipline refers not only to the elimination of negative actions or conduct which may block your advancement, but also the development and exercise of affirmative behavior which will enable you to improve yourself as a person. Some will find it difficult to do what is necessary to achieve success when one is easily distracted by activities that are pleasurable or require little or no dedication. If you are to make genuine and sustained progress, it will take continued effort, focus, and commitment. Begin this routine of discipline and personal will-power by concentrating on developing the following four habits:

- *Set aside quiet time daily for reading, contemplation, and practice. It is necessary to forge habits and a routine if you are to advance. Make it your nature to listen carefully to others, respecting their point of view, and thinking through your response and then expressing yourself in a clear and reasoned manner. This will allow calmness and tranquility to flow into your life.*

- *Take control of your emotions and actions ... especially anger, selfishness, jealousy, laziness, envy, arrogance, and overindulgence. Learn to rule them or they will certainly rule you.*

- *Lead a healthy lifestyle. Exercise, watch your diet, and make a vow of moderation. You will sleep deeper, feel stronger, reason more rationally, be happier, and your body and mind will function at a much higher level.*

- *Respect the religion, customs, lifestyles, and politics of others. The whole world is inhabited by people who hold varying viewpoints. As beliefs concerning these topics run deeply and seldom change, engaging in heated debates related to these matters will likely accomplish little other than stirring up emotional responses. As much as it is desired to have everyone participate in this philosophy, it is undeniable that some will utterly refuse to make the ideological change necessary to become an Ascender ... one who rises above.*

Taking charge of your thoughts and focusing on the challenges required can be difficult without a supporting well organized and defined methodology. Fortunately, just such a useful and systematic guide can be found in this book.

"You must be willing to give up what you are, to become what you want to be."

Orrin Woodward

"Things do not change; we change."

Henry David Thoreau

Eight factors that will determine your peace, health, happiness and prosperity as well as the person you become next year or five years from now.

1. *The knowledge you acquire and the skills you obtain.*
2. *The daily goals you set and habits you devote yourself to.*
3. *The food you eat and the lifestyle you follow.*
4. *The people you associate with and the behavior you display.*

Your action or inaction on these will determine the quality and nature of not only your future but that of your family, your community and your world!

Part I

NEOTERIC HUMANISM

B egin your inquiry into this unique variation of Humanism by reading and becoming familiar with its aspirations, its principles, its goals, and its mission. Should you find yourself in agreement with its purpose and conclusions, then I encourage you to review and assess the eight-step process that follows. There you will learn more about this philosophy's methodology, its mind-set, and intention. As you move deeper into this text, I will attempt to answer several of your questions that will no doubt develop. Some of these queries are best resolved with short stories, so in Part II, you will encounter a collection of parables that I hope will achieve that end. Finally, in part III, you will discover meditations, mantras, and prompters that will assist you in this quest should you desire to partake in and live by the tenets of this philosophy.

Why is this way of life important and why should you participate? Consider this ... with your everyday actions and deeds you make an impact in this world. The choices you make affect not only yourself but every one of us. Your actions contribute to the way we live and interact with each other. The consequences of your decisions either improve the human condition or contribute to its decline. Abiding by the principles of this philosophy will assist you in making the proper choices and will help in resolving important decisions. Therefore, if you yearn to make a positive impact in our world, your first decision should be one of beneficial involvement. An engagement that necessitates your contribution to life in a constructive and principled way!

"Individually we are one drop. Together we are an ocean."
Ryunosuke Satoro

"It is not more bigness that should be our goal. We must attempt, rather, to bring people back to ... the warmth of community, to the worth of individual effort and responsibility ... and of individuals working together as a community, to better their lives and their children's future."
Robert F. Kennedy

Examine the first mantra you will encounter in this philosophy that is titled ... **BING**! Bettering oneself will bring about favorable outcomes that will transform our world into a safer, wiser, healthier, and happier place.

It is my belief that ...
As I **B**etter myself ...
I will **I**mprove my family and community.
As I improve my family and community ...
a **N**ew vision for people will evolve.
As a new vision for people evolves ...
I **G**ive hope and optimism to the future.

We must acknowledge that to change the world we must first change ourselves. In doing so, we help others see and then hopefully pursue a new vision for a better world. The best way to achieve long-term progress in the human condition is by altering one's heart and character by infusing desirable values, principles, and endeavors. The dilemma you'll encounter when attempting to change the outside world, without first reinventing yourself, is that you will still be the same person you are now even when the new future you desire to create comes about. You will continue to have the same lack of focus and purpose, negativity, and bad habits within you. So, when this new society eventually arrives you will still be unhappy and lacking direction because your inner-self is still oozing with your old nature and character. Therefore, start changing yourself now or you will find your old enemies beating at your door creating even more problems and conflicts in your life ... and our world.

But "Why?" you might ask, would I want to transform myself if I'm comfortable with the way I am? This is a very good question. However, consider the rationale of this philosophy, that for a person to truly enjoy a fulfilling and complete life ... it will almost always involve moving towards excellence or perfection. Like the efforts of a musician whose life is spent studying and practicing to improve their musical abilities or the surgeon who constantly updates his skills to operate with more confidence and achieve better outcomes. Consider the teacher who takes on-going classes to improve themselves as educators or the artist who burns their freshly painted canvass and starts over again. As one moves along this pathway towards the ideal of manifest perfection, their efforts are rewarded with fulfillment, optimism, purpose, and a sense of well-being. We all have within us the opportunity to become better as individuals. It is our choice ... we can swindle or be truthful; we can be cruel or we can be kindhearted; we can be stingy or be generous—we can decide what kind of person we wish to be… Over a given amount of time, however, our thoughts and actions will shape us; each choice we make etches itself, deeper and deeper, into our inner character and will finally reveal who we genuinely are. Choose to become a better individual!

> *"An arrogant person considers himself perfect. This is the chief harm of arrogance. It interferes with a person's main task in life - becoming a better person."*
>
> Leo Tolstoy

> *"If you chase anything in life chase the things that get you excited about living. Chase the things that give you hope, happiness and a glimpse of a better life. Chase the things that make you want to be a better person. Chase the things that inspire you to think, create and live joyfully. Chase the things that reinforce in your soul that you can make a difference. "*
>
> Shannon L. Alder

Definition and Key Aspirations

Neoteric Humanism is dedicated to improving the quality of life in the here and now. Its participants will accomplish this by openly offering their talents, resources, time, and effort to forge well-balanced, educated and competent individuals, solid family units, stronger friendships, closer communities, and a better world.

What separates Neoteric Humanism from other various forms of Humanism is worth noting here. First, the adherents participating in this philosophy may choose to be part of a religious persuasion or they may opt not to be. The religious or non-religious aspects of one's life, while doubtlessly significant to that individual, will be kept as a discreet matter as it relates to Neoteric Humanism. Secondly, one's political affiliation is of no real concern either. It does not matter if one is a Conservative, Liberal, Independent, or of another group. Lastly, the national background or culture of an individual is also of no consequence. This philosophy will not insert itself into the personal choices of individuals relating to their belief in a particular religion, their political persuasion, or lifestyle preference. Continuing with this elucidation, Neoteric Humanism will also never associate with any hate factions, vile radical gatherings, or die-hard evil activists. What Neoteric Humanism does concern itself with are the issues and desires that enhance the welfare and progress of humanity in our world. As long as those aspiring to be part of this pursuit abide by the laws, ideology, and mission of this philosophy, almost any religious, political or social interests they may choose to participate in, outside of these associations meetings, gatherings, and activities, are entirely their own affair.

So, how would one characterize this ideology? I would put forward the following portrayal. … Neoteric Humanism is a practical and useful philosophy that considers humankind to be insightful, sensitive, judicious, and intellectually sentient. We as a species, are conscious beings who have the knowledge, the capacity to reason, and the free will to act with foresight and influence on possible outcomes. It asserts that people have within themselves the ability, competence, and the will to create a complete and positive way of life. Neoteric Humanism is unique in that it welcomes individuals who may also choose to pursue a spiritual life as well as a worldly one. It recognizes the importance of tradition, faith, and the need for hope in people's lives. For many, to enjoy a complete, full, and happy life, it must include their religious persuasion. Therefore, while religious activities will not be practiced within this association's workings or gatherings, it is perfectly acceptable to engage in them in other settings. Neoteric Humanism, with its step-by-step methodology, provides an ideology and guide for anyone, religious or not, who wishes to lead a valuable, rewarding, and gratifying life which in the end will produce a wiser, kinder, more well-rounded individual … and a better world!

Neoteric Humanism has four key aspirations. This philosophy will encourage each individual to act upon its 2nd mantra **KUPP**: It is my purpose and goal to …

Know and improve myself.

Understand and be of service to others.

Practice kindness, truth, and fairness … and

Produce a positive impact with my life choices.

(1) To Know and improve myself:

This philosophy invites you to remove yourself from the outer world and look inward. The one who looks only on the outside is like a boat without a rudder. He or she who sets aside time to look inside learns best how to chart their way. Those who first organize and then plot a course towards the improvement of themselves will advance much more quickly and experience greater success.

The essence of this statement to "Know and Improve Yourself"… involves discovering your underlying core values … discarding the negative qualities and adopting new positive ones. If an individual can be true to a set of positive core values, there then exists a compass to guide them through their entire life. One must take time to seek out these positive ideas and incorporate them into one's core values. Therefore to know and improve one-self apply the essential fundamentals of **SEEK**:

Practice …

Sensible reasoning to assess situations wisely and then draw prudent conclusions that fashion sound, rational, and appropriate choices and actions.

Expertise and competence by attaining valuable attributes, capabilities, and experience of a professional person or of a system, which is useful and appreciated by others.

Engagement by exhibiting attention, curiosity, and interest that shows you are truly interested in and value the feelings and opinions of others.

Knowledge and verification by empirical and sensible methods regarding the validity of any plan, conclusion, or proposition.

Abide by prudent virtues, rise and resolve to use **<u>SORD STRENGTH</u>**: Learn …

Serenity: Do not let mishaps or unavoidable situations anger or enrage you.

Organization: Let all your activities, work and desires have their place and time.

Restraint: Avoid extremes. Be careful to avoid overindulgence in all things.

Disposition: Embrace both your serenity or another's tranquility or character.

Simplicity: Adhere to modesty and humbleness.

Tenacity: Don't give up, accomplish what you have planned and resolved to do.

Rightfulness: Do what is reasonable, equitable, and fair in an impartial manner.

Efficiency: When-ever possible, engage in something useful or beneficial.

Neatness: Maintain a clean body, clothing, one's belongings, and dwelling.

Geniality: Speak with kindness and that which will lift up the spirit of others.

<u>T</u>hriftiness: Be generous, but do not unwisely waste your resources, assets, or time.

<u>H</u>onesty: Do not cheat, deceive, bear false witness, or commit foul deeds.

(2) <u>To Understand and be of service to others</u>:

To understand others, it is important to recognize that we are all different in our past experiences and backgrounds. Use this awareness as a guide to comprehend and empathize with others. Service and charity to our fellow man will bring about positive change for the better. Just as in winter, the warmth of the sun makes the morning frost melt, service, and having compassion will lessen despair and conflict and bring about joy, trust, and harmony.

Why is having "compassion" a vital component? First, consider the Latin roots of this word which literally means "suffering together". Feeling what another human being is experiencing will give you a sense of urgency that may not otherwise exist. However, while feeling another's pain and distress is highly motivating in trying to relieve it, the far more important attribute of compassion is sharing not only in another's suffering, but participating in their hopefulness and joy. Think about this … if we are singularly driven to eliminate another's suffering, even though that is a worthwhile objective than <u>we will only be there</u> for each other when there is an urgent situation or hardship. However, if we are determined not just to ease another's suffering but to take steps to increase and share in their jubilation and gaiety than we will come together as one true community. To understand and be of service to others show …

LOVE:

Listen and encourage individuals to become more determined, hopeful, and self-assured in their dreams and endeavors. Celebrate their successes!

Observe and focus on all relevant details, before fashioning conclusions, suggestions or rendering opinions.

Value and respect the feelings of all individuals and attempt to understand the full significance of what they are attempting to communicate, create, or achieve.

Empathize and contribute by sharing in the feelings of what another person is going through and then doing what you can to offer assistance or a possible solution.

3) To Practice kindness, truth, and fairness.

Practicing kindness is imperative. The words you use, comments, and remarks you make and the actions you choose will establish the quality of the world we live in. When you emphasize kindness, you become a pleasanter person and your world becomes a nicer place. Acts of kindness help pave the way to a happier life, to greater contentment and well-being, to cultivating a more loving and caring family and to making a positive impact in this world. To practice thoughtfulness and compassion, remember to apply …

KIND:

Keep silent until you have fully evaluated your thoughts, emotions, and words.

Instill in your words calmness and composure while being gentle with the truth.

Notice if you deviate from this and correct your attitude and mindset immediately.

Determine the most considerate and positive response before speaking or acting

Following a pattern of truth and objectivity means adhering to the facts, details, and circumstances of a given situation or issue. Utilize these to determine what is ...

TRUE:

Trial: What is the occurrence, statement, or issue to be addressed?

Research: What are the details and facts that are or can be known?

Understand: Comprehend and examine all rationales, claims, and opinions with both neutrality and impartiality.

Educe: Bring forth truth by using these standards combined with reason and common sense to justify and satisfy your conclusions.

To harness fairness and impartiality means both knowing what is right and then doing what is right. It means complying with the habits of ...

JUST:

Judge: Determining that which is fair, reasonable, honorable, ethical, and good.

Uncover: Learning from your own personal faults and mistakes and taking advantage of the occasion to improve yourself.

Steadfast: Establishing superior ideals, control, and discipline for your daily conduct and then not faltering, even when the situation or circumstances are difficult.

Truthful: Selecting words that are accurate and sincere yet are measured with kindheartedness.

4) and **P**roduce a positive impact with my life choices:

True fulfillment and happiness are not achieved through self-indulgence, but rather from a commitment to improving the world around us. It is necessary to comprehend that how we lead our lives inter-connects us with each other by trillions of unseen strands. This web, created by our choices and actions, runs to and from and between us and transforms the world we live in. As a result, those who bring tranquility and cheerfulness into the lives of others also bring it unto themselves. In view of the fact that how we live our lives interconnects and influences all others in this world, it is of great consequence how we make those selections. Fortunately, one of life's greatest gifts … is free will … or our ability to make discretionary decisions. Free will and choice, is, of course, the power to select one avenue of action from a set of various alternatives available to us. It is great because it allows us the opportunity to create the life we desire and grants us the possibility to experience true contentment. This gift, however, does come with some weighty strings attached. These strings are known as personal accountability and responsibility for the actions we take. … Understand that life does not stand still; it ebbs and flows like a listless and sleepy ocean and at other times like a raging torrent. Yet how we enter and plot a course through this body of water with our decisions will lead us closer to or further away from our goals. It would be considered wise, by almost any captain, to frequently stop and examine where one is in the ocean of life and ask: Am I doing all I can to achieve my objectives and arrive at my preferred anchorage or port? If the answer is no then what actions can I take to move more in that direction? The gift of free will offers us the option to steer our singular vessel and opens the possibility to control or determine our final destination.

Considering that every day we make an untold number of decisions … how can we be sure we are choosing the soundest course? … Produce a positive and constructive impact with life's alternatives by practicing …

<u>NAVIGATE:</u>

Nurture a contemplative mind and candidly deliberate your options when deciding on an important direction to pursue. Whenever you are faced with a significant life alternative, you may find that one of the ways is easy to take, but that might be the only advantageous thing about it. So, consider your options carefully. You may find that one route is seductive because it is effortless and undemanding … whereas another may make you a better individual. I would advocate … that you choose the option that makes you a better individual. As Harry Emerson Fosdick wrote, *"He who chooses the beginning of a road chooses the place it leads to. It is the means that determine the end."*

Adopt a positive attitude. Life can certainly be tough and problematic but our daily activities can be made much sunnier by altering our mind-set. No matter how gloomy the situation is, if you look hard enough for something positive, you will find it. However, if you spend all your time grumbling and protesting, you will never find anything constructive and affirmative? Consider the reality, that what we pursue is what we usually end up finding. Thus, if you pursue a positive and upbeat outlook, you will eventually find it. On the other hand, if you search for something to whine about, you also will surely find that. Choose to search for the positive. No matter the situation, maintain a positive frame of mind and choose to believe something constructive and affirmative can and will happen.

Visualize and separate your Needs from your Wants. Wants are unappeasable and limitless. We want to be and do everything under the sun. But how can we do and become anything if we want to do and become everything? Therefore, eliminate those that are illusions and concentrate on meaningful aspirations that you have the time for. Determine your priorities and focus on your most important goals. If you run out of time before getting to the secondary objectives, at least you will have completed the most important ones.

Invent a new you. If you can't change your circumstances change yourself. Change means reinvention. Every time a major event happens in your life—the switching of careers, the breaking up of a serious relationship, moving to a new city, or losing a loved one—in most cases, we discover that we must reinvent ourselves and become a new individual or risk never reaching our full potential. But what many people forget is that you must choose reinvention. You must consciously forge a new path deliberately and with foresight. If you wait for your future to find you, you may become lost in confusion or sadness. You must take control of your future instead of letting your uncertainty or pain choose for you. Reinvent yourself by creating a new vision for your future. Imagine the future that you want and how it will feel to be in that new place. Picture yourself walking away from the past and into the future. Put it down like a scene from a movie: where you are living, who are your friends, what your career is, how you will be spending the day, etc. Then surround yourself with visual reminders of the life you'd like to create. It can be anything that reminds you of what you're moving toward. Use pictures, books, or internet articles, anything that keeps your focus on the future life you want to create. Finally, now that you have a vision of where you want to be, break it up into workable tasks. What do you need to do, every day, to create that vision? Look on a career builder web site? Meet new people? Search for that new place to live? It must be specific. Make a list of everything you need to do and schedule a day and time when you'll do it. Then do it and commit to keep doing it, one day at a time. Never give up … as expressed by C. S. Lewis … *"You're never too old to set another goal or dream a new dream."*

Goals and actions have consequences. Use your head and make intelligent and wise conclusions. Not every decision we make involves a moral or ethical choice. Sometimes it's just a matter of choosing between foolishness and intelligence. For example, if an individual offers to play Russian roulette with a handgun, don't take them up on it. That would be ludicrous. So if you want to make the correct decision, in many situations, just avoid the alternatives with signs that say ILL-ADVISED or FOOLISH and stick to those that say SENSIBLE or RATIONAL. Remember; be sure to check the signs before you start along any new path. In addition to the routes of SENSIBLE or FOOLISH, there is yet another intersecting cross trail, and it leads nowhere. It is the footpath of non-action. Whenever we face choices and refuse to decide, that refusal becomes our decision. By refusing, we turn over control to fate, and instead of sculpting our lives; we decide to drift wherever the sea and currents will take us. Unless there is a logical reason for not making a decision, this route should also have signs saying DO NOT ENTER.

Associate with good and great people. Look around you. There are good and great people everywhere you look … champions, sponsors, supporters, allies, enthusiasts, and patrons. Guess what … they're all rooting for you. They are rooting for you because they want you to win. They want you to succeed and be victorious. Regrettably, you are also surrounded by losers, people who want to drag you under and see you fail. They are rooting against you. Many are for you. Some are against you. How this life event turns out all depends on you because you will choose who you will mix with? This decision you make will increase your odds of success or your odds of failure. So … be very careful which people you choose to involve yourself with!

Think before you leap! Don't jump into something impulsively; use some fore-sight or circumspect when making a decision. In other words, we should know what we are getting into before we commit ourselves. Aesop's fable about the fox that is unable to climb out of a well and persuades a goat to jump in makes the point well. … Aesop's Fable: *"The Fox and the Goat"* … *One day, a Fox fell into a deep well and couldn't climb out. A thirsty Goat soon came to the same well, and seeing the Fox, called down to ask whether the water was good. Pretending to be happy (and not in despair), the Fox lavishly praised the water, saying how delicious it tasted, and encouraging the Goat to come and join him in the well. The Goat, thinking only of his thirst, stupidly jumped into the well. As he drank, the Fox informed him of the difficulty they were both in and suggested a scheme for their common escape. "If," said the Fox, "you put your forefeet up on the wall and bend your head foreword, I will run up your back like a ramp and escape, and then I will help you out afterward." The Goat agreed and so the Fox leaped upon his back. Steadying himself with the Goat's horns, he safely reached the mouth of the well ... and took off as fast as he could! When the Goat complained of the Fox breaking his promise, the Fox turned around and cried out, "You old goat! If you had as many brains in your head as you have hairs in your beard, you would never have gone down without making sure there was a way back up. Only a foolish fellow exposes himself to dangers from which he has no means of escape!"* Look before you leap!

Employ your inner voice ... or gut feeling. After due consideration of the "Old Goat" above, trust your intuition to explore a fresh opportunity. Every great achievement starts with the decision to simply try. Trust that little voice inside your head. Believe in your inner abilities. You have everything you need within you to become the best possible version of yourself. Believe that you "can do it". Don't let false opinions or negative viewpoints prevent you from moving beyond yourself. And definitely don't get distracted by other nay-saying fear-mongering individuals who won't support you anyway. Remember, it can often be difficult to grow into your superior self, but it's a calamity to let fear stop you. Therefore, recognize that fear doesn't exist anywhere except in your mind. Be the stronger person who is both fearless and brave. Pursue your endeavors and set your rudder for your targeted destination. Never let fear steer your present or determine your future. ... Remember, one day you will cease to exist. The question you need to ask yourself is: Are you choosing to live your life the way you want to right now? Take a moment and reflect on this question. This is your time and your life is happening at this very moment. Give yourself a fair chance ... time doesn't wait for anyone ... so don't waste it!

> *"Remember your dreams and fight for them. You must know what you want from life. There is just one thing that makes your dream become impossible: the fear of failure."*
> Paulo Coelho

The Quest Wheel and its Four Quads

The primary aim of this philosophy is to improve our natural, ecological and social habitat by first, enabling the Completeness, Safety, Contentment and Well-Being of you … the individual. The guide that follows offers a step-by-step process to attain this state by pursuing the Quest Wheel and its Four Quads. These Four Quads being: Wisdom, Integration, Security, and Harmony **(W. I. S. H.).**

<u>Completeness, Safety, Contentment & Well-Being</u>

W I S H

<u>W</u>isdom, <u>I</u>ntegration, <u>S</u>ecurity, and <u>H</u>armony

W <u>W</u>isdom: Your ability to make sensible choices and reach rational conclusions or decisions based on the sum of things known.

I <u>I</u>ntegration: Remaking of yourself by abiding by the eight steps of this guide and carrying out this philosophy's goals and mission.

S <u>S</u>ecurity: Finding yourself amply prepared, skilled, supported, and comforted in times of need or engagement.

H <u>H</u>armony: Knowing that your life and the lives of those around will enjoy peace as a result of your character, actions, and deeds.

Wisdom and Integration

Civilizations throughout history have possessed a great passion for wisdom. From the East, you can learn from the teachings of Buddhism, Hinduism, Islam, Confucianism, and Taoism. From the West, you can examine the philosophy of the Greeks, study ancient Egyptian tablets, and refer to the Old and New Testaments. In fact, the Greek word philosophy literally translated means "love of wisdom".

When I speak of wisdom, I am referring to gaining individual wisdom. This achievement of individual wisdom is said to be attainable, in a variety of ways, from one particular belief system to the next. Even though there may be disagreements on which of these paths may be the best, they all agree on one point; that gaining individual wisdom is desirable and a worthwhile goal for the individual to pursue.

So, if wisdom is a quest worth pursuing, how do you choose which teaching and pathway to keep to; and then, how do you measure your progress? From my perspective, I believe you should adhere to whatever faith, belief, or methodology that passionately touches both your heart and mind. Therefore, it would be beneficial to expose yourself to all of them and then come to a conclusion on which, if any, is best suited for you. My viewpoint is that you can pursue one or more parallel paths at the same time. That is why I say you can be a Neoteric Humanist and also a Christian, Jew, Muslim, or atheist … simultaneously. Being one does not necessarily negate the other, as long as both paths are heading in the same direction and complement each other. … This point having been made, for the balance of this segment, I will be discussing wisdom and integration as it relates to adhering to the ideology and methodology of Neoteric Humanism.

Defining wisdom is a relatively complicated task as it can be expressed in so many different forms and ways. The best short explanation of it, though incomplete, would be that attaining wisdom is your ability to make sensible choices and reach rational conclusions or decisions based on the sum of things known. This would also incorporate the ability to make reasonable judgments and take the most appropriate action even when the facts are unclear and the outcome entirely unpredictable. The totality of individual wisdom is of course, much more complex than this. People throughout their life have a wide range of various and divergent experiences. These experiences can make two independent individuals come to widely different conclusions when presented with similar situations. One may respond by turning right and upwards and the other to the left and down. Is one wrong and the other right? Not necessarily! What may be an appropriate response for one individual may be inappropriate for another based on past outcomes, observations, the culture, and the history that one has been part of. It is easy to understand that there may be more than one way to approach a problem in what each would consider a wise way. Therefore, wisdom is a blend of one's acquired knowledge and particular life events and experiences. These will both, of course, influence one's future choices. When an individual reflects on past knowledge and experiences plus past outcomes, this will impact upcoming deliberations and actions. For example: What are the odds of success in a particular situation? What are the potential downside results? Will this advance one's objective? Should others be involved in this decision? Will this make the problem better or worse? Is this the best possible solution? Is this choice unbiased and just? What if nothing were done? Will there be a second opportunity if this option should fail? … This kind of questioning on which is the wisest choice continues until time either runs out or a reasonable plan of action can be reached and agreed to by all parties.

Individual wisdom develops and evolves with time and will change with every new day happenstance. It's an ever-shifting stream, stockpiled with acquired life experiences that help us make better choices. Choices based on the entirety of our knowledge, encounters, and individual perception. While not an easy concept to define or explain, wisdom, or the lack of it, will often expose itself by one's choice of words, behavior, or actions. As I'm sure, through our life experiences, we have all experienced or witnessed individuals who have exhibited both wisdom and foolishness. ... So, how does one acquire greater individual wisdom for oneself?

One way to move further toward individual wisdom is through the absorption and practice of worthy principles and values and then integrating them into a person's everyday life. This involves a commitment to:

1. Identify "what are" the best values and principles to live by and then Integrating oneself into a unified whole reflecting those values and principles.
2. Putting these values and principles in practice every day.
3. Reviewing your daily behavior and
4. making adjustments and improvements.

Remaking one's character with a combination of values, principles, culture, history, and perspective will provide a framework that will assist in future decision making. So ... what would constitute a worthy set of values and principles to live by?

This remaking encourages sticking to the sixteen values of **PRAISEWORTHINESS:**

- **P**ersistence, by the individual, to become the best they can be.
- **R**etaining a clean mind and a healthy body through one's activities.
- **A**dapting a positive, peaceful and optimistic mental attitude in all things.
- **I**nstilling one's character, behavior, and actions with virtue and goodness.
- **S**eeking prosperity … through new abilities, skills, and knowledge.
- **E**ngaging in self-discipline to work for long-term rewards.
- **W**illing to help, assist, or benefit others.
- **O**pening your mind to the truth no matter how unpleasant.
- **R**emoving the anxiety and fear to be a creative and/or a unique individual.
- **T**ransforming your frame of mind by taking personal responsibility for your choices and actions.
- **H**olding a sense of wonder and appreciation of all that life has to offer.
- **I**nformed so that one is organized, self-reliant, and prepared.
- **N**aturally exhibiting the desire to deal honestly and fairly with all people.
- **E**xpressing both common sense and courage when facing the unknown.
- **S**haring your good fortune and helping others attain their goals and happiness.
- **S**ubmitting to moderation and self-control in all things you do.

All the decisions we make on a daily basis involve a choice of what is most "internally" valued by us. That is to say, by what we feel deep inside, not just the words or actions we choose to use in public. To truly judge one's values, one must examine their character and behavior when as they say … "No one is looking". That is where the real values of a person lay. Why is the development of these desirable values and characteristics of the individual so crucial? It will take this kind of wise and judicious individual with sound values and principles to help forge exceptional institutions, enable sensible laws, and bring greater advancement to our society.

Become a more valued individual by adhering to the four habits of **GOAL:**

1. **G**aining worthy ethics, values, principles, and morals through engagement with honest, constructive, optimistic and virtuous people.
2. **O**btaining by individual study and academically as many positive and desirable characteristics as possible.
3. **A**cting and practicing with effort, the character, behavior, and attitude that will one day enter and dwell within one's deepest, truest self.
4. **L**earning deep meditation and self-analysis of your inner-being with a commitment to improve and better yourself.

The point I want to make here is that the attainment of individual wisdom, positive values, and principles do not need to be left to chance. They can be developed intentionally through proper exposure and dedication to the right people, activities, habits, studies, and ideology. This proper exposure and dedication can be found within this methodology and practice of Neoteric Humanism.

Use this four-step process when seeking to formulate intelligent and fair-minded conclusions and judgments ... employ **WISE:**

Weigh all the information provided as to its accuracy and if it is verifiable to the best of your knowledge?

Individually is it generally acceptable to all? Is this the best decision for the majority of people involved while still endeavoring to preserve the interests of the minority?

Success may not satisfy all parties concerned, but will it still be acceptable ... even if they all don't get everything they desire?

Equitable in that everyone participating should receive some advantage as not all situations have an equal or win-win result.

Security and Harmony:

If one could call forth a powerful and wise genie from a magic lamp and could ask him to grant them two wishes on the most essential things they will need for a happy life, the genie would no doubt have Security and Harmony at the top of his list. Why? ... Because this wise genie knew that Security and Harmony are the basic prerequisites to facilitate Peace, Health, Happiness and Prosperity. The advantage of safety and tranquility is that it allows one to attain better health, amplified optimism and greater prosperity as they are the crucial building blocks for the preservation and advancement of a civilized world. A world deprived of security and harmony will certainly fall apart and return to a long past era in which the strong prey on the weak and the dominant gang of the day rules. Therefore, having security and harmony is an obvious and necessary demand of a community and a logical path to continue for the betterment of humanity. This means dealing with disputes and resolving conflicts legally, fairly and peacefully to further the general welfare of each individual as well as the wellbeing of the populace as a whole.

Security and harmony provide indispensable dividends to society. They are a necessary platform for the creativity of individuals, the development of the economy and the progress of culture. This dynamic two-sum is needed for the long term safety and prosperity of neighborhoods, communities and society. No country can develop properly or grow economically without nonviolent coexistence among its population within and around its borders. This means that the nations who will advance the fastest in the world will be those with the best security and safety and those having both peace and harmony thriving within them. However, building this harmony and security will involve a wide range of effort by diverse actors in government and civil society at the community, national, international levels. This will be needed to address the root causes of conflicts and violence and to ensure that people have freedom of fear from lawlessness, war and serious conflicts. Good governance and the rule of law are essential requirements to ensure that justice, resources and services are made equally available to all the people. They are there to guarantee freedom from fear and violence, and emphasize the respect for law and order as a cornerstone to society's progress.

Fulfilling harmony and security implies much more than just the absence of physical violence. While most often the search for them is seen as an end to armed conflict or the enforcement of stability within the state the absence of physical violence should be only the beginning. It should be a quest not only for tranquility, but for the individual's right to have freedom of knowledge, speech, religion, thought, and movement.

The freedom to pursue one's own vision of fulfillment and the freedom to elect leaders and officials who will represent them and be responsible for satisfying the best interests of society. This crucial objective is inextricably intertwined within the context of global involvement. Hence, worldwide expansion of these ideals is fundamentally related to processes of global political, social and cultural advancement.

This means addressing the drivers of internal and international methods for establishing these desirable objectives is going to be a long-term and complex task. Conflicts between people and nations have multiple motives, take place under various political systems, are often locally initiated but do not always stop at a countries borders. Therefore, answers to creating global peace, health, happiness and prosperity require the commitment of people, officials, states and institutions at many levels. Leaders need to be made aware locally, nationally and internationally of the need to integrate these ideals into political, social and economic initiatives and corresponding policy decisions if there is to be substantial progress and abundance for all.

Of course, living in harmony with others is easier said than done, especially in a world filled with conflict, catastrophes, and differing opinions. You may find it a struggle to feel in sync with people close to you and with society at large. So ... What to do? One good way to develop one's personal civility and good nature is by sincerely opening up with family, friends and neighbors. Deal with any disharmony you encounter by first reevaluating your own behavior and actions, than practice being open-minded and generous to everyone you meet and by giving back to those in your community. ... This will give you a much stronger and deeper connection with others!

To obtain greater peace and harmony abide by the eight points of

ENVISION:

- **E**liminate choices with negative consequences. Say NO to bad or unethical options. Breaking the law or causing harm can result in a lifetime of undesirable after effects.
- **N**urture constructive solutions to obstacles, be open-minded and free of bias.
- **V**olunteer for a worthy cause bigger than your specific personal desires.
- **I**nstill joyful and positive thoughts in your mind throughout the day … smile.
- **S**eek out people who are ethical, good-humored and who make you feel good.
- **I**nvolve yourself with people. Try such pastimes as chess, bridge, golf, tennis, etc. Read and share books, organize group visits to artistic or music venues.
- **O**vercome the enticement to associate with those who make bad choices and are reckless in their temptations as they will contaminate and corrupt you.
- **N**ourish everything that is positive, good, noble, or virtuous.

Internal harmony is achieved by practicing thoughtful reflection. External harmony and security are accomplished by setting goals, building strong supportive relationships, and acquiring skills and knowledge. The world we live in is constantly being altered and is in an ongoing flux of modification. Each minute of each day something new is being created, altered, removed or eliminated. This is the way of our world. It is our curse and our blessing. Sometimes the change is good and we are glad and sometimes the change is unpleasant and we are sad. This persistent transformation does not mean we throw up our arms and lament "what will be, will be". We, unlike other species, have the ability and foresight to influence our circumstances and to formulate plans based on possible outcomes. There can be no denying that plans and goals may fail but when they succeed, do we not feel harmony and greater security? Therefore, set goals and make every effort to attain them. Do try to pay off your home, set aside money for retirement, buy insurance, and set up an educational fund for your children. ... We, as intelligent beings, have the capacity to learn a profession, a trade, and new skills or to perhaps take on a new career. Ask yourself ... would not gaining knowledge and proficiency in medical remedies, CPR and first aid, disaster readiness, home safety drills, foreign languages, communication methods, and techniques of self-defense add a degree of self-confidence and security to one's life? These are all things within our control. All one needs to do is research, plan, set aside time, and follow-through. Attaining new skills, preparations and knowledge are very powerful tools in building self-assurance, confidence, security and tranquility.

Finally, and most importantly, one must recognize the four most essential benefactors you must bring into your heart and everyday life if you wish to achieve more security and thus more harmony. These four types of wonderful people, when all else fails, and the world is collapsing around you, are the ones most likely to hold true, be dependable and strong for you to the very end.

If you desire greater harmony and security ... nurture, protect, respect and love those valuable and marvelous individuals noted in

SAFE:

- Your **S**pouse or significant other with whom you share your life.
- Your **A**llies and friends who are true and actively supportive of you.
- Your **F**amily members who are reliable and trusted.
- Your **E**xternal support groups who are dependable and kindhearted. (For example: Church, Temple, Mosque, HUB, Associations and Clubs etc.).

In your time of great need or hardship, it will be your loved one, your family, your true friends, and those in your support group who will stand by your side and will offer to defend, support, or do anything they can ... for you.

"The superior man, when resting in safety, does not forget that danger may come. When in a state of security he does not forget the possibility of ruin. When all is orderly, he does not forget that disorder may come. Thus his person is not endangered, and his States and all their clans are preserved."

Confucius

Vision and Objectives

Over the next few decades, we will witness numerous unsettling and dramatic developments. Technology will begin merging with humanity, an ever-growing population will compete even more forcefully for limited resources, disasters and tragedy will be mixed with new discoveries and many reasons for optimism. The possibility of doomsday scenarios will intensify side by side with opportunities to grasp a new golden age for human progress. This is the world we live in … and it is our actions that will tip the scales for better or worse. What will you do? You can simply accept whatever befalls you and your family or you can make a conscious effort to weigh the scales in humanity's favor? Faced with this uncertain future, an individual should decide which life path offers the best hope for both personal and wide-ranging success. This crucial choice, I believe, should be one that leads toward the completeness, safety, contentment and well-being of not just one individual, but for all people. Only when the welfare and serenity of all individuals is treated with equal opportunity to fulfill common goals will our world share peace and the bountiful fruits of a new golden age.

Neoteric Humanism provides the vision, the objectives, and the way to help us move toward this optimistic future. It offers personal meaning and significance to human life by laying out a shared ideology that will focus, unify, and direct its adherent's actions. This focus, unity, and effort will bring forth a bright ray of hope that will illuminate a pathway to a brighter future for all humankind.

Aspirations and Ambitions of NEOTERIC HUMANISM ...

- Notes that an ideal human population for planet earth would be somewhere between 2 and 3 billion people. That when our population exceeds these thresholds many problems and crises arise that may cause enormous suffering and corresponding ecosystem destruction. These dangers include the possibility of war, mass starvation, overwhelming poverty and deadly pandemics. Neoteric Humanism acknowledges the only rational hope to control this trend is to practice, promote, and teach methods of birth control and family planning around the globe.
- Encourages the promotion of the arts, sports, competitions and nature's beauty so it may be enjoyed and experienced by all. It champions all efforts to develop and support these endeavors to bring excitement, joy and challenges into our daily lives.
- Observes that one's health care is generally best provided by a competition between wellness contractors depending on which ones provide the best service and lowest costs. This being said, it also supports the idea of a government-sponsored safety net for those who are mentally or physically deficient, abused or abandoned, and those involved in serious catastrophic situations or those born with severe pre-existing conditions.
- Teaches individuals to live by the highest standards of ethics, morality, and personal responsibility. That following these principles will lead to greater harmony, trust and good will within the community.
- Emphasizes the importance of green spaces, clean air, unspoiled land, and unpolluted water. It holds a

deep appreciation for the wonders and splendor of nature. It will energetically back widespread efforts for conservation, recycling, the expansion of state and national parks, and the protection and preservation of wildlife and scenic marvels. Neoteric Humanism also comprehends the need for compromise in the development of energy, industry, and commerce, but believes a diligent and thorough effort should be crafted to keep these sites as natural and pristine as possible before, during, and after its utilization.

- Recognizes the need for an educated, informed and fully participating citizenship to best maintain a government by and for the people. It supports and believes in the inalienable right of the individual to Life, Liberty, Equal Rights, Fair and Impartial Justice, and the Pursuit of Happiness. That this is best achieved in a Constitutional Republic containing a Bill of Rights and three branches of government (Executive, Legislative and Judicial) each with effective checks and balances on each other. These should all incorporate the principle of Meritocracy to achieve the best results.

- Insists the best way to generate a healthy and prosperous standard of living for its members and the world is through continuous education and skill-building. This aim will be advanced by expert training events and by staging multiple ways to gain knowledge.

- Contends that completeness, safety, contentment and well-being in one's life are found by coupling personal talents and passions with an innocuous occupation and life mission. A blending that benefits not only the individual himself but also one's community.

- Holds and asserts that it is not humanities destiny to live and prosper only here on earth, but to explore and move beyond Humankind's mother planet. It supports continued efforts in space exploration and the natural progression of our species to other man-made habitats and/or suitable terrestrial bodies.
- Understands and supports the importance of fellowship between the adherents of this philosophy. It will encourage projects and activities that will form strong bonds between families, members, and friends. Neoteric Humanism also comprehends that to truly fulfill its purpose, a concentrated and sustained effort must be made to solicit new members, educate and motivate current members, and increase public awareness of its goals, mission, and ideology. This will entail personal and ongoing efforts through multi-media, publications, and one on one individual contact. It will require perseverance and dedication particularly by the initial participants and supporters if there is to be a fulfillment of the ambitions and objectives desired.
- Maximizes results by the use of reason, facts, laws, and the scientific method combined with creativity and imagination thus providing the best basis for setting objectives and solving problems. Final decisions are to be carefully balanced with ethical, ecological, social, and economic values before being entrusted for action. Truth, fortitude, and each person's unique and varied spiritual beliefs will provide the strong motivation needed to contend with hardships, obstacles, and setbacks. ... In addition, it maintains that even though technology and new discoveries are vital keys to human progress and development, feasibility

and capability does not imply social or cultural desirability.

- **A**dvocates "free thought" and encourages the unending questioning of basic assumptions and convictions. It promotes the search for "truth" as the best means to move humankind forward. It is opposed to all forms of radical hate and prejudicial dogma and doctrines that hold back, distort or deny knowledge for personal gain or power.
- **N**urtures the idea of a common 2nd language for humanity. A simple, reasonable, and agreeable 2nd language, <u>not</u> to replace a native tongue, but one to advance greater understanding between nations and cultures. This implies employing a language such as Esperanto or a similar version … should it be created. Until this becomes a reality, affiliates will be urged to learn and practice those languages most beneficial for their own place and time. Neoteric Humanism deems that knowledge and appreciation of additional languages will help promote mutual compassion and goodwill between people. It also maintains that it will assist members and attending novices in attaining a higher level of satisfaction and success in both their personal and professional lives.
- **I**dealistically and by characterization, is non-violent. However, as a matter of caution and vigilance, it will encourage members to participate in lessons of self-defense. It also contends that preparedness will be further enhanced by supplementary instruction in basic survival techniques, first aid, and personal security. Additionally, it advocates that as soon as possible, families create an emergency plan and maintain four months supply of appropriate food, water, medicine,

suitable supplies, tools, and equipment. Being ready for any disaster will lead to a greater sense of self-assurance and well-being.

- **S**tresses that one's body and senses are the components that allow people to live and experience life. That this philosophy's adherents should strive to eat and drink nutritious foods and avoid partaking or limit that which may degenerate the body, dull the senses and weaken the mind. It believes in the ongoing development of one's physical and intellectual potential and will promote activities for this specific purpose.

- **M**aintains that it is best to have tax-financed free education from kindergarten through the 12th grade and low-cost federal loan subsidies for college, trade schools or similar programs. But, this free or low cost funded education should be tendered only to those who attend to gain knowledge, useful skills, and who display effort and respect to the instructors, education centers and other students. It is the position of Neoteric Humanism that education is best offered as an earned privilege, not a right. It advocates freedom of choice for students and their parents to pick the schools which provide them the best learning and/or training prospects for their future. Finally, that church and state are best kept separate in government-run institutions. Parents who choose a well academically qualified private education facility for their child's schooling may ignore this. All tax dollars to chase the teaching, skill building or preferred school of their choice.

New ways of thinking have the power to be either uplift-
ing or degrading. They provide the passion to change the way
you view and act in this world, either in a negative or positive way. … How are the experiences and opinions that shape
your thoughts now affecting your inner-nature? How are they
influencing those around you? How are they altering your
immediate environment and surroundings? When you think
about the above aspirations and ambitions, do you see the
possibility and opportunity of your making a quantum shift
for the better … in your life? … In the lives of those you care
about? In this world we live in? The answer to these questions
is … yes! You can start doing it right now!! The only one holding you back … is you!

The Eight-Step Process

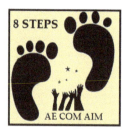

As we labor through life's daily challenges, we are fortunate to have many dynamic religions and philosophies to help guide us. If we eventually decide to choose and pursue a particular belief system, or world view, it is one of the most important choices we will make in our entire lives. This decision is supremely important because it will not only influence our daily action ... but will also shape, forge, and transform our inner being. As asserted by the poet, Alexander Pope, *"As the twig is bent ... the tree is inclined."* With this insightful thought in mind, it is an appropriate time to illuminate each of the eight steps of this guide, beginning with acknowledgment. In doing so ... please remember and consider the wise words spoken by Pocahontas *"Sometimes the right path is not always the easiest one!"*

Step #1 ... *Acknowledgment*

Fulfilling the necessity of Acknowledgement requires four personal actions ... to Understand, to Resolve, to Desire, and to be Non-judgmental. First ... it is essential to comprehend the entirety of this philosophy. Secondly, it is imperative to have the focus and willpower to do what is required. Thirdly the heart to do what must be done and finally to abstain and withhold one's judgment. In other words, maintain an intellect enlightened by analysis, a resoluteness which nothing can check, an aspiration which cannot be broken, and a commitment which nothing from the outside can poison. To complete this first step, one must examine all the facts to ascertain their validity. This is crucial, for if an individual does not truly believe something, then it will be impossible for them to move rationally and enthusiastically in that direction. Once this inquiry and analysis have been performed and one concludes that ... what is said is the <u>truth</u> ... then one should logically and without delay, alter their mindset and life to live in harmony with this reality. ... So, what are these truths I speak of? If one is to pursue an enlightened, constructive, and positive way of life, then one should be in agreement with the following four affirmations:

1. That there is perpetual change, for the better or worse, in the foreseeable future and habitat of humankind.
2. The above being true, to improve the human condition, one must first strive to fashion themselves and their families with wholesome values, habits, and lifestyle. That they must be actively involved and proceed as responsible citizens, custodians, and humanitarians. Above all, that they must make every effort to formulate reasonable, responsible, and wise choices.
3. That one must be cognizant that the decisions made today will have consequences not only for themselves but for future generations as well.
4. One effective way to move in this positive and beneficial direction is by obeying the methodology, goals, and principles of the above-mentioned guide and actively practicing the ideology of Neoteric Humanism.

If after study, contemplation and deliberation, both heart and mind validate the truth of what has been stated, then you are ready to proceed. Remember, the first step is acknowledgment. Once you internally accept the truth, it will open the door for change. By choosing to proceed through this doorway with the power of truth, you will be armed with the necessary strength to begin and complete your journey.

Why is this power and armor of truth so essential? To begin with, to establish yourself as something new, you must first relinquish your prior conceptions and overcome your fear. Why? Because the truth is life-altering. It threatens the status quo and it makes you see things differently. It brings about change and as human beings, we are fearful and apprehensive about change. As children, we are born as a blank slate, but by an early age, this slate becomes imprinted with family and communal ideals, norms, and customs. These ingrained survival and social skills are drilled into us from the very beginning, as the world we live in, is a hard and unforgiving environment. Our parents and teachers impart to us what is right and what is wrong, what to believe, and what not to believe, what is acceptable, and what is unacceptable. This process brings to a community a feeling of conformity and safety. Society encourages this because it brings individuals a feeling of contentment, and security, as well as, a daily pattern to support and live by. Truth, on the other hand, may require change and people are uneasy about change. Why? ... Because seeking the truth requires us to ask questions ... questions that may make us uncomfortable and for which we don't have easy answers. One great truth of life is that we all live in an ever-changing and uncertain universe; a universe in which sometimes facing the truth is quite frightening. Consider this ... good, decent, and law-abiding people die every day from both bizarre and often very ordinary events. That is a fear-provoking thought and it is definitely a depressing and unsettling fact of life, but it is also true. … Truth arrives when you accept that no matter what pattern of living you are now following you are not as safe and secure as you might think. You are not safe because life, the earth, the solar system, and our universe are forever transforming themselves. By letting go of the imaginary security and control you think you have, you will begin seeing everything as it actually is! Yes, the truth is that this world that we inhabit is a precarious place and is in constant turmoil. … Nonetheless, each of us does have the power and capacity to produce an impact on our day-to-day activities and influence the human condition and its advancement. For you to accomplish this initial step, however, <u>it is necessary to shed off your existing shell</u>. You must have the courage to acknowledge this reality thus allowing your transformation to begin. Within all of us is a dynamic and robust being, one who is ready to leave the old cocoon behind and take on fresh challenges, a new purpose, and a willingness to improve oneself, one's family and community, and thus provide a new vision to make our world a better place.

Step #2 … _Education_

To move forward along this path, you will need to expand your mind by intensive inquiry, research, and assimilation of knowledge. This should include, but not be limited to, an examination of history, law, the sciences, philosophies, religions, political systems, the arts, languages, life skills, and literature. Establishing ongoing education brings with it new and fresh perspectives about our world and helps develop one's character. It brings about a sense of unity with society and inspires a desire and responsibility to participate in it. Learning makes an impact inside the whole person ... body, mind, and spirit. It instills a love of discovery that will guide your life and encourage creativity and new passions. New knowledge expands your way of thinking and facilitates your understanding of the interconnectivity of systems, the human body, families, neighborhoods, communities, countries, the earth, and the universe. A broad and diverse education is something that cannot be taken away; it becomes an intricate part of you. It brings wisdom, self-confidence, curiosity, and inspiration. This lifelong pursuit will, over time, increase your perspective, insight, and awareness. Set aside time daily to pursue this undertaking and do so in a calm atmosphere with little or no distractions. Study in-depth and evaluate alternative and contrary opinions. Read, watch, and listen to all you can on a variety of subjects from a wide array of diverse sources. Do not straightaway accept all you read, see, and hear as fact. Verify and question all conclusions and be constantly aware of embedded prejudice and bias.

One way to commence this education process is to explore the types of "Read or Review" homework sections introduced on page #178 in this book or by starting with those topics beginning on page #181. Understand that this is only a suggested collection of subjects and not at all a complete archive of what one should attempt to gain familiarity with. This is, after all, an ongoing process, and these reading recommendations will in time, no doubt, need revision.

A parallel course of education that you should explore ... is through the arts. The arts have proved to be a wonderful source of honesty, beauty, and meaning. Artists have an amazing ability to unlock our imagination and stimulate our minds to either contemplate or re-evaluate ideas and concepts.

Through their work, they enable us to see our surroundings and the human condition perhaps differently. In doing so, we may see or realize a certainty we may not have comprehended before. Artists raise questions and compel us to think or maybe examine further. A skillful writer, for example, may have a keen sense of verse that could be a powerful force for good or at the very least awaken us to an unseen or unspoken truth. Artists will often go out of their way to create something simply to stir up the public's emotions. For some these sensations will bring delight and to others, they will bring disdain. In either case, they frequently force us to see things differently and in doing so, expose or accentuate a veiled reality. The arts, with their novel perspective and vision, open our imagination to beauty and evil, to the possible and improbable, to falsehoods and the truth. The arts are a gift to all of us to both enrich and influence our lives.

Art is not only beneficial to our society but also the artist's themselves. Composing music, writing a dramatic piece, painting on a blank canvas, or even writing a poem or book, forces the individual to think in unconventional ways. It frees them to imagine, dream, and even to sense things differently. This proves to be internally helpful as it has a propensity to unlock an artist's intuitive and creative impulses. This being so, they become freer and more engaged and will perceive realities and meanings that possibly might not be grasped in any other way. From another perspective, the art that a person may choose to pursue could be viewed as merely the beginning of much more important work; … this work being, how this <u>individual</u> chooses to lead their <u>own</u> life and what kind of legacy they will leave for generations to come.

Using observation and a "living it" approach is still another means to acquire knowledge. This kind of education encourages direct individual involvement and participation in activities such as, attending seminars, political meetings, cultural events, and artistic performances. Materially building a house, hitching a ride across the country, or riding as a passenger in an old WW I plane is a "living it" experience. These types of experiences leave a much deeper impression than simply reading about it or looking at pictures in a book and trying to imagine what it's like. The "living it" approach is hands-on real-life education. How to handle money and finances, learning to play an instrument, or painting a picture are all learning opportunities. Growing a garden or raising a crop can teach us how to cultivate, identify, harvest, and preserve. Changing the oil or coolant in your car, maintaining or replacing your battery, or topping off fluids all teach hands-on auto care and maintenance. Experimentation is also a type of observation. It is based on the use of the scientific method as a means of discovery. Here one creates an experiment to prove or disprove a hypothesis or educated guess. Do not let the word "scientific" throw you off track. Experiments might include such things as using unusual ingredients in food preparation, a strange chemical in cleaning, a new kind of fertilizer in gardening, or anything that may help one learn and discover. This is an approach we used daily as children but tended to forget as we got older. Children are naturally curious, they find out that limes are sour and candy is sweet by tasting. They are inclined to dip French fries into chocolate ice cream to discover if they like it or not. They are pre-wired to try new methods that may allow them to jump higher, throw farther, or run faster. Experimenting teaches us to rely on our own personally gathered evidence rather than on an authority, i.e. a textbook, expert, teacher, or parent. Most of us live in an authoritarian world and have made a conscious decision not to learn new skills or try new ways. We have come to rely on others for nearly everything we do or need to be done. If we do not change our ways, our dependence will continue to grow and we will have even less understanding or ability to do for ourselves. The importance of individual observation and "living it" experiences are crucial as they provide an understanding of how true learning takes place. While information can be remembered, if taught through books, true understanding and the ability to use knowledge in new situations requires the kind of learning in which one justifies conclusions by direct experience. The justification for "living it" learning is that it allows one to build not only understanding but also the ability to inquire; in other words, to become free and independent thinkers. Thus, because people become better educated, they are more self-reliant and able to resolve problems using their individual abilities.

An additional "living it" method is by participating in and making a study of sports and games. This is not only stimulating and pleasurable but it also helps build self-esteem, good health, and confidence. At the same time, it provides a great mental exercise for the developing mind. Games and sports enhance awareness, resilience, and resolve, as well as, aiding in the improvement of creativity, perception, and memory. Most importantly, it facilitates the ability to analyze a situation, learn how to make difficult decisions, and to solve problems. Games and sports teach the rewards of attention and focus as well as providing immediate consequences for carelessness and miscalculations. Few learning methods provide such quick feedback for success or failure. Just one slip in concentration can lead to a simple error, this simple error perhaps causing the loss of the game. Only a focused and persistent player will sustain consistent and positive results. … Why is this so critical? With the introduction of the internet, e-mail, and computers, information is pouring in faster and faster. This new technology and its evolving software are rapidly changing the essential skills needed to succeed in society. Information that took months to track down a few years ago can now flow off the internet in just a few minutes. With such easy access and tremendous volumes of data, the ability to choose effectively among a wide variety of options is even more imperative. In all aspects of business, home, and one's social life you must increasingly be able to respond quickly and judiciously. An individual must now be able to wade through and synthesize vast amounts of information. One must learn to recognize what is relevant and what is irrelevant. People also need to acquire the skills necessary to learn new technologies and modes of operation quickly as well as to solve a continual stream of problems typically associated with them. This is where learned gaming skills are particularly effective. By their very nature, sports and gaming present a whole set of wide-ranging problems. Except for the very beginning of the game, each move or choice creates a new situation. For each new circumstance, a player tries to find the best alternative by calculating ahead and evaluating future possibilities. Throughout this process, more than one choice usually exists, just as in the real world, where more than one option is frequently present. Players must learn to decide on a course of action, even when the answer is ambiguous or difficult. It teaches the importance of planning and the consequences of decisions. It clarifies how to concentrate, how to win, how to think logically, and ultimately how to more skillfully cope and deal with real-world problems.

Extensive travel is yet another means of education that involves learning without the presence of a traditional classroom. The things we see and come into contact with during traveling influence our very core. The lessons we learn from such encounters can create a greater impact on our lives than anything taught or described through books and lectures alone. The food you taste, the music you hear, the friendships you make, and the exotic locations you visit all become part of you. This combined with the climatic differences you are subjected to, the culture you come to understand, the faiths, celebrations, and rituals you experience transform your perception of the world. The insights gained from comparing and contrasting these builds bridges and a greater appreciation of each other. Travel gives the individual a new kind of educational learning … a total emersion type of encounter. Such full exposure helps us to face life with more empathy and open-mindedness. Every winding bend along the traveled road leaves within us a new smell, taste, vision, or impression. You are gathering new insights and understanding every moment you are there. Even if you travel the same route, season after season, you will find that every trip is distinctive and that every outing varies from the last. The essential point here is that just by exposure, you are acquiring an enhanced world view. Do other traditional teaching methods offer such an opportunity? Traveling is a marvelous adventure that allows people to discover things in a unique way. It is a perennial source of learning that transforms and influences people and their perception. The value of traveling is if for no other reason, an opportunity to absorb the fact that our world has many distinctive inhabitants and is wonderfully diversified. That there is more than one way to do things and that the earth's various cultures have a great deal to offer in this regard. That by traveling, there is much knowledge and wisdom to be gained, and the differences we find there are very much … the spice of life.

To supplement the above methods of learning, you should also attempt to build an affiliation with other members and supporters of Neoteric Humanism. By connecting with them individually, or as a group, you will find fellowship, encouragement, and support as you continue on your journey. During this time, you should also try to limit or cease association with all those people who are counter to or are a negative influence, in your evolution. Understand that you cannot help but be affected by the actions, customs, and way of life of those around you ... for the better great! ... For the worse ... best to steer clear and avoid!

Finally, set aside ample time for siblings, parents, and grandparents to discover and research your family roots. By knowing your own history and actively living in the present, you will be better able to chart a reliable course for your future. Be a good record keeper and custodian of a family diary and add new chapters to it often. Make a point of discussing with your sons and daughters your family genealogy and keep it up to date with personal records, notes, and memories. Prepare now to pass on this heritage to the next generation. Over time, for your heirs, it will become cherished.

Step #3 ... *Character*

One's authentic character resides within the true self. To develop this true self into a superior and virtuous character requires one to adhere to a set of fundamental laws and to live by a code of desirable traits. Why is this necessary? The cause of many of our troubles today is a failure of the individual to live their life based on the rule of law, wholesome behavior, virtuous honor, and decent values. You don't have to look far to see the consequences of this lack of moral fiber and integrity. Schemes abound that steal millions from charities, retirement accounts, or government funds. Our elected officials are frequently exposed selling out to special interest groups. Corporate executives, on many occasions, are convicted much too often for misleading or lying to their stockholders. We read about our most trusted members of the clergy who are caught abusing children or stealing out of papal coffers. More and more we hear of students in our schools who favor cheating over obtaining an honest grade. We have employees who don't think twice about stealing from their employers and employers who unfairly exploit their workers. Society is teeming with those who make conscious decisions to rape, destroy, and pillage when our social systems break down. We are living in times in which the lack of virtue and good character is creating a culture full of thugs, thieves, liars, and cheats. Our society is in crisis and the moment is now to pick up the banner of honor, virtue, and moral character to forge a better future.

Following the philosophy of Neoteric Humanism, its principles, values and tenets will help accomplish this in several ways: First, by ascertaining what is true. Secondly, what is genuinely desirable, and will enhance our world. Thirdly, creating a natural desire to do what is necessary. And finally, fulfilling that desire and achieving the goal or aspiration.

This process will involve more than a commitment to social ethics. It will include lessons, and discussions on one's integrity, honesty, personal responsibility, and reputation. It will explore life's negative and destructive forces such as hypocrisy, self-deception, and selfishness. The objective will be to look at life's demons square in the face and learn how to cast them away. Organized activities will encourage behavior that emphasizes civility, kindness, and honesty. They will articulate tales that reinforce goodness, moral character, and desirable virtues. These teachings will involve one's inner nature, as well as, one's mindset. It is hoped that these experiences will inspire the individual to become aware, that it is they themselves, who shape the quality of the life they will lead. … This brings to mind a fable I'd once heard regarding a young Native American boy who asks his father about a very disturbing dream he has been having. He describes his dream to his father as witnessing two great wolves, fighting to the death, over his heart and spirit. One wolf has silver fur, green eyes, and is evil; the other wolf has golden fur, brown eyes, and is good. He asks his father which one of the wolves he thinks will win. The wise father thought for a moment and replied, *"Whichever one you feed, my son"*. ... Have you examined your life recently and considered which wolf ... you are currently feeding?

It is your actions, from this day forward, that will determine who you will become. Set aside time to reflect on unkind deeds or poor behavior performed in the past and pay special attention to the motives or people that prompted you to do them. If possible, apologize, or in some way make amends for any wrongdoings done to those involved. This action may not be openly accepted by those offended, but they will internally welcome your regret and remorse. What's more, this being an uncomfortable and painful task, it will help you avoid repeating the same mistakes in the future. ... Now ... let yesterday die! Rise above the mistakes of your past! Make a pact with yourself, from this day onward, to live by the 4 Fundamental Laws, the noted Desirable Traits and 16 Pursuits that you will uncover in this guide. There are essential qualities to be acquired and a lifestyle to be altered if one wishes to better oneself. It will take repeated effort, enduring vigor, and continuous dedication if one desires to make genuine progress. Bear in mind the words of Ralph Waldo Emerson: *"Watch your thoughts, for they become words. Watch your words, for they become actions. Watch your actions, for they become habits. Watch your habits, for they become your character."*

Fill your "**Personal Mindset Well**" with these Desirable Traits and Fundamental Laws.

The Desirable Traits:

I will be ...

- **F**aithful and dependable.
- **A**ccountable and ethical.
- **W**ell-groomed and mannered.
- **N**ovel and free-thinking.
- **Q**uality focused and guided.
- **U**nderstanding and tolerant.
- **I**nclusive and charitable.
- **L**oyal and trusted friend.
- **M**indful of behavior and deeds.
- **E**ducator and student.
- **D**iscerning and judicious.
- **S**eeking of truth and wisdom.
- **T**ruthful yet kindhearted.
- **O**ptimistic and cheerful.
- **P**unctual and prepared.
- **C**lean in mind and body.

The Fundamental Laws:

Do ...

- not commit or contribute to **M**urder.
- not commit or contribute to unjustified **I**njury.
- not commit or contribute to foul **D**eeds.
- tell, under oath, the absolute and complete **T**ruth.

Step #4 ... *Occupation*

How will you occupy yourself in the time life has allotted you? What path will you choose to stay on? Will you select a spiritual quest? Will it be one of service in the military or possibly as a social worker? Will it be a political, entrepreneurial or an artistic ambition that will be your calling? Maybe something else or perhaps, some combination of the above. This is a critical decision, as this choice will likely consume a large part of your waking day. So, how does one make such an important decision? What should the criteria be? Most people desire to do something in life that offers greater meaning as well as money; something that imparts a sense of worth in what they do and in themselves. An occupation wherein the doing is as significant as what gets done and the making as valuable as the service or the product completed. In essence, a way of life that fulfills the needs of the body, the intellect, and the spirit.

Resolving this question also demands that you understand another aspect as well. That the decision you make will not just influence your world but that it will also transform and define who you are as an individual. What you do in this life ... will shape, mold, and change "who you are". The fact that "what you do" shapes and defines "who you are" necessitates that you select an occupation that facilitates rather than obstructs your inner spirit and intellectual progress. You need to grasp that it will be impossible for you to transform your inner self into a better person if your choice of service or livelihood conflicts with this evolution. It is easier to believe that juggling balls of fire would cause no harm, than presuming that one's occupation will have no impact on what you become! Therefore, it may be necessary to alter your livelihood, if you long to be in harmony with your emerging self. Finding and combining significant work with a beneficial and meaningful mission will not only advance you along the way but will add greatly to the satisfaction of your daily activities. If you can merge a worthy purpose with a career or service that you truly love then you will achieve fulfillment, joy, and success.

Unearthing a livelihood and purpose that will set you on the right path ... Begin by determining if your current career or existing pursuit matches your core interests, personal beliefs, desirable values, economic needs, and the skills you have acquired. Ask yourself these sixteen questions, and then commit your answers to paper.

1. What topics do you primarily enjoy reading or learning about?
2. What are your favorite types of entertainment, hobbies, or activities?
3. What media themes do you find yourself tuning in to?
4. What issues do you like conversing about with friends or co-workers?
5. What type of volunteer endeavors do you favor?
6. Which contacts bring you the most joy? Which brings you the most anxiety?
7. What were your favorite jobs and preferred school subjects?
8. What would you like to see yourself doing 10 years from now?
9. What were the happiest moments in your life? What was your worst?
10. What would you eliminate out of your life if you could?
11. What comes to mind when you sleep and dream? What keeps you awake?
12. What if you become rich, what would you do with your wealth?
13. What would you like to be remembered for after you die?

14. What are your political, religious and social values?
15. What undertakings have brought you the most success?
16. What endeavors do you think you might do well at given the opportunity?

Examine your answers. Do you see a certain behavior or note specific trends in more than one aspect of your life? What information do you see repeated that seems to reveal a particular pattern? What appears to be your longest lasting interest?

Use this information to paint a self-portrait by completing these eight statements:

1) I am mainly interested in …
2) I believe most in …
3) I most value …
4) For a good life, I feel I need …
5) Commitments and responsibilities I must consider are …
6) To feel I have fulfilled my life's purpose I need to …
7) I can do this or these things well …
8) This choice conforms to the 4 Fundamental Laws and Desirable Traits …

If you are currently employed are you fulfilling these eight statements? If it does, you're probably in the right career. However, if you still find a nagging voice in your head than perhaps your current career is not satisfying your core desires and values, then it's time to find a better fit. Remember … one's future harvest is always shaped by the seeds sown today!

Reflect on whom and what you are and what it is you desire to be. … Therefore, before you begin or continue on with your current vocation, it would be wise to allow sufficient time to turn inward and discover what the answer to this key and crucial question would be. It will be necessary to look deep inside yourself, to search for your passion, and to review your strengths and talents. It is, within your heart and mind, where you will uncover your genuine desire and true calling. It is here where you will find the purpose and enthusiasm that will become the nucleus and essence of your life's passion.

To initiate this process, proceed to Step #5 below and learn more about meditation. Keep in mind … it will be difficult to discover your life's aspiration and correct path if you never take time to ascertain who you actually are. Meditation and reflection will help you find what moves your spirit, as well as aiding you to recall your past joys, achievements and successes. This time of introspection will assist you in searching your memory for those moments of being so caught up in something that you forget about everything else; that feeling of getting so lost in an activity that time had no importance and your day ended with a smile. Consider these things as well as those that will make a positive impact not only in your life but in the lives of others. This will guide you to a livelihood or pursuit that you will genuinely enjoy, one that will increase your fulfilment, and lead you to a life of supreme satisfaction.

Step #5 … _Meditation_

Meditation is a method of focusing one's mind and is a technique which has been practiced for hundreds of years. It originally was used to help individuals obtain a deeper understanding of the sacred and mystical forces of life. Though it is still used for that purpose today, it has evolved and is now more commonly used for relaxation, pursuing a healthier lifestyle, and for deep reflection and contemplation. Just about anyone can practice meditation. It's simple, inexpensive, and it generally doesn't require any special equipment. While best practiced in a calm and quiet setting, you can meditate just about anywhere — whether you're out for a stroll, sitting on a park bench, traveling on an airplane or taking a cruise on an ocean liner.

Below are a few methods of meditation you might consider utilizing:

- Guided meditation. As the name implies, this method is led by a guide or teacher. Sometimes called guided imagery or visualization, this type of meditation invites you to form mental images of places or situations you find relaxing. While utilizing this process, you are encouraged to use as many of your senses as possible, such as smells, sights, sounds, and textures. Tranquility or introspection is the goal.
- Mantra meditation. In this technique, you silently repeat a calming word, thought, or phrase to prevent distracting thoughts. When you do this form of contemplation your purpose is to achieve a deep state of relaxation, awareness, reflective practice and self-examination.
- Mindfulness meditation. This method of meditation is based on being mentally awake and having an increased awareness of living in the present moment. You focus on what you experience during contemplation, such as the flow of your breath. You are allowed to observe your thoughts but you let them pass without evaluation.
- Qi gong. (chee-Kung) This practice generally combines meditation, relaxation, physical movement, and breathing exercises as a way to restore and maintain poise and balance.
- Tai chi. (TIE-chee) This is a mild form of martial arts. In Tai chi, you perform a self-paced series of postures

or movements, in a slow graceful manner and is another method to maintain stability and body control.

- <u>Yoga</u>. In this method, you perform a series of postures and controlled breathing exercises to promote a more flexible body and a calm mind. As you move through poses that require balance and concentration, you're encouraged to focus less on your busy day and more on the moment.

Generally, for "at home" meditation sessions, it is best to set aside a special place and time, without distractions, for self-examination and general reflection. This should be performed preferably for 10 to 20 minutes daily, in pleasant surroundings, in solitude, or with like-minded people. The classic methods above, suggest that you initially focus entirely on one thing, such as your breathing, a movement, image or sound. This allows your mind to drift away from the daily demands and obligations that are constantly trying to fill and dominate your life. With repeated and determined effort, the goal of clearing your mind, "to think of nothing", does occur and the process of meditation begins to take on its special form and energy. The result being awareness, serenity, calmness, and eventually an opening up of yourself to new insights. Consider your meditation routines as an adventure into self-discovery. After all, do you want to live your life without truly knowing who you are ... or who you might aspire to become? If someone asks you who you are and what you do, will you simply give your name and toss out a job title? Does this express what and who you truly are? Are you the same person you were 10 years ago, 10 days ago, or 10 minutes ago? Will you be the same person you are now 10 minutes, 10 days, or 10 years from today? Meditation will gradually increase your awareness of who you are, what is important to you, and how you should be living your life.

This thought process has other values as well. In addition to greater mental, physical, and emotional energy you will experience enhanced calm and tranquility. You will begin to perceive the world as a more supportive and enjoyable place. Through focus and relaxation, you will begin to lead a more centered and happier existence. You may also find that your practiced meditation may be useful if you have a medical condition, especially one that may be related to stress. Life gives no guarantees but my understanding of the rewards of meditation indicates many possible positive and welcome outcomes.

Even though these advantages aren't definitive as of yet, meditation may be very helpful for such conditions as:

- Body aches, pains, and fatigue
- Anorexia and eating disorders
- Anxiety and nervousness syndromes
- Asthmatic breathing problems
- Mental depression
- Drug and alcohol abuse
- Stress and high blood pressure
- Sleeping disorders

Meditation should not be used as a replacement for traditional medical treatment, but it may be useful in addition to other forms of healing or therapy.

A final form of meditation that I would highly advocate for those engaging in the methodology of Neoteric Humanism is located in Part III of this book. The routine offered in this section is designed specifically to assist those wishing to reflect exclusively on Neoteric Humanism … this guide … or this philosophy's components. ... Life is a passage of stages, do not get lost in the daily routine, and neglect what is truly important. Alertness, reflection, wisdom, and action are of supreme importance. Ignorance, waste, and lost opportunities are the great offenders of our existence.

Step #6 ... _Assimilation_

How do you know when you have attained this stage? You will know when you find that you are naturally conducting yourself as the truly "new individual" you have become. This is the subtle juncture at which the pursuit has ceased to be simply a philosophy to be examined, studied, and contemplated. It is here, where you have completed your transformation and have started living your new way of life. You have accepted the methodology of this guide and the ideology of Neoteric Humanism. You recognize and abide by the demands of the Fundamental Laws, are living by the Desirable Traits, and progressing in the Pursuits A-P. You are making an ongoing effort to improve yourself, are being of service to others, and are participating in this philosophies suggested activities. The realities of daily living and your purpose are now clear. You understand your significant place in this world as well as your goals, mission, and responsibilities. Having reached this point, an individual is normally well qualified to request initiation into the Inner Circle*. When the prospective candidate feels they are ready, they should immediately attend to and pursue this admission. It is also possible that an existing Inner Circle member will seek them out and speak to them about this very meaningful and beneficial opportunity.

---

*   To enjoy all the rights, benefits, and privileges of Neoteric Humanism, one must be initiated into the Inner Circle. See page #158 "Benefits of being in the Inner Circle?"

I feel it is important to reaffirm, that the process and completion of assimilation does not mean one renounces their religion, national background, culture, or political standing. Assimilation of this nature involves combining and blending of parallel paths. Try to visualize this as a well-ordered symphony or perhaps a "musical melody". A musical melody of individuals, each with their unique special tone, yet organized into a pleasing and harmonious whole. This analogy holds true, as dissimilar members keep their unique cultural norms and traditions while at the same time sharing the common values, goals, and the mission of Neoteric Humanism. Hence, one individual may be Latino, an atheist, and a conservative yet another, Anglo Saxon, Jewish, and a liberal. If for example, you are Latino, you keep and enjoy your cultural identity. Black beans and rice, pasteles, and pork during the Christmas Holidays, ... turkey, mashed potatoes, and dressing at Thanksgiving. English spoken at work and Spanish when at home. The Fourth of July ... as well as Cinco de Mayo. Do you have to be Americanized or speak only English to be a Neoteric Humanist? Of course not! Do you have to like cheeseburgers more than sauerbraten or gyros? Absolutely not! ... So how do you conclude when one has achieved this step known as assimilation? It is accomplished when one has completed and is adhering to the lessons of this guide up to and including step #6.

Let me make one additional point regarding assimilation. As our society moves forward into this and the next century, it will inevitably become much more diverse both demographically and culturally. The reality of this change is that a variety of ethnic, political, and religious factions will make up an ever-increasing share of the population. This change is certain to bring with it a multiplicity of new challenges within the makeup of this philosophies gatherings as it grows. These challenges will require mutual understanding, acceptance, and shared respect for each other. In the long run, it is hoped, issues like these will be replaced by a diverse group of young people who will forge their own sense of identity; one that will include the populace as an amalgamation of many nationalities and cultures. ... Whatever this blend may be, they must feel free to embrace their customs and traditions, as well as the methodology, goals, and mission of Neoteric Humanism. (E Pluribus Unum)

Step #7... _Initiation_

Having completed the first six steps of this guide, the act of initiation consummates a very important transition for the individual. Having been found suitable and worthy to join, initiation formally declares the initiate to be an official member of the Inner Circle. This person has completed the required pledges and commitments and has willingly accepted the Inner Circle obligations. The new initiate has been accepted and bestowed with all the advantages and privileges of the Neoteric Humanist fellowship. He or she has passed all challenges to accomplish this quest and is ready to experience the full advantages of belonging to the Inner Circle. ... Having become a formal Inner Circle member this individual will begin to experience feelings of completeness, safety, contentment and well-being. The initiate has officially become a valuable, important, and constructive enabler of a much larger mission. One meant to enrich, not only their life, but that of their family, their community and the world.

At this point, an inquisitive mind might ask ... what happens during initiation? What are the pledges, obligations, and responsibilities one gives and commits to? What are the advantages one can expect to receive? ... Becoming part of the "Inner Circle" is necessary if he or she is to take full advantage of this philosophy and its rewards. Once one has committed themselves to complete the steps of this guide, it is only a matter of time before initiation and full admittance become inevitable. This key stage of initiation allows an individual to join with others at the very core and heart of the association. It is here that a person becomes much more than just an occasional guest participating in organized activities, classes, and events. Initiation is the moment at which the individual, who has fully adopted the steps of this guide, is now ready to merge with the like-minded and committed Inner Circle. It is at the conclusion of this ceremony that one is officially and publicly welcomed as a recognized member of this central hub. The "new you" has formally arrived and has merged with the nucleus and mainstay of the Neoteric Humanist community. It has been firmly established that the initiate is qualified, suitable, and has been presented with the most sought after rights and privileges that the Neoteric Humanist fellowship can offer.

To obtain these rights and privileges, it is necessary for the prospective member to make commitments, vows and to take on specific obligations and responsibilities. While making these dedications, the future member will, in turn, be receiving similar promises from those of the Inner Circle as they take on obligations and responsibilities to the inductee. The particulars of these pledges are openly revealed later in this book so that the new initiate fully understands and becomes familiar with the oaths and promises involved. The ritual, in and of itself, is not a spiritual, mystical, or religious experience. It is treated, however, as a very serious occasion and solemn affair. This rite of passage will utilize special symbols, terms, and actions that are intended to illuminate an idea or concept related to the philosophy of Neoteric Humanism. The precise details of these vows, obligations, responsibilities, and advantages are disclosed and reviewed by all the participants several days prior to the actual ceremony. ... See page #149 "The Initiation Ceremony" for details.

Step #8 ... *Motivation*

Feeling alone? Worried about what others will think? No one is around to help encourage you as you proceed? Will you still persist? Will you be able to stay focused? Will you remain bold and steadfast in adhering to this guide and its principles when nobody around you cares? ... If you are to advance along this path ... you must learn to motivate and encourage yourself. If you keep waiting for someone else ... you will never set yourself free ... to become who you yearn to be.

Staying motivated is difficult ... so keep in mind these eight psychological issues you should acknowledge regarding your **ATTITUDE:**

1) Accept that your loved ones may not share your dreams or this philosophy.
2) Tantrums and complaining will get you nowhere if your family and friends show no interest.
3) Throwing a "Self-Pity" party won't work. Nobody wants to attend them anyway.
4) Imagining and embracing your future can be difficult. It's up to you to do it with enjoyment, enthusiasm, and with confidence.
5) Tranquility knowing the principled legacy you will leave behind. Keep these positive thoughts forefront and constantly in your mind.
6) Utilizing and practicing a habit of "Self-Talk" will help you advance. ... You must talk it, act it, and live it!
7) Developing an environment and an ambiance that motivates you is vital.

8) **E**ffective outcomes will only come from good mental habits and physical routines!

You must comprehend that to improve your life you must change your behavior. You cannot change your behavior until you alter and redefine your life's vision. You will not alter your life's vision until you become irritated and unhappy with your present situation. This unsatisfactory situation is what will fuel your motivation, it is what will power your focus, it is what will influence what you pursue, it is what will determine the life vision you believe is worthy of your effort. What you do daily from this day onward will create the future you want … or the future you dread.

> *"You cannot control what happens to you, but you can control your **attitude** toward what happens to you, and in that, you will be mastering change rather than allowing it to master you."*
>
> Brian Tracy

Everything is difficult at first. Refuse to stay in your comfort zone. Many will fail because they won't make necessary changes. They weaken and don't change jobs, towns, or relationships. They never have the courage to take on the challenge. One must be willing to deal with some discomfort if they are to rise to a new level in their lives. Do not be the one who breaks their focus. Do not be the one who wastes valuable time and energy. Do not be someone that lets life pass them by. Remember … if it's not challenging you … it is not changing you! As stated by Mike Murdock … *"When you want something you have never had, you have to do something you have never done."*

"Letting go is the willingness to change your beliefs in order to bring more peace and joy into your life instead of holding onto beliefs that bring pain and suffering…"
                                                    Hal Tipper

Beyond this … it is critical for Neoteric Humanism to expand its membership in a swift and ongoing manner. Participation and growth are essential as this philosophy requires a broad support group if it is to survive and prosper.

It is imperative, that this expansion continues rapidly and steadily so that it will eventually reach a self-sustaining level. Members must exhibit enthusiasm, knowledge, approachability, and persistence if prospective new affiliates are to become involved and ultimately a supporter of this philosophy. I find the following quote, by Peter Singer, especially inspiring to keep in mind as one moves forward:

"By working to improve the world, one thing is certain: you will find plenty of worthwhile things to do. You will not be bored, or lack fulfillment in your life. Most important of all, you will know that you have not lived and died for nothing because you will have become part of the great tradition of those who have responded to the amount of pain and suffering in the universe by trying to make the world a better place."

With the above quote in mind, if one is going to make the world a better place they will need the help of others. One should always be alert for opportunities to add new members and building closer relationships. As with all things, this philosophy will either grow or fade away. It is a fact that, other than change itself, there is no sustainable status quo. The nature of life itself is all about transformation into something else. Growing never means staying the same. Living, without growing and changing, is simply disappearing in small stages. Even with death, there is change through collapse and a return to the earth. On the other hand, when something is alive, robust and growing, it gains strength and vigor. Imagine, if you would, a Giant Redwood Tree … with one of its seeds gently falling down into the fertile earth. The following spring, with the warmth of the sun, it pushes out through the soil and begins reaching toward the sky. It grows taller and more powerful creating longer branches and more leaves with each passing year. The larger the tree grows, the more it is able to sustain itself. Its limbs get thicker and continue rising upward towards the nourishing rays of sunlight. It is nature's way, and a fact of life, that trees, and all living things must change and grow. To deny or inhibit growth is to open the door to the beginning of its end. Each season, the tree must conquer more space, gain greater height, generate fresh cones, and push its roots deeper into the soil. Such will be the future of Neoteric Humanism as well. It needs to grow and ever increase its adherents and participants. Just as the tree becomes stronger and more durable as it grows larger, so will this philosophy flourish and become more robust by the continuous enthusiastic motivation exhibited by its members.

It would be easy to daydream and imagine Neoteric Humanism as it might grow to be, but to actually give reality to that dream; one requires a well thought out plan of action. How should one go about this? The way to engage the community, families, and friends, is not by trying to lecture or recruit them. That kind of approach typically puts people on the defensive and closes their minds to fresh ideas. It is much better to simply be a purveyor of information and then let them decide to investigate it on their own terms. When it is pursued because of personal choice and interest, they will be more receptive and open to new concepts and viewpoints. Once they understand how participation will help them and their families, there is a greater probability they will be persuaded to become members. Once again … one should regard this undertaking as an effort to simply educate and enlighten those around them. This can best be accomplished by personal example, success stories, publicity, involvement in the community, invitations to activities, and by one's individual enthusiasm. If they cannot or do not appreciate its value in this way, then perhaps they are not good candidates to pursue? To assist in this challenge, commit to memory the positive attributes that this philosophy advances.

This philosophy offers many worthwhile **<u>BENEFITS</u>** to an individual by:

- <u>B</u>ecoming more culturally aware and involved in the lives of others.
- <u>E</u>ngaging and promoting art, nature, virtue and kindness in our world.
- <u>N</u>oticeably growing stronger, healthier, and more physically fit.
- <u>E</u>nhancing the human condition and joining others with a similar mission.
- <u>F</u>orming meaningful and close family, friendship, and community ties.
- <u>I</u>nwardly achieving greater expertise, knowledge, wisdom, and contentment.
- <u>T</u>eaming with others for mutual support and protection in times of hardship.
- <u>S</u>ocially becoming more valued and appreciated by those around you.

Beyond affirmative and meaningful information and the sharing of positive activities and events, there are several ways to encourage a prospective member and express to them that they are welcome and wanted. Let's assume a visitor accepts an invitation to an association event. They should be:

- greeted warmly and with a genuine smile.
- kindly introduced to others who are there.
- politely escorted to where they need to go and provided with answers on any questions they may have.
- presented with a friendly host to look after them and their needs during their visit. One who will advise them where restrooms, snacks, drinks, comfortable chairs or other facilities may be located.

All an individual can do is be pleasant and attempt to enlighten the prospects of this philosophy's mission and goals. One can only try to lead them to the welcoming spring water flowing with the hopes and aspirations of this undertaking. However, it will be entirely their choice … and their decision … to fill their cup … and partake in it.

Now is the time to become an **ASCENDER:** A person that …

Accepts this guide as an effective means for improving oneself and *Acknowledges* this truth by working to better themselves and improving our world.

Seeks continuous *Education* in knowledge, wisdom, abilities, and skills.

Creates a superior *Character* and employs it to ultimately illuminate and define who they are as an individual.

Engages in a suitable and un-soiled *Occupation* for their livelihood or career.

Nourishes their mind with *Meditation* which will lead to greater understanding, performance, and well-being.

Dedicates themselves to do all things necessary to fully integrate and *Assimilate* into a better person and openly helps others to do so as well.

Employs and adheres to all the steps necessary to attain *Initiation* into the Inner Circle so they may fully profit from this philosophy.

Recognizes and relies on *Motivation* to reach their individual endeavors and the fulfillment of the mission aspired to in this philosophy.

> *"I long to accomplish a great and noble task, but it is my chief duty to accomplish humble tasks as though they were great and noble. The world is moved along, not only by the mighty shoves of its heroes but also by the aggregate of the tiny pushes of each honest worker."*
>
> Helen Keller

If you aspire to become an <u>ASCENDER</u> *it's important to stay on the right path to achieve the results you desire. This can be accomplished to a large degree by undertaking the Sixteen Pursuits A-P and filling your "***Personal Mindset Well***" with their goals, ideals and values.*

The Pursuits A-P

As an ASCENDER, I will …

(1) A̲c̲t̲ ̲w̲i̲t̲h̲ ̲a̲b̲u̲n̲d̲a̲n̲t̲ ̲l̲o̲v̲e̲ ̲a̲n̲d̲ ̲k̲i̲n̲d̲n̲e̲s̲s̲.̲ ̲I̲ ̲w̲i̲l̲l̲ ̲t̲r̲a̲n̲s̲f̲o̲r̲m̲ ̲m̲y̲ i̲n̲n̲e̲r̲ ̲n̲a̲t̲u̲r̲e̲ ̲i̲n̲t̲o̲ ̲a̲ ̲b̲e̲n̲e̲v̲o̲l̲e̲n̲t̲ ̲a̲n̲d̲ ̲c̲o̲p̲i̲o̲u̲s̲ ̲s̲p̲i̲r̲i̲t̲.̲

Abundant Love and Kindness is the inner character and disposition we hope to achieve. However, this should not be confused with those who advocate u̲n̲c̲o̲n̲d̲i̲t̲i̲o̲n̲a̲l̲ love and kindness. This often spoken appeal to unreserved support, devotion and dedication can be very difficult to achieve and even harmful under many circumstances. Unconditional love and kindness as it is commonly known and professed, is problematic, if not impossible to attain. To begin with, those using this term demonstrate an absence of understanding of what this expression truly means. When we think of unconditional love and kindness, we generally conjure up impressions of a mother and fathers love say for their child, or perhaps the love of a brother or sister. While this may be true for most families it is usually predicated and observed by only those with no outstanding issues, quarrels or conflicts. When using the terms abundant love and kindness, as stated above, I am referring to the love and kindness we show in most every-day situations when caring for the good cheer and well-being of another person. However, this action of doing a good deed or act from one individual to other does not mean it should be unconditional. The drawback with unconditional love and kindness is that it can break down under numerous situations or conditions. As much as you might truly love and care for a person who is also a liar, cheater, physical or mental abuser, or person with alcohol or drug problems, your providing unconditional love and kindness, isn't healthy or beneficial for you or the person you are trying to help. Therefore, when I refer to displaying an abundance of love and kindness what I want to articulate needs to be expanded on. When one provides love and kindness, under these circumstances, there must be given in return, mutual respect and redeemable action, not simply an acceptance of "you must put up with me, my activities and behavior, no matter what I do." Understand, that giving an abundance of love and kindness doesn't mean always giving people what they want or always accepting what they do, particularly when done at your expense, pain or suffering.

In these situations, Abundant Love and Kindness means this:

1) Being aware and conscious of the needs of other people, while at the same time establishing limits and boundaries.
2) Doing your best to fulfill these needs only when you are able to do so without causing harm or distress to yourself or others.
3) Exercising open communication by letting other people know your sentiments and position so that together you can work out the best outcome for all involved.
4) Sharing power. No one single person should be able to do and get everything they want at any time they want for this will lead to anger and embitterment by others.

Live an Abundant and Kind Life by:

1) Giving in a way that is fair, big-hearted and helps the most people.
2) Smiling and being open with a "yes I can and will do" attitude and follow through.

3) Being generous with your time, knowledge, skills and resources.

4) Always looking for opportunities to help or be of service to others and building new and closer relationships.

"The richest man is he who lives simply but has an abundance of love and kindness to give away."

Debasish Mridha

(2) **B**ring the earth's natural beauty into this world and maintain and care for all things of value. Where Nature and Industry must co-exist, preservation, protection and reclamation will be my focal point.

Having the desire to beautify the world and safeguard nature can certainly feel like an overwhelming undertaking. However, there are actions that you as an individual can do to make an impact. Begin by looking at your personal household and determine ways to introduce nature, reduce waste, and begin making sensible and local marketing choices. Then expand these efforts outward by finding opportunities in your local neighborhood and community. This expansion can be maximized by educating people with e-mails, phone calls, and fliers of area beautification projects and eco-friendly events among your friends and family. Consider starting or joining with other nature-loving advocates promoting policies that protect the environment and rebuild and restore those areas, centers and parks we visit and reside in with family and friends.

Below are eight community ideas for preserving and safeguarding nature:

(1) Promote parks and green zones. Champion well thought out green zones in your community to enhance

public places. Planting trees, shrubs, and flowerbeds can change a dull or unsightly space into a flourishing and friendly retreat. Be mindful that there must also be a maintenance program formed as part of this overall plan. This will keep your initial efforts looking good and something all can enjoy for years to come.

(2) <u>Recycle</u>. If your neighborhood has a recycling program ... do your part and participate. Recycling saves resources and reduces the amount of waste going into our landfills. Take some time and research which parts of your community do not have recycling containers available. If your community does not have a recycling plan, be the initiator and take steps to begin one.

(3) <u>Create a neighborhood swap</u>. Some people grow tasty vegetables; others grow delicious fruits, beautiful flowers, or fashion tempting arts and crafts. This gathering permits the exchange of foodstuffs and goods within a localized area perhaps eliminating a trip to the grocery store or a retail outlet. A swap of this sort also allows opportunities to barter one thing for another on items we may otherwise want to throw away. You will find you are not only doing a good thing for mother-nature but you may also develop new friendships and find partners with similar aspirations.

(4) <u>Conserve energy</u>. Use weather stripping and caulking on all windows and doors. Insulate well your attics and floors. Purchase and maintain appliances that are energy-efficient. Use a programmable thermostat and light timer to conserve energy when you're less active. Use natural lighting whenever possible, and consider installing skylights in darker areas of the house. Switch to energy-efficient lightbulbs. Be aware that chargers

for your electronic devices are constant energy users, even when your device is unplugged.

(5) <u>Think through your ways of transportation</u>. Before you fly, consider driving. If you can drive, consider carpooling or taking a train, bus, biking, or walking. If you must fly, try to fly non-stop, as this will use less fuel. Consider walking anyplace less than a mile away. Try biking to nearby destinations. Look into trying to work by telecommuting.

(6) <u>Utilize native trees, bushes, and flowers</u>. When you use plants that are native to your area, you'll be working with the local ecology rather than against it. Native plants help with water conservation because they require less to perhaps even no irrigation. Furthermore, localized diverse plantings that bloom for multiple seasons will help support your local bee and bird populations. Avoid using commercial pesticides.

(7) <u>Participate in a community cleanup</u>. Trash is not only an eyesore to the public; it often damages or devastates the natural home sites and habitats of birds, fish, and other creatures. Help out by joining with others, or start a local group yourself, and begin cleanup events in your community.

(8) <u>Consider how you shop for groceries</u>. Can you buy in bulk and reduce the amount of packaged goods you may eventually throw away. Make an effort to reduce your use of plastics and disposable convenience types of products.

Taking good care of things of value may feel like a challenge. This is particularly the case if an individual is dealing with issues of low self-esteem. Taking a stand to value your life and your things are possible even if difficult to do at first.

One way to begin this process is to take good care of your sur-rounding habitat. Look after and maintain your abode so that it's clean and orderly. Create an environment for yourself so that you're dwelling feels welcoming, and warm. Make it a place that exemplifies who you are and all that you value. This might be particularly important if you've ever experienced homelessness. Which-ever is the case, you need to care for it in such a way that it exemplifies the care that you want to give to yourself. Even though sometimes it might be difficult to care for ourselves, we can begin by caring for what surrounds us. Do you play a musical instrument? Are you an artist? Do you collect butterflies or coins? Are you an avid reader? Looking after your personal belongings with care can be a great les-son in learning how to care for yourself and others. It's easy to let things age, to ignore the fact that they're getting soiled, dirty, or broken. It's easy to just accept that that's the way it is. However, there's a certain feeling that you can bring to your belongings that will also bring positivism and order to your life. … It's not always easy to do something we've never done or felt before. But that's never stopped people from achieving these things in the past. Learn to love and care for yourself, start with small steps … learn how to care for and value your surroundings, personal belongings, and relationships.

"Gardens are not made by singing 'Oh, how beautiful,' and sitting in the shade."

Rudyard Kipling

"Clearing clutter—be it physical, mental, emotional, or spiritual—brings about ease and inspires a sense of peace, calm, and tranquility."

Laurie Buchanan, PhD

(3) <u>Create a home and mobile emergency kit and keep a 4 month supply of food and provisions within my abode.</u>
    Learn basic first aid and CPR. Check with local organizations that offer knowledge and training on essential emergency treatment and vital medical skills. Remember, even limited knowledge and practice could mean the difference between life and death if someone is injured or ill. Always keep a first aid kit handy at home, in your vehicle, and where you work.
    Therefore, create an emergency kit and practice "First Aid" skills. Then, should a safety or dangerous emergency arise set in motion …

HELP:

<u>H</u>azard – Make sure you are not putting yourself and others in danger.

<u>E</u>nlist – Call out for help and assistance. Call 911 or designate someone nearby to do so.

<u>L</u>ook and listen - Is the distressed person conscious? Examine for breathing, beating, and blood. Check for a drug, alcohol, poison, or allergy connection?

<u>P</u>erform – Should the person be choking, implement the Heimlich maneuver. If the person's airway is clear of obstructions and they are not breathing or their heart has stopped beating employ CPR or the use of a defibrillator? If bleeding is observed, apply pressure and wound bandages as needed to reduce blood loss.

Keeping a "First Aid" kit on hand and learning First Aid Skills.
It is vital to have a well-organized, fully stocked, and readily available first aid kit accessible at all times. This kit should contain items and supplies suitable to manage a variety of emergencies, depending on the location or activity.

Four reasons why learning "First Aid" is important?

- Learning "First Aid" enhances the public's well-being: Knowledge and training in first aid creates a feeling of reassurance and security between individuals. Having this valuable skill, hands-on experience, emphasis on prevention and a focus on preparedness makes the public, families, and friends feel safe, knowledgeable and protected thereby reducing the number of and severity of accidents.
- Learning "First Aid" will save lives: An individual who has been trained on how to handle medical emergencies is in a position to offer immediate action and a skilled response rather than waiting for help to arrive. It's also simple common sense that a trained and well-informed person is more steadfast, self-assured, and has more self-control when placed in stressful circumstances.
- Learning "First Aid" improves the likelihood of less pain and suffering. A qualified first aid responder, who is active on the scene, can relieve or lessen the discomfort by implementing established calming and medical techniques. Waiting for an ambulance or EMT takes time and a knowledgeable first aid responder can make use of that time to make the patient as comfortable and pain-free as possible.

- **Learning "First Aid" can stop events going from bad to worse.** An experienced responder can supply skilled practices that will help keep the patient's injury or illness from worsening while medical assistance is on the way. Many situations could arise that would call for immediate action in which life or death will be determined in a matter of minutes. Being trained to provide proficient first aid is useful not only to oneself, one's family and community but also society as a whole.

Prepare yourself and your family for adversity:

As you and your family may not be together in one location when a calamity hits, it is vital to have a plan in place beforehand. It is also a good idea to have a preloaded and ready emergency supply kit that contains the essential components you may need in a crisis. Since there are numerous types of calamities, such as fires, river overflows, economic crises, biochemical dumps, terrorist threats, or unexpected explosions, the planning you do now will be extremely valuable should any of these unforeseen misfortunes assault your family, home or neighborhood. An important piece in your initial planning and preparation should also involve your locating and being networked into dependable forewarning organizations and alarm systems. Taking time to set up a family communication arrangement should be high on your list as well. Allow an evening once a year to get together with household members and take into consideration both family and pet needs. Determine what additional training, equipment, and supplies are needed or desired. During this annual get together, it would be a good occasion likewise to check on current school and workplace plans so everyone knows how to best communicate with each other should an emergency arise. … Then … practice … regular practice can enhance reaction time and limit anxiety and fear in a genuine crisis.

Organize a mobile emergency backpack, which is simply a collection of basic items you may need in the event of a crisis that involves immediate movement. Prepare your emergency pack well in advance of a calamity so you will be able to survive without assistance for a bare minimum of 3 days. Both the Department of Homeland Security and FEMA offer excellent instructions on how to organize and what to include in your pack. Review their suggestions and then modify them to meet the individual needs of you, your family, and your pets.

In addition to having a short term emergency plan, you should also begin storing provisions and add-ons for a prolonged situation. Your objective should be a 4-month strategy of survival for your entire family including any pets. This is a project that you can build slowly as your finances allow and should be based on canned and well preserved food you already eat regularly. When you make your normal food supply purchases, buy larger quantities, and store the excess in a dry cool area. Rotate this extra food that is stored away based on a first in first out basis and build on it until you have an adequate supply. It's wise to choose foods you use all the time as you will not only be keeping your stock fresh but you will be using food that you would have eaten anyway. Avoid the retailers who deal in bags of commodity items that you are unfamiliar with, may be difficult to use and offer little in the morale-boosting department. A good rule of thumb to stick to in the beginning is concentrating more of your effort on canned foods that don't require cooking, water, or special preparation.

Here are eight good ideas to get you started. … How to be **PREPARED**:

- **P**roactively begin by building your supplies based on your family's everyday needs and preferences. Choose foods that they will not only enjoy but which are also high in calories and nutrition. … Be sure to include a manual can opener.
- **R**etain all supplies, food, and water in a safe and accessible location.
- **E**stablish a system for each food and drink category by rotating supplies, first in … first out, to keep stored food as fresh as possible.
- **P**rocure powdered or dry juices, milk, and soup as all are great to have on hand for long term storage, but remember they will necessitate stockpiling considerably more water. Make sure to include items that may be bartered, such as cash, silver, gold, alcohol or fuel.
- **A**llow a mixture of comfort foods, such as candy, cookies, instant coffee, hot chocolate, tea bags, and high-energy foods, such as peanut butter, jelly, crackers, granola bars, nuts, and dried fruits. Don't forget condiments: Salt, pepper, sugar, spices, etc. , as well as family personal products that may be needed over a long period of time.
- **R**emember food for infants, elderly persons, or persons on special diets. Include any medications that may be needed daily.
- **E**quip your provisions with a "Coleman" like cooking stove, fuel, waterproof matches, pots, pans, dishes, cooking utensils, flatware and clean up supplies. Don't forget warm and waterproof clothes, work boots, gloves, and tools you may need. Consider

adding at least one adult hazmat suit, also known as a decontamination suit. This is a piece of personal protective equipment that consists of an impermeable whole-body garment worn as protection against hazardous materials in a toxic environment.

• Download DHS and FEMA emergency broadcast information on your telephone, computer, and/or listen to your radio to understand what is currently happening.

When a family prepares in advance for a crisis you gain two important things, peace of mind and independence. Once you are no longer dependent on others for shelter, food, water, and heat you will sleep much better because you know your family is safe and will survive. To top it off, you are now in a position to help and assist your friends and neighbors as well. … That's what makes preparedness so essential!

> *"It is an eternal obligation toward the human being not to let him suffer when one has a chance of coming to his assistance."*
>
> Simone Weil

(4) Develop intimate ties with good family and friends.

When all is tallied, it is good family and friends who are the true source of our security and joyfulness. When you develop strong relationships with these, you have people who always will care for and support you. You know they will always be there for you no matter what, just as you would be for them. It is a mutual bond formed so each can count on the other and each can be trusted with anything. When you are surrounded by good family and friends, your world is a better place.

Having good people in your life is important because human beings are social creatures and need one another's contact and interaction. We need others for support and comfort, just as we would comfort and support them in return. Whether you are making a career change, a move to a new city or just getting over a difficult breakup, it's much easier when you have your good family and friends there to help you. These are people who will boost your self-worth and self-confidence no matter what situation may arise. They will provide you with a sense of protection and security because you realize that they are going to stand by you regardless of what you are going through.

These individuals are very important because they love and understand you. Human beings have emotional needs, the fulfillment of which is essential for mental well-being and happiness. Everyone needs love, understanding, and a feeling of belonging. These are people who understand you inside and out and know what you've been through during your life. They provide you with enduring friendship, ongoing enjoyment, and the warmth of fitting in. These same good family members and friends will also provide you with strong moral values which will give you the strength to avoid doing something that may be unethical or illegal through peer pressure. Therefore, if you possess a strong perception of what is right and wrong due to the values you have been raised on and/or associated with, you are less likely to go along with any bad influences in your life.

Your retaining good family and friends furnish your life with a solid foundation. Regardless of where you move to, or are making changes in your life, you can feel confident that someone always has an open door for you. You are never left abandoned out in the cold because you know someone always cares for you and has your back.

Principled family and friends play an important role in raising your children. These wholesome and nourishing individuals can assist you in raising a healthy, honest, and ethical child. It won't be some unknown persons whom you hope are providing the proper care and nourishment for your child; you will have people you trust and who will love and protect your child. If you find you have to deal with a personal issue or you come down with an illness, family and friends will be there with open arms. Caring for and raising children can be hard, tiring, and complicated; having trusted, loving and reliable allies on hand will greatly ease your mind.

Having close ties with good family and friends that you can discuss things with helps you make better decisions. You will have a trusted source you can rely on for honest opinions and who may have valuable wisdom from past experiences. Making decisions on important or critical issues can be difficult, and you may feel confused about which way to proceed. Having someone available to talk to and get their input on will greatly help you to choose the best alternative or make the right decision. The advantage of having these valuable people in your life are numerous and important and will help you to achieve all of your dreams and goals.

(5) Educate myself and support the best schooling possible for future generations. I will first Generalize my skills and knowledge then I will Specialize and perfect my expertise in an innocuous occupation. I will promote Meritocracy.

A life of learning and continuing education can improve our appreciation and perception of the world around us, present us with further and better opportunities and enhance our quality of being. It can heighten our self-assurance and certainty; make us more open to changes and our approach to solving problems. It can help us create a more satisfying life, as well as re-evaluating our way of thinking and viewpoints … plus it can also just be … very enjoyable.

There are two principal reasons for continuing your education: 1) personal growth and 2) professional opportunity. One does not necessarily eliminate the other as they are often interconnected and directly impact each other.

Education for Personal Growth:

There does not need to be a precise purpose for continuing one's education since knowledge for the sake of understanding can be a very satisfying undertaking. There are many reasons why an individual would want to pursue personal growth:

- You may want to expand your knowledge or skills regarding a special interest or activity that you find pleasurable.
- You may want to acquire a completely new skill that will improve your ability or handiness. For instance, perhaps you want to gain some electrical or plumbing expertise.
- You may want to investigate the history of China or indications of child Autism.
- You may elect to go back to college simply because you enjoy a certain subject and desire to become more knowledgeable on the topic.

Education for Professional Opportunity:

Opportunities in our professional life are directly linked to our knowledge and ability to do the job. Continuing education not only keeps one current with existing trends but opens the door to new and possibly better employment prospects. Make a note, however, that being knowledgeable alone is not necessarily the key to getting the particular job you are seeking.

Employers are looking for more, such as having good people skills, the ability to be part of a team, the desire to learn, your contribution to the bottom line, follow through on projects, your stability, and the likelihood of staying with the company.

If you are currently unemployed then use this time to your advantage. Continuing education can pay-off with fresh career options that might not otherwise have surfaced.

If you are currently employed, make time for company-sponsored courses, updates or training events and constantly work on your professional knowledge and skills as you will not only become better at what you do but more valuable to your current or future employer. An individual who can offer more expertise will be of more importance and worth not just to their employers but also to clients. Know-how and skill are often looked upon by companies as the fundamental characteristics of a good leader and can lead to roles as such. Of course, from strictly a monetary perspective, the more highly skilled and knowledgeable a worker is to a company the greater are the opportunities for promotions, bonuses, and salary increases. ... Keep in mind that you'll do much better and contribute more to the world as a specialist. Recall the words of Adam Smith, *"There are three things that make us more prosperous: the freedom to pursue our own self-interest; specialization and freedom of trade."*

> *"Rising living standards - depend first on specialization: on letting people concentrate on what they do best and trade with others who specialize in other things."*
>
> Virginia Postrel

(6) Follow both an active and prudent lifestyle as well as a healthy diet. In healthcare, I will stress personal choice in my medical services yet will also espouse a government sponsored public safety net for those less fortunate.

Health, Fitness, and Well-Being: The combination of routine physical fitness, living a wholesome lifestyle, and maintaining a hearty nutritional plan and the effects they will have on your well-being are nearly impossible to separate from each other. The persistent danger of numerous health issues caused by a poor diet, flawed personal choices, and lack of regular exercise is something everyone should be very conscious of. Understanding this, if one wishes to achieve a healthy, safe, and physically fit life it will be necessary to make significant adjustments to your daily life and in the everyday choices, you make. With the exception of some important lifestyle changes, these adjustments do not have to be extreme to start with, and they should be things you normally would enjoy and look forward to doing. The essential conclusions here ... is your determination and resolve to improve your lifestyle choices, health and fitness, and well-being on a regular basis ... even if it's a little bit at a time. Just bear in mind ... sooner is better than later!

Start by allowing some time to review your current diet and adjust it to the parameters of your daily recommended nutritional needs. Do your research as dietary requirements for people of different ages, sexes, and activity levels vary from one person to the next. As a rule of thumb, a 2,000-calorie diet and no more than 65 grams of fat per day is the normal standard. Bearing this in mind, taking in fewer calories, and losing some weight will make being active easier, and will tend to motivate you to work even harder on attaining good health. Consider altering your diet by consuming whole, unprocessed food for a good balance of vitamins and minerals, fiber, and other essentialn nutrients and avoid excess sugar and unhealthy fats.

Regardless if you're attempting to lose weight, sustain weight, or just want to live a healthier lifestyle, here are four nutritional tips that can help you maximize your health, fight disease and improve your well-being.

* Fill your nutritional regime with Antioxidants: Antioxidants can be found in many colorful fruits and vegetables and protect the body from the damage that can be caused by free radicals within our body's cells.
* Load yourself with Vitamins and Minerals: Vitamins and minerals can be found in whole grains, low-fat dairy, lean meats, fruits, and vegetables and help provide basic organ function, energy, and vitality.
* Control Serving Sizes: Rather than eating large meals three times a day, try grazing on multiple smaller and healthier meals. It will keep you satisfied throughout the day and help maintain your energy levels.
* Substitute Unhealthy fats with Healthy fats: Your body needs some healthy fat for peak energy and function. Choose unsaturated fats and foods with key fatty acids, like Omega-3 and Omega-6, that provide heart health and joint lubricating properties.

Although healthy eating habits are crucial for optimizing nutrition for overall wellness, consistent physical exercise is an extremely important component. Exercise not only strengthens the body and helps you release toxins, but it also facilitates nutrient metabolism and allows your body the opportunity to maximize the impact of all those healthy nutrients you give it. ... There are several key factors associated with improving physical fitness and mental well-being. These four primary and essential actions and components are:

(1) Stretching: Taking time to stretch your body will increase your overall flexibility.

(2) Cardiovascular/Aerobic Conditioning: Beneficial aerobic activities are exercises that raise your heart rate and maintain that level for a minimum of 20 minutes.

(3) Strength and Weight Training: This helps you burn more calories and build up muscles thus reducing the risk of a fall or injury.

(4) Physical and Mental Relaxation: Allowing time for physical and mental rest is crucial to give the mind and body time to recuperate and work efficiently.

A well thought out health and fitness plan will take several important factors into account. It should involve regimented exercise, diet, and nutrition, as well as time for mental and physical rest. For most people who generally get very little exercise, adding more activity to their lives can begin by simply walking more. Others might take up a new activity such as Karate, Judo, Swimming, Biking, Tai Chi, Dancing, or Hiking. Those who already have a pastime such as golf may add more active elements to it, such as forgoing the use of a golf cart. The important thing is to eat right and get moving!

Make it part of your routine to see your doctor on an annual basis and make sure you are current with all your vaccinations. Vaccines help protect you from serious infectious diseases throughout your life — from the time you are born, through adulthood, and finally into old age. Vaccine schedules are organized by age. These begin with infants and young children, then preteens and teens, continued by adults and senior citizens. Some people who are at an increased risk for certain diseases may need additional inoculations or treatments. For example: Gay or bisexual individuals, health care workers, military personnel, people with health conditions, those that travel, and people who inject illicit drugs. To prevent getting a sexually transmitted disease, or STD, always avoid sex with anyone who has genital sores, a rash, discharge, or other symptoms. The only time unprotected sex is safe is if you and your partner have sex only with each other, and if it's been at least six months since you each tested negative for STDs. Otherwise, you should: Use latex condoms every time you have sex. Avoid sharing hot tubs, baths, towels, or underclothing. Get a vaccination for hepatitis B and keep in mind that people who are drunk or on drugs often fail to have safe sex. Lastly … consider postponing or not having sex. Remember; some diseases are not yet curable and if you become infected will be a challenge for the rest of your life. Vaccines for preventable ailments and sickness as well as being cautious with your personal life choices will lead to a happier life._

(7) Greet failure with a renewed dedication to succeed.

Failure is unavoidable. Sometime in your life, it's guaranteed that you will fail at something. So, "Join the club" … everyone has failed at one time or another and so will you! In fact, if you read the history of famous people such as Bill Gates, Henry Ford and Thomas Edison you'll find that they, too, failed and failed over and over again. Nevertheless, it was just such failures that produced the inspiring stories of these same individuals who struggled yet never gave up. They labored relentless and finally they fulfilled their dreams and triumphed!   Think of failure as the breeding ground for your future success. Failure openly displays that something needs improvement or change … that you've made an error or have done a process incorrectly. This way, the next time you come across the same or a similar problem, you'll know what to do or how to handle it better. Dealing with failure in such a manner will make you stronger since you know that when you hit future obstacles, as you certainly will, you can and will overcome them. This is how you should respond to failure when it is encountered. It shouldn't defeat or crush you. It should be deemed a "wake-up call" to make necessary adjustments. You then proceed forward with even more determination to achieve your purpose or goal.

Four lessons to be learned from failure: The first valuable lesson that you will gain … is the actual **experience** itself. Failure, as much as it hurts, is an important fact of life. Failure is one of life's great teachers; it forces a reevaluation of ourselves and who we think we are. Through our suffering we become more human knowing that we ourselves are not perfect. This understanding makes us more capable of compassion, empathy, and kindness, as well as creating within us the fortitude and courage to accomplish great things. The experience forces us to reflect on the focus of our life and our priorities, in the process hopefully transforming and improving our future-selves into better individuals.

The 2nd lesson we gain is **knowledge.** Failure brings with it important firsthand knowledge and discovery. That knowledge can be employed in a future attempt to conquer the very failure that caused so much trouble or pain in the first place. The knowledge gained from past failures is actually essential for potential victory. When Thomas Edison failed nearly 10,000 times to create a practical electric lightbulb, he gained the knowledge of just one more avenue that didn't work. It was the accrued knowledge acquired from thousands of failed attempts that ultimately led to his success. Another example is Steve Jobs who was a wildly successful innovator in his time. He pioneered the computer, phone industry and was the CEO and co-founder of the first company to be worth over $1 trillion with Apple. But what obstacles did he have to overcome to get to the point in his life where he became known as an icon of human progress? Jobs was introduced to obstacles from his very birth. He was born to a young, unwed graduate student who decided to put him up for adoption. Later, at an early age, he dropped out of college and ended up sleeping on the floor of a friend's room. To survive he would gather and return Coke bottles for the 5 cent deposits in order to buy food. ... Not deterred, he started a company in his garage with a friend, where eventually, ten years down the line, it would be worth over $2 billion. Even with this great success, it was during this similar time that he was fired by the same company that he had founded. Stung and hurting with that enormous let down and betrayal he was still able, with his acquired knowledge and experience, to start two new companies named NeXT and Pixar. Pixar would go on to become one of the most successful animation studios on the planet and NeXT would eventually be bought by Apple, thus enabling Steve's trumpet return to his former company. ... Success!!

Lesson #3: is **fortitude**. Failing in life helps to build determination. The more we fail the tougher and more driven we must become. In order to achieve success, we need to incorporate grit and additional resolve into our mindset. Because, if we think that we're going to be successful on the first try, or even the first few tries, then we're sure to set ourselves up for continued letdowns and disappointments. Embracing and nurturing fortitude into our lives can help us in many ways. Fortitude helps lead to success by setting the process up to eventually being triumphant. Therefore, it is understood that success will not happen immediately or even in the short term, but only with an immense amount of hard work and sustained effort.

Opportunity is lesson #4. When you fail, you may suddenly realize that the present career, direction or track you're on is not the right one for you. Do not ignore this; this is opportunity knocking on your door. This could be an occasion for you to seek an alternate route, pathway or set a different course to discover new possibilities. If you hadn't failed, you might never have considered pursuing different avenues. You'd just continue on down the wrong road. Life is devised for us to experience failure and change as well as growth and improvement. Once you understand what failure is, and how it benefits rather than defeats us, you'll liberate and open your mind to experience the world of opportunities that failure offers us.

> *"Success is going from failure to failure without losing enthusiasm."*
>
> Winston Churchill

> *"It is impossible to live without failing at something, unless you live so cautiously that you might as well not have lived at all, in which case you have failed by default."*
>
> J.K. Rowling

(8) Honor and protect my family and teach my children to be good, fair, and kind as well as to exhibit gratitude and forgiveness. I will educate them on the greatness of a Constitutional Republic and the value of Life, Liberty and Justice for all.

Instill in your family honor, dignity, and respect. Begin by gathering all members together and discovering what are their views and perceptions of honor, dignity, and respect. What one member may consider normal and okay, another might feel is a sign of disrespect, ridicule, or of being improper. Therefore, if you want to treat your family with honor, dignity, and respect, start by finding out from them what they consider these values to be, and how they themselves would like to be treated.

One error some make is creating an issue or stress by comparing their spouses or their children to other individuals and making them feel that they are inferior or not up to a set of higher standards. A mistake of this type demeans your partner or child and may cause him or her to falter even more by generating low self-esteem. This then may make it harder for them to relate to you emotionally and consequently cause problems forming and maintaining a loving bond within the family. If you want to treat your spouse or children well, you must see each as a distinct person, with unique qualities, and an individual personality. When you view them as being one of a kind, you will consider him or her as a special person, with the honor, respect, and dignity they deserve. You will feel a greater willingness to give them the approval they desire, and you will see them for who he or she truly is, and not simply as a replica of someone else. Also remember, it is easier to take criticism when you are alone with your spouse or son or daughter. When other people are around, it makes it more painful and extremely embarrassing for them. If you want to act toward your spouse and children with honor and respect, you must refrain from such behavior. In its place, use constructive criticism of him or her only when you are alone. ... On the flip side, always make him or her look good in the eyes of others. Praise their merits to other people, and talk about only their positive sides when you are with your colleagues, friends, or family members. Make it a guiding principle not to expose their weaknesses or shortcomings in public. This is important to you as well if you want to be treated in the same manner and with the same respect. It is an action that creates within family members a sense of honesty, truthfulness, and integrity that becomes closely tied in with their family identity.

Not only will they try to do the right thing because it is good in and of itself, but because they want to live up to and preserve their family's reputation for ethical and respectable behavior.

<u>Ideals Worth Instilling In Your Children:</u>

<u>#1 Honesty:</u> A tried and true way to foster truthfulness and honesty in your children is to be honest and truthful yourself. Your children take their cues from you, so it's important that you try to avoid any kind of deception, even a seemingly innocent one. Never, for example, say something like "Let's not tell Mommy we got ice cream this afternoon or tell Daddy you want pizza tonight so I don't have to cook." Let your children hear you being truthful with other people.

Another method to encourage honesty is by not making a big deal when your children lie to you. Replace that action with a way for them to tell the truth. Reassure them that you won't get mad and ask them to be honest and think about what they are saying for a minute, and then ask them … "OK … now let's start over." If they admit to their fault, be gracious, limit the punishment if any is needed, and emphasize how much you value their honesty. In doing so, you will have taught your child an important lesson: Being honest isn't always easy or entirely painless, but you will always feel better if you tell the truth.

<u>#2 Being Just:</u> An effective method to instill in your child a genuine awareness of being just, would be to urge them to carry out some action to correct an offense or damage they may have just created. Asking them to just say they are sorry lets them off too easy without compelling them to actually consider the harm they have done. Your child

needs some time to reflect on their actions and then make reparation in a positive way. Your job is to assist them in thinking of a way to make amends to those who were wronged. Urging your child to take on such an action, teaches them the importance of treating people justly. It will also help guide them in the future by acting toward people they meet every day in a fair and ethical way.

#3 Dedication and Commitment: Dedication and Commitment are principles that should be nurtured at every opportunity. It is best achieved by not over praising simple accomplishments and by giving your children direct critical feedback, handed out in a gentle and thoughtful way.

Dedication and Commitment can also be encouraged even further by challenging them to do things that don't come easily and then cheering them on for their efforts. Telling them "Way to go! ... That was hard but you did it!" is positive recognition and reinforcement and children will become even more determined to keep trying and taking on new challenges.

#4 Consideration and Love: Teach them to think about others' feelings. Should your child act in an inconsiderate way correct them immediately. Don't shout at them ... that is never helpful. What you should do is ask them why they did what they did and then offer a better way to behave. If for example, they are with their friends and they dominate a game without giving their friends some equal time ... rectify it.

Another illustration would be taking note of what other people do. When you witness a person being inconsiderate explain to your child why that kind of behavior is wrong. Tell them what the proper thing to do would've been. For instance, if people were standing in line for a movie and others tried to cut in ahead of them … you would point out that it was in-considerate; the respectful thing to do would've been to wait behind those already there. Small examples like these help a child learn the value of being considerate. Over time, children see that actions can make another person smile or feel better and that when they are kind to someone, that person is also nice to them. This reaction inspires future acts of thoughtfulness and that exactly is the result we are looking for. … Demonstrate your Love and Care to your children often and with feeling. Let your child see your love and care for family members and the important people in your life. Speak to your kids about how much you love and care for their grandparents, aunts, uncles, cousins, and close friends. Express your affection for them in a multitude of ways: Give hugs and kisses whenever you get a chance. Write a love note and place it under their pillow. Tape a heart to the bathroom mirror for them to see when they brush their teeth. Say "I love you" to your child whenever you get the chance. The more hugs and kisses you give, the more your home will be filled with love and warmth.

Fostering Kindness:

Abraham Herschel, an American rabbi and one of the lead-ing Jewish theologians and philosophers of the 20th century wrote *"When I was young, I valued clever people. Now that I am old, I value kind people."* We all feel better and our day becomes brighter when we are treated with kindness and respect from others, and this becomes even truer as we advance into our golden years. As we travel along life's highway and we begin to see the end of the road approaching, the desire for kindness and greater harmony in our life replaces the craving we once had for material possessions. In our youth and into mid-life it was the pursuit of success, the big house, the new car, private schools, being in fashion, and that vacation of our dreams. As one gets older this is gradually replaced by a yearning for contentment, kindheartedness, and a sense of well-being. This transformation of mindset is both uncomplicated and simple because the passing out of kindness doesn't cost a thing or take much time to do. It does not necessitate extravagant research, planning, or training. Kindness can be as easy as a friendly smile, a gracious word, a warm handshake, or a helping hand. It also seems that there is a real connection between the well-being, cheerfulness, and health of individuals who extend kindness. Perhaps it is hard to be unhappy, discontented, or unwell when one is offering kindness towards another human being. Being thoughtful and considerate is recognized and appreciated by people throughout the world. Even if you don't speak the language in a country or culture you are visiting, your unspoken acts of kindness are easily conveyed. As Mark Twain once wrote, *"Kindness is the language which the deaf can hear and the blind can see."*

Does being kind truly help people? ... Yes, absolutely! It can provide new hope to someone's soul and thus encourage them to change a negative filled existence to a positive one. It can elevate someone from the dark pit of hopelessness and misery and shine a light of bright optimism strong enough for them to give life a second effort. It can encourage a person to be more self-assured, courageous, and upbeat. In today's busy world, we often take too lightly the potency of a genuine smile, a friendly word, a sympatric ear, a gentle touch, or a simple act of thoughtfulness. ... What's more, it benefits you as well! Showing kindness to someone exposes the warmest spirit in one's inner self and makes one's own life happier and more gratifying. At the end of life's road, when time has run out, people may forget what you've said and they may even forget what you've done for them but they will never forget how you made them feel. ... It may be hard to gauge the value of acts and deeds of kindness but its effects are contagious as one good act given to another often passes on to the next. As spoken by Amelia Earhart *"A single act of kindness throws out roots in all directions, and the roots spring up and make new trees."*

Eight easy Roots you can throw out ...

- If you are in a long line, invite the person behind you to go ahead of you.
- Drop off combs, toothbrushes, blankets, pillows, etc. at a local shelter.
- Offer to carry someone's groceries.
- Pay anonymously for a soldier's or police officer's meal.
- Give your mail carrier a paper cup of hot chocolate or cool lemonade.
- Bake some cookies and deliver them to a nearby fire or police station.
- Check "yes" to become an organ donor.
- Ask others what you can do to help them.

If you pay attention, you will notice small acts of kindness and generosity performed every day by people everywhere. All you have to do is change your mindset and look for opportunities to practice it and pass it on.

"Today I bent the truth to be kind, and I have no regret, for I am far surer of what is kind than I am of what is true."

"Treat everyone with politeness, even those who are rude to you, not because they are nice but because you are."

"Love thy neighbor and if it requires that you bend the truth, the truth will understand."

Robert Brault

<u>Protect your Family:</u> There are many ways to provide safety and additional security for your family. Below are a few ideas for you to consider.

<u>#1 Place a bell or buzzer on your entry doors</u>. Home invasions are rare but can be devastating when they happen. Having a simple bell or buzzer to chime when people come and go gives you a heads up each time your home threshold is passed. These few valuable seconds give you a chance to evaluate a potential threat. If there is a real threat to your family have a plan in place for defense, a safe room, a baseball bat, or a gun if that is your personal choice. If you choose to possess a firearm, make sure anyone utilizing such a weapon is trained and practiced on its use and that it is stored in a child-safe area.

<u>#2 Install and maintain several Smoke Alarms</u>: Mount smoke alarms on every level of your home, outside every sleeping area, and in each bedroom. Replace conventional batteries at least once a year, even if alarms are wired directly into your home's electrical system. If your alarm is more than 10 years old, you should install a new one. Create and practice a home fire escape plan with two ways out from every room. Place toddler safety barriers around hot areas such as fireplaces, stoves and heated appliances. Invest in electrical outlet, door and cabinet child safety products. Consider adding new and advanced types of safety products as they are developed.

#3 Establish a safety plan for the unexpected: Talk with your family regarding what everyone should do in an unantici- pated emergency such as a flood, tornado, hurricane, or other severe and dangerous situation. Discuss taking cover within your home, a large building, move to higher ground, or even evacuate if need be. If you are caught outside in an electrical storm, do not stand under tall trees or telephone poles and if heavy rain, stay away from deep swiftly moving water. If you are on a lake in a storm, get off the water and stay off the water until such conditions are far far away.

#4 Learn basic self-defense: All family members should learn and be prepared to protect themselves if they find themselves in a situation with no other alternatives. This is elaborated on in greater detail later in this book.

(9) Inwardly purify and cleanse both my mind and body of toxins, additive substances and negativity. Purification of the mind and body is a prerequisite to awaking the senses and transforming one's health, temperament, and charac- ter. Lucidity of the senses and physical being directly affects an individual's ability to "mentally and bodily " face the certainty of truth. Without cleanliness of mind and body, one cannot experience truth, and without truth, there can be no growth in an individual's well-being, disposition, and nature. ... To begin this procedure, initiate the physical and mental cleansing activity. This involves performing the nec- essary Purification Process. ... Start with a bath or shower ... or at the very least use clean fresh water to thoroughly and ritually wash your hands and forearms, mouth, nose, ears and eyes. The purpose of this routine is to prepare your mind and body to enter an attentive state of mindfulness as well as to become receptive to new ideas and insights. The bathing of the hands and arms signifies that one's touch must be virtuous, honorable, and ethical. The washing of the mouth symbolizes the purifying of the tongue and the elimination of offensive and toxic speech. The swabbing of the nose is to allow fresh and clear breathing of uncorrupted thoughts. The wiping of the ears represents one's readiness to accept words of truth. The rinsing of the eyes is to carry away confusion and allow a genuine vision of what is sensible, just, and right. ... <u>The goal of this purification is to symbolically wash away undesirable covets, bad habits, and adverse attitudes.</u> It is a way of offering a clean slate to learn new ways of thinking and to begin laying the foundation of a superior and better individual.

In this process of purifying one's mind, understand that there is no issue or negativity that cannot be changed or cleansed. This practice and methodology is one that involves the intimate workings of the mind and spirit. It is our mind and spirit that creates and brings forth all our external actions. Therefore, the purpose of this exercise is to eliminate that which generates negativity combined with a new focus on producing that which is positive. ... One purifies the mind and spirit by implementing the detailed techniques described in both the Purification Process and Cleansing Action.

At this stage, loosen and relax your body, have no contact with any toxic substances or entities. Eat a light snack, perhaps have a cup of green tea or similar drink and then clear your mind of all other distractions.

To bring about the Cleansing Action, one must first perform the Purification Process explained above and then locate a comfortable spot to sit down. When you are ready, centered, and attentive, focus on quieting your mind ... complete the process of a Cleansing Action by performing the four steps of ...

<u>WASH</u>:

1) **W**iden your mental faculty and engage in genuine deep thoughts of "Heartfelt Contrition". Repentance from the deepest part of your spirit for any harm you may have done throughout your life. Acknowledge the mistakes you have made and the hurt you may have caused. Accept sole responsibility for your actions and do not blame others. Tell yourself that if there is to be a change to become a better individual, it must happen with you right here and right now. Say to yourself that "I regret from the bottom of my heart any wrongs, bad deeds, mistreatments, and offenses I have done in my life. Form this day forward I will do no more harm."

2) **A**nnounce a self-affirmation by saying out loud "I am changed and renewed ... I reject all negativity and toxic substances and entities from my past". Take command of your attitude by saying out loud, "I'm in control. From now onward I will make a positive impact with my life choices". Should you have a tainted bad thought enter into your mind, throw it out. This thought is like a burglar who has entered your home. Why should you consciously allow a robber to remain in your house when you have the absolute power to throw the evil character out? When a negative thought enters into your mind, seize that thought and throw it into the trash where it belongs. Do not give your mind a chance to wander, <u>immediately re-focus and begin reciting and absorbing the Desirable Traits and the Fundamental Laws.</u>

3) **S**hift yourself now into the advanced "Proactive Phase." At this point, you are actively planning and preparing positive measures for the future. It is also a time for making amends for past ill deeds. It is during this period that one commits

themselves to accepting responsibility for their past behavior. It's a time for you to face reality by admitting to your wrong-doings, repaying your debts, repairing damage caused, and doing your best to heal injured relationships with others.

This stage is more than just making time to say you're sorry, although an apology is usually a good first step. It's actually about making restitution, in other words, doing your best to mend your past behavior or repair what has been damaged. Simply apologizing rarely serves to set things right or negates a past harmful deed. In fact, words alone may make things worse unless they're backed up by action. You must demonstrate a changed behavior that shows you understand your error, regret its harmful consequences, and will not repeat it. This is also a good time for self-reflection about being more open and forgiving to others who may need to make amends to you.

4) Habitually practice a firm and rock-solid pact with yourself that from this day forward you will be a person of sound character and a doer of good deeds. Make a compact with yourself that you will behave in all things with integrity and will be a positive influence on others you meet. When you speak outwardly, do so with a clean thoughtful mind and a civilized tongue. You have purged your mind, body and actions of all negativity and maliciousness and will now work only for what is good and right. Repeat this vow: "I swear to abide by this pact I now make with myself. That there is no longer any space in my mind, body, or spirit for anything but love and kindheartedness, forgiveness and wisdom, joy, and compassion. That I will be that better person I aspire to be".

By adhering to the above actions you not only help improve our world but you continue to cleanse your spirit and reinforce your inner positive being ... thus becoming a new and better you. ... Be that principled individual ... by never breaking this vow. It is this determination and commitment that will give you the strength to change.

Understanding how the Mind operates.

The mind works day and night and as much as we may want to control it, it almost always is filled with unhealthy and blemished thoughts. This element of the brain we recognize as the dreadful, unreasonable, and impulsive demon many phycologists refer to as the "id". Even when we attempt to keep it peaceful, calm, and quiet, it lays in wait in its cage filled with hate, jealousy, hypocrisy, lust, temptation and other contemptible qualities. One may try to cast-off and discard these thoughts, but they endure in all of us and continuously call this demon to come forth out of its cage. This is the malicious component of the brain. In contrast to this, there is what phycologists refer to as the "superego" component of the brain. The "superego" is the ethical, virtuous, and moral part of the mind. It works to remind us of the goodness, decency, and integrity we also incorporate within ourselves. It can bring forth feelings of shame and embarrassment for causing grief or distress in the life of others. One could easily regard this function of the brain as an individual's conscience of what is right and what is wrong. In other words, it's that inner voice reminding people to be good. In a way, it could be thought of as an internal angel that is infinitely pure, moral, and upright. It is here that feelings of kindness, love, devotion, goodwill, charity, forgiveness, and other desirable qualities reside. Finally, we come to the third and final component of the brain that phycologists refer to as the "ego". This is the "decision making" part of one's personality that evaluates and chooses what to do. Its responsibility is to strike the perfect balance between the desires and impulses of the demon and the morals and virtues of the angel. The "ego's" aim is to recognize the realities and certainties of the world and to ignore the fallacies and illusions. It's much like the old story of having an evil demon sitting on your left shoulder and a principled angel sitting on your right. The demon is speaking into the left ear suggesting shameful desires and the angel is speaking into the right ear counseling virtue while your "ego" is in the middle as the mediator. This mediator works to direct our improper and destructive urges into more acceptable practices and behavior. In this way, an individual's personality is fashioned by their ego. It refines one's behavior and makes us more socially acceptable.

So how then do we use this information to cleanse the mind and positively influence your character? ... To begin with, avoid people, places, situations, and thoughts that may sway you in a negative or undesirable way. Removing negative thoughts and influences can be difficult, especially if you are surrounded by undesirable individuals or if you have created a substructure of adverse behavior. Nevertheless, through understanding and determination, you can reverse these patterns and set in motion an emphasis on being positive. By changing who you choose to devote your time with and how you choose to utilize that time an individual can unlock countless opportunities to find both jubilation and fulfillment. ... Unfortunately, there is very little you can do about the harmful influences of your past. You must simply acknowledge how they motivated you and make a decisive effort to overpower them going forward. Regrettably, some people we know and care about can also be a detrimental force in our lives. This doesn't mean you should entirely eliminate being near or around them, it just means you should limit your contact with them. If they say or do negative things, try to offset those by saying or doing positive things. Look inward and direct your "ego" to resist the undesirable onslaught with self-affirming and constructive thoughts. If the situation gets out of hand or becomes too hard to handle, then simply ... walk away. A good idea is to carry a copy of this philosophy's "Wallet Prompter" close at hand to deal with adverse influences. Recite from it over and over if necessary. Voice encouraging affirmations out loud to your "ego" whenever you need it by saying "I am renewed ... I reject all negativity and toxic substances and entities in my life". Vocalize optimistic feelings in the morning to start your day on a good note and concentrate your power on positivity throughout the day. This means repeating phrases that start with "I can", "I am" and "I will". For example: "Today, I will promote only positive actions", "I am in complete control of my choices", "I can and will overcome any negative thoughts". One must utilize four basic principles: (1) purify one's mind and body, (2) give up all malicious things, (3) nurture all things good, and (4) act appropriately thereafter.

Now build a strong physical foundation.

To begin with ... do no harm. Do not smoke or indulge in substances that are destructive to the mind and body or which are addictive. If you drink alcohol, do so in moderation.

Smoking: Every cigarette or vapor you smoke damages your breathing and scars your lungs. Smoking compromises the immune system, making smokers more likely to have respiratory infections. Smoking is addictive and also can cause disease, including Crohn's disease, chronic obstructive pulmonary disease, osteoporosis, cardiovascular disease, and arthritis. Additionally, the more cigarettes an individual smokes, the higher the risk for diabetes and many forms of cancer. If you don't smoke or chew tobacco, don't start. If you do ... quit.

<u>Drugs</u>: Drugs have been very good as servants for the betterment of mankind but they can also be terrible and demanding as masters. There exists a fuzzy boundary between routine or temporary use and actual addiction. Only a small number of addicts are truly able to distinguish when they traversed that border. Many addictive drugs start out very innocently until you find yourself suddenly hooked. These addictive types of drugs may fulfill a perceived need. For instance, they may be taken to soothe or invigorate a person, make them more self-confident, manage panic attacks, escape reality, or relieve pain. Be aware, however, dependency is something that usually sneaks up on you, as your drug use gradually grows over time. Increasingly, getting and using drugs becomes more essential to you. As your drug use becomes a priority, you are more likely to miss work or school and you may end up slacking off or being absent on your family obligations. Eventually, your ability to stop using is no longer an option ...you are now the slave and the drug is the master! ... To preserve a beneficial equilibrium in your life, you need to avoid these temptations, engage yourself with wholesome individuals and groups, and learn to feel good about your life without drugs. This requires strong self-control, steadfastness, and also compels an individual to commit themselves to develop and pursue a healthy lifestyle.

To develop this healthier lifestyle, begin by changing your eating habits to include a wide variety of fruits and vegetables and try to include these items: Blueberries, Lemons, Apples, Beets, Carrots, Avocado, Leafy Greens, Broccoli Sprouts, Garlic Flaxseed, Turmeric, Basil, Cilantro, and Herbal Tea. Those specifically named above offer either antitoxins, beneficial nutrients, vitamins, or assist the body to work in the most efficient manner and cleanse the body of impurities. ... Don't forget to drink plenty of water to flush toxins out.

Exercise! Walking 30-minutes a day several days a week will help maintain a healthy weight and reap rewards such as lowering the risk of heart disease, osteoporosis, diabetes, and hypertension. Over the course of a week, also try to work in at least 150 minutes of moderate aerobic activity or 75 minutes of vigorous aerobic activity or a combination of both. Do strength training exercises for all major muscle groups at least two times a week. Aspire to do a single set of each exercise, using weights heavy enough to tire your muscles after about 15 repetitions. Making this part of your regular routine by cleansing the mind, the body and building a strong physical foundation will keep you on the right path to becoming the better individual you desire to be.

(10) Join with others in resolving the needs and goals of our community, our country, and our world. I will cultivate and encourage new Neoteric Humanist Membership.

When endeavoring to be of service to society, you will have greater success and much more fun when you join together with others with similar desires and goals. Many such organizations are voluntary nonprofit groups whose members meet regularly to perform charitable works or raise money for their designated causes. Organizations that fall under this category are groups such as Rotary, Kiwanis, Lions, Elks, Altrusa International, Junior Chamber International, Civitan International, Sertoma, National Exchange Club, Optimists, Zonta, Quota International, Hands-on Network and DoSomething.org. These are all worthy non-profit organizations and being part of one or more of any of them would be a worthwhile venture.

Being a member of a non-profit group and participating in its activities has many rewards. You get to share your desires and goals with others who have the same aspirations. You acquire current and on-going information while forming positive and lasting relationships. You have the prospect to do good deeds, improve our world, and limit suffering. It's also an opportunity to foster closer ties with other neighborhoods, communities, and perhaps even those in other parts of the world.

Below are some ideas you might want to consider to help people in your locality. … Please note that, before starting a particular project, it's a good idea to make sure that you have identified and decided on a specific goal. It's important to clearly define what it is you wish to accomplish so that you can (1) measure your success and (2) make adjustments along the way if they are necessary to accomplish your objective. So … Be the leader, organizer or energetic participant and …

- Clean up trash from local neighborhoods and open spaces.
- Start a campaign to renovate a local playground or raise money for a new one.
- Ask people with knowledge and skills to teach community classes.
- Create a tutoring group to help struggling children at a local school.

Another way to be of service and to participate is through politics. Anyone who is of legal age and a citizen will be able to involve themselves in one way or another. A very easy and important way … is to simply exercise your right to vote. Voting is by far the most common yet critical form of political involvement. Informed and educated voting makes sure that the politicians that are elected are the politicians that we as citizens want. This is a vital and dynamic responsibility as it allows us to impact how and who governs our communities and country. Voting affects nearly every aspect of our lives including health care, education, the environment, law and order, taxes, the military & defense, businesses, and employment. It is therefore imperative that you partake in an informed and educated manner as your vote contributes to the way our republic functions and evolves.

If there is a special issue or problem that exists, you can also start your own sponsorship or movement to generate a solution. By bringing such an issue or problem to light it will raise awareness of the matter so that other citizens will understand it better as well. It will likewise convey this to the attention of those in charge and hold them accountable as to how they respond to it. Possible forms of political activism you might choose include nonviolent parading, writing letters to your representatives, or joining an advocacy group. By continuously working for solutions relating to an issue, it will increase the chances that the problem will be addressed and hopefully resolved satisfactorily by the leadership in our government.

Promoting Membership in Neoteric Humanism: Reading the information contained here may be illuminating but written content alone is not likely to produce the results you want when hoping to influence an individual's mindset or personal views. While the material in this text is useful, there is no opportunity to have an open discussion, clarify a point or question, and/or receive a response in return. This book simply provides a one-way flow of information regarding the principles, ideals, and vision of this philosophy. It's the people you meet with, associate with, and speak to that allow for real communication to take place. As people are social creatures, the message and vision of Neoteric Humanism will resonate more with others when you make polite and respectful observations, ask reasonable questions and offer sensible explanations and they, in turn, have an opportunity to be heard, respond and digest what is posed. Below are a few ideas on how to share this philosophy:

(1) If in school, talk to fellow students, teachers, club members, and others.

(2) Steer the conversation to a person's religious beliefs or their philosophy on life.

(3) Recite a Neoteric Humanist Mantra before a meal with family or friends.

(4) Hold a free car-wash or host a Red Cross event in a local subdivision or nearby park. Wear themed t-shirts with some stimulating statements / pictures on them.

(5) Always look for ways to demonstrate helpfulness, kindness and generosity.

(6) If you are creative, use your talents to spread the word through your art or ability.

(7) Say provocative phrases. Instead of saying "Have a nice day" say "Paco, Sano, Felico kaj Prospero" … "Peace, Health, Happiness and Prosperity" or as a response to "Have a nice day" reply "Al vi ankaŭ" … "To you as well" in Esperanto.

(8) Leave Neoteric Humanism pamphlets or literature at various locations.

Just keep in mind that you are promoting beneficial ideas, you're doing good deeds for the community and you are helping to make our world a better place!

(11) <u>Keep a stable budget, invest wisely and live modestly.</u>

Setting up a stable family budget is not necessarily to re-strict spending. It is principally a means of defining your goals and providing a system to show you where your money is going and making sure it is going to the right places. When setting up your budget it is imperative to track every expense every day. You can track your expenses by using a simple pocket pad and pen and saving your receipts. Next, orga-nize a filing system in your residence with defined categories (Gas Heating, Electric, Mortgage, Telephone, Water & Sewer, Income, Taxes, Medical, Business Meals, weekly Business Mileage, Business Lodging, Donations, Miscellaneous, etc.) and place your receipts and notes there. After tracking your expenses for a few months, what do you see? Are you mak-ing ends meet? Are you consistently overspending on some things? Are you saving enough? A good rule of thumb is a 60/20/10/10 plan. 60% on necessary expenses, 20% on what you desire, 10% put aside for emergencies, and 10% for long term retirement savings. Of these, pay yourself first and bal-ance out your lifestyle and expenses with what's left. Live modestly, invest wisely and guard overspending and you will sleep well at night and be ready to take advantage of oppor-tunities when they arise. Avoid the temptation to overextend yourself on loans and credit card debt. Not all loans are bad and can be good investments, such as a home or business in a good location. Just be careful to not end up real property rich and cash poor ... be judicious and sensible.

Live modestly and invest 10% in yourself first! You will need a large nest egg if you ever plan to retire one day. One good long term strategy for investing is allocating 45% of it in Stocks, such as mutual funds which will provide broad market exposure, low operating expenses, and small portfolio turn-over. 45% in Multiple Income Streams, such as commercial rental units or products, a product or service you can provide, or perhaps an enterprise you can develop and eventually sell, etc. 4% in Precious Metals or Art such as gold and silver or desirable in demand artwork. 5% in Collectibles such as classic automobiles, rare coins, desirable antiques, etc. 1% Cash to keep on hand taking advantage of opportunities you may come across. If you find you excel in one of the above areas by all means change the balance to complement your talents. Finally, start a side home business. This is not so much for the revenue as the ability to have write offs to lower your taxable income. Doing this will give you the option to write-off a home office, part of your utilities, postal and shipping costs, travel expenses, vehicles or mileage, insurance, advertising, telephones, donations, business conventions, etc. If you use these shrewdly and judiciously you'll find ways to tie in personal advantages, for example, vacation trips, leveraged into legitimate business expenses. Just keep records and receipts for what you do on an ongoing basis and file them appropriately.

One simple saying that has severed me well over the years is *"More is better than Less, Sooner is better than Later and Location, Location, Location!"* … <u>The most important thing is that you start early … time can your best friend or your worst enemy!</u>

(12) <u>Learn and practice multiple pragmatic languages</u>.

Be competent in at least one other language, such as Spanish, and become familiar with the basics of Latin, Greek, and Esperanto. … While Neoteric Humanism favors a 2nd world language, such as Esperanto, that all nations will agree to use in addition to their native tongue. It is clear that, in today's political climate, this is a dream that will take decades of negotiation as well as a strong effort from willing countries to accomplish. Therefore, understanding this, it is still exceedingly beneficial and often very practical to have the ability to communicate in at least one other major foreign language and to have a good understanding of the fundamentals of Latin, Greek, and Esperanto. In today's interconnected world and our ability to cross our planet in just a few hours, there has evolved a need for people to become proficient in more than just their specific counties tongue. Indeed, not learning a second language in this day and age will limit one's opportunities on both a personal and professional basis. Increasingly, if you are not at least bilingual, you risk living with the rest of humankind as a less successful and unenlightened citizen.

To be effective and prosperous on an international basis, businesses now need employees who can function in various cultures and who have a reasonable competence in at least one principal or dedicated foreign language. Such abilities are valued in many occupations; the cruise and airline industries, hotel and tourism markets, production in films, radio, and journalism, commercial offices with international customers, and also in other areas such as medicine, law, and government. The workplace has become a diverse world of many cultures and languages. Learning another language has become necessary if a person wishes to have a competitive advantage in their career options both today ... and more importantly tomorrow.

There are other compelling reasons to study and becoming competent in another language besides the occupational advantages.

- It is valuable for traveling and interacting with new people: With your new ability, opportunities will swing wide open for you around the globe. You'll be surprised how friendly and helpful people will be to you when you speak their national dialect. Just traveling through a foreign country becomes much easier if you can see, speak and write in the vernacular of that population. Exactness or perfection in fluency isn't essential when talking with the locals and learning about their customs. People everywhere will be pleased that you are at least trying to communicate in their particular lingo. It is in essence a verbal display of respect and appreciation to others in their own region and is a good way to open a dialog with them. Having good communication skills is one of the most important keys in understanding and relating to other people and their culture.

- It is good for your brain and well-being: Becoming proficient with a second language also enhances your retention of memories and improves your concentration and focusing abilities. Learning to become multilingual is like aerobics for your mind; it forces you to spend time and energy applying your brainpower to a new way of thinking. By utilizing this new way of thinking, it correspondingly boosts your problem-solving skills. Multilingual people also seem to have more overall commonsense, better decision-making aptitudes, and have a higher awareness of their surroundings. In addition, bilingualism may delay the effects of Alzheimer's and Dementia disease for many years and that multilingual speakers tend to be more creative than monolingual ones.

Studying and becoming competent in a second language is a whole new operating system for your brain and is set up with distinct rules, definitions, and meanings. This operating system makes your brain work hard developing additional pathways that will comprehend this new linguistic structure. As your brain assimilates these fresh insights and makes full use of this unique cache of concepts and ideas, it improves skills in both reading and speaking. This of course helps boost your self-confidence. ... Thus learning a new skill and enjoying your power to use it effectively is a great boost to your ego. Your self-confidence swells when a new skill is conquered ... and mastering an additional language will do just that.

There are, of course, several reasons why people desire to learn a second language. A teacher may want to have the ability to reach out to students of different backgrounds. Travelers may want to have a greater and deeper cultural experience or just want to feel more comfortable when venturing into a new country. Having knowledge of another countries language enables the bridging of social barriers and allows for a more personal connection. A bilingual individual has opportunities for business rewards as well as the potential mental advantages of learning an additional language. To top it off, you may just have a great deal of fun taking on the challenge, and knowing you've accomplished something not everyone can duplicate. If your native tongue is not Spanish, here are 8 reasons for picking it as your 2nd language. ... Consider those noted in **LANGUAGE** below:

(1) **L**earning Spanish will make other languages such as Italian, French, Portuguese, or even English much easier to understand or acquire as they have similarities.

(2) **A**cquiring Spanish as a 2nd language will improve communication skills and your enjoyment of Spanish art, music, literature, TV, and film.

(3) **N**ationally, in the U.S., millions of people speak Spanish as their first language and it is predicted the Latino population will reach approximately 130 million by 2060.

(4) <u>G</u>lobally there are roughly 400 million speakers. It is the fourth most commonly spoken language in the world (after English, Chinese, and Hindustani).

(5) <u>U</u>nderstanding Spanish is easier because it is spelled and pronounced logically.

(6) <u>A</u>dopting Spanish as a 2nd language is becoming a business necessity.

(7) <u>G</u>aining knowledge of Spanish is a valuable asset as it is one of the most widely dispersed language in the world.

(8) <u>E</u>ntering many countries and Islands on four continents you will find that it is the primary language. (**Europe**: Spain.------**America**: Argentina, Bolivia, Chile, Colombia, Costa Rica, Cuba, Dominican Republic, Ecuador, El Salvador, Guatemala, Honduras, Mexico, Nicaragua, Panama, Paraguay, Peru, Puerto Rico, and Venezuela.------**Africa**: Ceuta, Canary Islands, Melilla, Equatorial Guinea, Gabon (Coco beach area), Western Sahara.------**Oceania**: Easter Island.)

<u>Why learn the fundamentals of Latin, Greek, and Esperanto?</u>
What do famous people like Benjamin Franklin, Thomas Jefferson, and Theodore Roosevelt all share in common? They all understood the value of an education in Latin. Latin was a central part of an individual's schooling and was included as an important part of the foundation of a liberal arts education. Latin was the way scientific, religious, legal, and philosophical literature was written up until about the 16th century. Many of the prefixes and several of the roots of common English words are derived from Latin. Therefore, by knowing the meaning in Latin, if by chance you to come across a word

you've never seen before, you can make an educated guess at what it means. Many of the same advantages that come from the study of Latin also come from studying the ancient form of the Greek language. For example, take a look at the word Antarctica. If you were familiar with the basics of Greek or Latin perhaps you would notice that it comes from the Latin *arcticus,* "Arctic or Northern" and from Greek *arktikos,*" literally the region of the North Pole." Then, you may detect that *anti-* means against or even opposite, so the Antarctica is literally the "anti-North," also known as "the South Pole." Knowing Latin and Ancient Greek can give you insights into all kinds of things.

Know one Root, Know many Words.

Knowing one Greek and Latin root means that you know many words associated with that root. For Example: The Root: theo- = Definition: god. If you understand that any time you see the root, *theo-,* you're going to be dealing with "god" in some form. You'd know that words like theocracy, theology, atheist, polytheistic, and others all have something to do with a deity even if you've never seen or heard those words before. Knowing many roots can increase your verbal ability and intellectual capacity.

Know a Suffix, Know the Part of Speech.

Knowing a suffix or the "word ending" can often help you know how to use it in a sentence. For example, the Suffix: -ist = Definition: a person who... A word that ends in "ist" will usually be a noun and will refer to a person's job, ability, or tendencies. For instance, an acupuncturist is a person who performs acupuncture. A geologist is a person who studies or works in geology. A guitarist is a person who plays the guitar. A hairstylist is a person who works with hair.

Know a Prefix, Know Part of the Definition.

Knowing the prefix or the "word beginning" can help you understand the word itself. For example, the <u>Root:</u> a or an- = <u>Definition:</u> without, not. Anorexia means a loss of appetite for food. Amnesia means an inability to remember. Abacterial means free of or without microorganisms. If you understand a prefix, you'll have a better time guessing the definition of a word you may not have seen before.

Why is learning the fundamentals of Esperanto worthwhile? It is useful to study and practice because of its clearcut objective to serve as a common second language for people around the world. Esperanto does not endeavor to replace all other languages ...its sole purpose is to facilitate global communication. Consider this, would it not make more sense and be preferable to have tourists, businessmen, diplomats, and scientists from every country learn one common second language than learn all the major languages that they may be required to learn? It would render communication so much easier for everyone, where ever they may go. The individual mother languages would keep their special characteristics and unique attributes for natives to continue utilizing and retaining them. ... A further noteworthy advantage of Esperanto is that it doesn't come with any political baggage. In certain parts of the world, there are some prejudicial or partisan concerns that may arise when speaking in some languages such as English, French, or Chinese. Thus, speaking in Esperanto is totally harmless, unbiased, and non-political. Finally, Esperanto is very easy to learn and is helpful in teaching the process of learning languages. The new skills and techniques you learn by studying it can later be applied to the more complex and difficult languages. Acquiring the essentials of Esperanto is therefore the perfect training ground for learning the basics of other vernaculars and dialects around the world. ... If you would like to feel yourself a citizen of the whole world, then do learn Esperanto.

> *"The limits of your language are the limits of your world,"*
> Ludwig Wittgenstein

(13) <u>Maintain and practice restraint yet be proficient in self-defense</u>.

Use self-control to avoid physical conflicts. To avoid fights and physical confrontations first requires that you understand yourself. Become familiar with your inner emotions and discover what prompts you to engage. For instance, how easily do you get aggravated, and are their certain topics or situations in particular that initiate a response? What are your limits as to how much you can take without retorting or taking action? By examining this and recognizing what has elicited your response in the past will allow you to conceive of ways to control yourself in the future. Why is this important? In most cases, for a physical conflict to take place it takes two willing participants. You can't control what the other individual will do but the one thing you can do ... is to manage your response. In such situations, your initial reaction should be restraint, thus making a willful choice to not react to provocative actions, words or comments. On the other hand, if you feel you must reply, do so peacefully, calmly and with composure without being loud or vulgar. Then immediately create space between you and the instigator or simply walk away. Be aware that, when found in such circumstances, if you counter each and every remark you run the risk of getting yourself into a fiery exchange. It is in just such situations that one may find themselves very close to the brink of a physical confrontation. Here are several factors you should consider when this occasion may arise:

- In many such circumstances, individuals start yelling or speaking loudly because they feel frustrated or think they are not being heard or understood. Consider taking a moment to acknowledge the person's irritation or anger. Remain cool, calm, collected, and sincerely ask the person what it is that they are upset about. This recognition is likely to lead to further, deeper, and clearer dialogue in a more civilized and congenial manner. Thus having brought forth true interaction, the likelihood of physical conflict occurring will have been greatly reduced.

- Try to quickly determine if the other individual is in a reasonable, sensible, and sound state of mind. Perhaps you have crossed paths with someone who is dealing with a bad social, health, or economic situation. Maybe they have just lost a job or had a nasty fight with a spouse or lost someone they cared deeply about. Perhaps they are normally a good person but they can't handle alcohol or are reacting to some medication they are on. If this is the case, avoid any reaction as it is unlikely that they will be responsive and it could lead to greater aggressive behavior.

- Allow yourself a moment to cool down. If you feel worked up, exhale, and then take a deep breath. If the first breath doesn't make you feel calmer, continue taking deep breaths while you contemplate what to do next. This will help you relax and give you time to think about how best to resolve the conflict. Think to yourself, "I won't dignify those remarks with a nasty comeback. Or, say to yourself, "I will be the better person" or repeat the "KUPP mantra" or anything else that will let you focus on something different. Don't pay any attention to the instigator. Don't respond to anything they say and totally disregard any actions they may show. Repeat to yourself, "This is unpleasant now, but soon it will be over ... or this will just be a bad memory by tomorrow." Remember, a broken hand or black eye will take a lot longer to go away, not to mention the potential of paying for damages and all the explaining that will be required.

- Think about having a discussion. Is this a situation where a heart to heart conversation may help resolve an issue? Of course, a true dialogue involves listening and understanding on the part of both parties, so in this case, try to look at the occasion as a chance to communicate your point of view and acquire a better appreciation of theirs. Here, you will need to evaluate if you believe doing so will have the potential to end in a negative outcome. Ask yourself, "Am I running the risk of ruining my relationship with this person if we have a discussion?" or "Will this discussion likely lead to an escalation in hostilities?"

Most people are rational and will try and evade a conflict as much as possible, but there will always be a few hostile characters out there looking to cause trouble. It is always best to try and calm down what is going on and attempt to prevent it from becoming a brawl. Keep in mind that you have no idea how much experience and fighting ability your potential adversary has, nor can you be sure if they may or may not be hiding a weapon. Furthermore, there are legal considerations if things get out of hand. Do you want to spend time and money on legal fees and perhaps several days defending your actions in a courtroom? As you can see, there are many reasons to maintain self-control in order to prevent a volatile situation from potentially leading to physical violence.

When the above recommendations fail, <u>you do have the right to self-defense.</u>

> *"The general rule in the U.S. is that a person is allowed to use such force as <u>reasonably</u> appears necessary to defend themselves against an apparent threat of <u>unlawful</u> and <u>immediate</u> violence from another. In cases involving non-deadly force, this means that the person must reasonably believe that their use of force was necessary to prevent imminent, unlawful physical harm. When the use of <u>deadly force</u> is involved in a self-defense claim, the person must also reasonably believe that their use of deadly force is immediately necessary to prevent the other's infliction of great bodily harm or death. Most states no longer require a person to <u>retreat</u> before using deadly force. In the minority of jurisdictions which do require retreat, there is no obligation to retreat when it is unsafe to do so or when one is inside one's own home."*
>
> Wikipedia

The principal objectives of self-defense rulings are simple and basic. An individual should not face criminal charges or be penalized for injuring or killing another person if it occurs in cases of self-preservation. However, these same rules serve a second purpose in that they <u>limit the circumstances</u> under which it is legally permissible to harm or kill someone under the rule of self-preservation. These laws are written with a number of "reasonableness" clauses, designed to limit the conditions where it's considered legally permissible to greatly injure or take the life of another human being. This is another reason why resorting to violence is an absolute last resort. The self-defense rules are not an easy out or excuse when physical fighting takes place as they, can and do, end up in court.

There, you can be absolutely right regarding the law, but it will still be left up to a judge or jury to hear and determine your case. This will involve lawyers, time, and money for an event that will be an enormous inconvenience even if you are found innocent of all charges.

Nevertheless, keeping all the above reasons for restraint in mind, there are many reasons why you should go ahead and take self-defense classes. Of course, the first reason for learning self-defense is that it helps you acquire a special ability to shield yourself, your family, or friends from harm. In any fight you may find yourself, having a competent means of reacting or taking action gives you the opportunity to protect. If you should find yourself being suddenly attacked it is far better to already have the knowledge and experience on how best to counteract. This knowledge and experience will allow you to move quickly and effectively should just such a situation arise. Hopefully, you will never find yourself in that position, but if you are ... you will be prepared. You will know what stance to take, where to step, how to respond, and if necessary where to punch, jab, or kick your most effective body blows. Taking self-defense classes can prepare you for just such an encounter and, most importantly, raise the odds of less harm to yourself and loved ones ... and if need be survival itself!

Remember, that the reason for taking self-defense classes is to prepare you for any situation that could harm to you, your family or your friends. This also means that improving one's overall physical fitness is a key component of a successful self-defense event. If you find yourself in a position where someone confronts or attacks you, you need to be in good physical shape if you want to effectively deal with a threatening situation. Being bodily fit will empower your muscle reflexes, your mental abilities, and your actual response to an attack. So ... should you find yourself with no other option but to fight it is important to be ready and able by being in good physical condition and having taken classes to be well trained and prepared beforehand.

Keep in mind that even though you have no intention of being attacked, your attacker perhaps does and if so they likely have a plan. This training will help you to be aware of potentially dangerous areas and to at all times be ready. If it does, you will have the necessary skills and knowledge to protect yourself and others. ... Of course, one of the major gifts of taking self-defense classes is not only to help you protect yourself but they also build your confidence, improve your balance, develop self-discipline, help with goal setting, and ultimately molding you into a better person.

(14) N̲u̲r̲t̲u̲r̲e̲ ̲C̲r̲e̲a̲t̲i̲v̲i̲t̲y̲,̲ ̲I̲n̲n̲o̲v̲a̲t̲i̲o̲n̲ ̲a̲n̲d̲ ̲A̲d̲a̲p̲t̲a̲b̲i̲l̲i̲t̲y̲.̲ ̲I̲ ̲w̲i̲l̲l̲ c̲h̲a̲m̲p̲i̲o̲n̲ ̲r̲e̲s̲e̲a̲r̲c̲h̲,̲ ̲e̲x̲p̲l̲o̲r̲a̲t̲i̲o̲n̲,̲ ̲f̲r̲e̲s̲h̲ ̲d̲i̲s̲c̲o̲v̲e̲r̲i̲e̲s̲ ̲a̲n̲d̲ ̲n̲e̲w̲-̲ f̲o̲u̲n̲d̲ ̲p̲o̲t̲e̲n̲t̲i̲a̲l̲ ̲l̲i̲f̲e̲ ̲e̲n̲d̲o̲w̲i̲n̲g̲ ̲h̲a̲b̲i̲t̲a̲t̲s̲.̲

The three attributes above are the building blocks of a sound foundation that are beneficial to anybody no matter your background, health or age. Developing and nurturing these qualities is more essential now than ever before given that if you properly cultivate them they will impact your life in many positive ways. Let's review several reasons why these traits are so valuable:

To begin with, being personally involved in a creative activity tends to reduce an individual's overall stress level and anxiety. It is an action that permits us too fully immerse ourselves in the task at hand and lets us enter a state of artistic flow which furthers our well-being and mental health. While we are in this engaged state of mind we tend to forget our surroundings, the passing of time and feel removed from the worries perhaps going on in our lives. In this mindset our body produces "satisfying and upbeat" hormones which increases our "joie de vivre" and contentment. This feeling of being happy and at peace is a good state of mind for an individual to be in and is reason enough to partake in creative ideas, hobbies and projects.

Nonetheless, there are many more reasons to consider; creativity is one of the best tools to help you deal with daily problem-solving. If your creative talent is being well exercised, it will help you find the solutions to the difficult and complex issues you are currently facing. Using your creativity to find these answers will also help you more easily recover from other difficult situations and help build up your self-confidence as well. This ability will become even more important in the future as jobs, professions and trades are being replaced by automation and artificial intelligence. The desirable occupations that remain will be reserved for those people with novel and resourceful ideas and solutions. ... Creativity is a vital aptitude that has been indispensable to humans ever since we moved from drafty caves to wooden huts and now into our modern homes. It will be even more critical for us in the days to come.

Creativity propels and energizes innovation. As we have advanced as a civilization it has to a large degree been due to insightful inspirations that eventually led us to new and exciting innovations. These innovations were formed by thinking as has been said "outside of the box" and advance a new approach, idea or product that in some way improves the quality of our lives. Innovation is, in fact or reality, actually putting that approach or product idea into practical use. Innovation has been and always will be in demand not only by individuals but in companies of all sizes as well as many private institutions. People and businesses feel continuous pressure to produce something new either as a way to maintain their trade position or build on their current professional standing. This constant demand for "first, different, better or faster" drives companies and our society as a whole to repeatedly search for ways to fast-track and develop new advancements.

Creativity involves more than imagining and innovating, it's also about acknowledging uncertainty and the unknown. This involves an individual having an inquisitive mind but perhaps not having all the answers. It is their forging ahead with confidence and faith that "there must be a solution". In these types of progressive societies, people challenge the status quo and are open to fresh ideas. The old adage of "If it an't broke … don't fix it" does not exist. In fact, they more aptly say "If it isn't broke … break it"! This attitude helps recognize potential opportunities and also may possibly point out impending obstacles. This is an open minded kind of approach that should be encouraged so that people don't hold back their thoughts and opinions, but rather their input is sought after, nurtured and respected.

Creativity leads to innovation and this innovation necessarily involves risk and adaptability. Consider the words of Charles Darwin, "It is not the strongest of the species that survives, nor the most intelligent, it is the one that is most adaptable to change." Being a reasoned risk taker and having the ability to adapt is immensely important. Being adaptable means one is able to swiftly react to changing trends, modernism, disruptions, cultural swings, and so on. This ability to modify or change makes an individual more agile and responsive to any condition or problem they may face. The individuals, who can adapt by thinking creatively and with foresight, will be the ones who will carry their businesses and our society forward in the future. On the other hand, the ones who adhere to the way things have always been done will find themselves, their businesses and their careers in jeopardy. Are you adaptable? An adaptable person will have these valuable traits: They continue their education, they build on their skills, test new ideas, seek opportunity, find ways to be inventive; continually think ahead and never place the blame or failures on someone else. They stay curious, open minded, observe the methods and practices of others and stay up to date on contemporary issues and events. If you do not possess these traits, there are ways you can train yourself to be more adaptable:

1) Change Your Mindset. Forget the "We've always done it that way" way of thinking. Look at a change or challenge as an opportunity to improve, learn, and update your skills. It may make you feel uncomfortable and ill at ease but it will also likely open the door to creative thought as well. Keep in mind that, to attain this mindset, it also means you must always be open and alert to the various thoughts, ideas and opinions of others.

2) Become a Reasoned Risk Taker. Nothing happens and nothing improves unless something is actually done ... and this will involve risk. Taking risks is a key part of being adaptable. However, risk should always be tempered with reason and well thought out action. One good way to think things through is to discuss the risk you are taking with trusted advisors, team members and others who can offer perspective, suggestions and support. What-ever you decide to do, consider the words of Mark Zuckerberg, *"The biggest risk is not taking any risk... In a world that's changing really quickly, the only strategy that is guaranteed to fail is not taking risks."* ... To eventually be successful you must be willing to take risks!

3) Encourage Others to Be Open Minded. One of the best ways you can develop open mind-ness is to encourage the people around you to speak up and express themselves. This

creates a more accessible and approachable environment for those all around you, thereby further inspiring your own open-mindedness and that of others. It also serves as a means to shut down closed-minded and negative thinking by those unwilling to contribute and participate.

4) Embrace Learning and Skill Building. People who are curious and are open to new ideas are more likely to be adaptable. This means you need to engage in ongoing education and continually work on abilities and talents. Read books, magazines, articles and search the internet about new ideas and technologies. Take time to go to educational seminars and find out about current developments. Connect with colleagues and professionals and absorb knowledge, skills, and valuable experience that can be acquired from them.

(15) Openly advocate inspiring art, stimulating music, competitive games, and sports. I will employ reason, logic, strategy and the freedom of ideas and thought to solve problems.

Try to imagine our lives without these inspirational activities. Extremely dreary and unexciting isn't it? To the lonesome, these components give companionship in their solitary world. To the rich and famous, a way to express their success. To the defeated, a means to repair their soul. To the sick, a source of optimism and hope. To the depressed, a way to restore their joy. To worshipers, a melodious way of praying and expressing their passion. The arts, music, games, and sports make us feel alive and involved. The contribution of art introduces us to new viewpoints, novel perceptions, different beliefs, and innovative alternatives. Through it we find ourselves sharing a common thread with the rest of humanity and we might identify with an artist's purpose. Sometimes we may even hear an inner voice that speaks inside us and says "Ahhh … that is so true", perhaps simply "Beautiful" or even "Wow! … That's totally bizarre". Everyone translates art in their own particular way, adding in their individual knowledge and understanding and then explaining or interpreting it based on their unique and personal opinion. As we experience a piece of art, we tend to escape everyday realities and live in that moment where it is just us and the creation before us. To me, the true value of art is that it diverts our minds from common everyday life and exposes us to other possibilities. It is also during these moments, when the experience itself may actually make us feel more emotionally and physically rejuvenated. There are countless reasons why we appreciate art and we may truly never know all the reasons why. … We just know we like it and we want more of it.

> *"Arts education not only enhances students' understanding of the world around them, but it also broadens their perspective on traditional academics. The arts give us the creativity to express ourselves while challenging our intellect. The arts integrate life and learning for all students and are integral to the development of the whole person."*
> Dr. Terry Bergeson

The contribution of music influences us in ways that other sounds don't. Who doesn't have a story or account about a certain song or tune that moved us? Who hasn't had a time when the hair stood up on our arms, gotten the chills, or felt transported into another state of mind. Whether you were part of the crowd at a concert, listening to your radio, or just singing in the shower, there's something about music that charges us with emotion, from joyfulness to tears. Music makes us happy … makes us cry … we dance and celebrate … with and because of music. Music is life keenly sensed and experienced!

... It may cause you to settle down and relax or be rowdy, be cheerful or melancholy ... but in the end, it does have a real emotional impact. It can eliminate monotony and boredom, fatigue and weariness, and even help reduce stress. Listening to music means we have a heart and feelings and it helps rejuvenate us physically, mentally, and spiritually. The famous philosopher, Plato, made the following observation about the value of music. *"In order to take the spiritual temperature of an individual or society, one must mark the music."* ... As individuals, we have the power to both create our own music and support others who produce that which we love. Music is a powerful resource and an essential part of being alive ... and thus should be fully and deeply integrated into our daily living!

The components of games and sports involve us, prepare us, and inspire us. The human species has been strengthened and held together by its need and desire for communal collaboration. Individuals learn important rules on how to conduct themselves at home and in public through our social interactions with others. Playing games and sports provides a great way for us to learn the admired and valued guidelines of society and also allows people to test their worth, skills, and talent against each other. By participating in this kind of competition, we are able to see just how good our knowledge and skills are and what improvements we need to make to enhance our abilities, competence, or understanding. Simply by playing games and sports people sharpen their mental and physical skills and the experience helps develop future strategies. These elements inspire and motivate us. Exceptional athletes and top-notch gamers demonstrate the advantages of competition by giving us the fastest, the greatest, brightest, and most dazzling achievements in their areas of expertise. Connecting with such people, or even merely being a spectator, not only causes us to elevate our desires and goals but also supplies tremendous motivation to pursue our own individual hopes and dreams.

(16) Practice family planning by using contraceptives or abstinence to prevent an unplanned pregnancy. I will advance the ideal of a balanced world population based more on the quality of life than quantity.

Promoting and utilizing family planning is an essential strategy that will help introduce harmony and economic stability in the world today. In several countries, overpopulation remains the primary cause of malnutrition, deforestation, civil unrest, and a range of societal problems. There are maximums and boundaries on our planet that, if exceeded, will touch all of us in a negative manner. We must recognize that there is a tradeoff between "quantity" and "quality" of life for humankind. With new developments in science and technology, we could continue to add more and more people to our planet but what will we sacrifice in doing so? Do we want to crush nature, our wildlife preserves, and add even more pollution and poverty to our world? Acknowledging that a larger and ever increasing population threatens our quality of life means that promoting and utilizing methods of birth control will be extremely important in helping manage this unique place we call earth.

So what does it involve? Family planning, by our philosophy's definition, means essentially choosing to only have a limited number of children and also avoiding pregnancy at unwanted times. Some of the best family planning practices include birth control pills, condoms, other comparable choices, and abstinence. As discussed later in this book, abortion is not a desirable, tolerable or defensible form of birth control.

The four main advantages of family planning can be found in ...

ROLE:

1) **R**etaining stability in a family's financial affairs. Using a birth control method allows the timing of a new child to fit in with a family's economic situation. This means that birth control enables avoiding times of monetary difficulty and also permits occasions for building a nest egg that an unplanned pregnancy might not allow. This is no doubt one of the greatest poverty preventers available to an individual or a family. Being able to time a pregnancy allows people to finish education or career training so that they are better able to provide for a new arrival. It also allows them a choice in determining how many children they can afford to take care of properly. In addition, it permits a woman or family to practice safe sex if she/they choose never to have children or may have some health or medical condition that a pregnancy would complicate.

2) **O**ptimizing the odds that all the children in a household are ones that are desired. It also helps spread out the ages of offspring within a family. Children who are born closer in age to their siblings may have a higher risk of adverse birth weight and an earlier than desired delivery. These can result in unnecessary exposure to childhood health issues or even the possibility of death.

3) **L**ivelihood serenity and contentment are enhanced by lowering the stress of raising more offspring than had been planned for. Not only this, if a mother and father can plan the timing in which they desire to have a family, then they

can opt to take advantage of a business and/or skill building prospects. The family will then have opportunities for saving more money for a good home, providing the children with a better education and just fulfilling their household needs and desires.

4) Enables healthier and better educated young people to enter the workforce. With healthier and well-schooled young people joining the workforce it may also facilitate an increase in a countries GDP and reduce the number of dependent people draining government fiscal and economic resources. This translates into higher-quality schools, domestic infrastructure, national defense, standards of living, healthcare, and on and on.

Why is there a global need for contraceptives?
     Millions of women of reproductive age in developing countries who want to avoid pregnancy are not using modern contraceptive methods. The reasons why include the explanations noted below:

- a narrow or no selection of contraceptives are available.
- limited or no easy access to contraceptives, particularly among experimenting young people, and poorer sectors of populations.
- concerns about potential side-effects of contraceptives.
- social upbringing or religious disapproval on using contraceptives.
- deficient quality of knowledge or services that are accessible.

<u>What birth control methods are available today</u>?

A. Reversible birth control

- An Intrauterine Device (IUD) is placed in the uterus for birth control.
- Using Condoms helps prevent pregnancy and also helps protect against sexually transmitted diseases.
- Nexpanon is an implant inserted under the skin of the upper arm and can prevent pregnancy for up to three years.
- Using an oral contraceptive (The Pill) for birth control. Taken correctly, it is 99.9% effective. The O Pill, no doctor prescription needed.
- Appling a contraceptive Patch that releases hormones through the skin for up to 7 days.
- Receiving an injection of (Depo-Provera) protects against pregnancy up to 14 weeks.
- Use of a small contraceptive ring (Nuva Ring) that contains the same hormones as The Pill.

B. Permanent birth control

- Vasectomy is a (Sometimes reversible) surgical birth control option for men.
- Tubal ligation is a surgical procedure during which a woman's fallopian tubes are blocked, tied, or cut.

C. Miscellaneous methods

- Spermicides such as foams, jellies, tablets, creams, suppositories, or dissolvable films may be used by women to prevent pregnancy.
- Women can practice the Rhythm Method by learning to recognize the days they are fertile and abstaining from sex before and during those days.

What help is currently available?

In the United States, Title X family planning clinics provided through the U. S. Department of Human Services, Office of Family Planning and Office of Population Affairs have filled an important role in ensuring access to a comprehensive range of family planning and related preventive health services for millions of low-income or uninsured individuals. Title X is the only federal grant program dedicated solely to providing individuals with wide-ranging family planning and related preventive health services. The program is designed to provide access to contraceptive supplies and information to all who want and need them with priority given to low-income individuals. All services are available on a voluntary and confidential basis.

Internationally, the Bill Gates Foundation's Family Planning program is working to bring access to high-quality contraceptive information, services, and supplies to millions of women in the world's poorest countries. The foundation's support includes assessing family planning needs, particularly among the most vulnerable populations, identifying access barriers and funding gaps, and fostering coordination among governments, partners, and donors. It also works to increase funding and improve policies for family planning, create public-private partnerships to expand contraceptive access and options, develop innovative and affordable contraceptive technologies, and support further research to close knowledge gaps.

<u>Who presently provides family planning / contraceptives?</u>

It is important that global family planning is widely available and easily accessible through cultural midwives and other trained health workers to anyone who is sexually active, including adolescents. Midwives are trained to provide locally available and culturally acceptable contraceptive methods. Other trained health workers, for example, community health workers, also provide counseling and some family planning methods, for example, pills and condoms. For methods such as sterilization, women and men need to be referred to a medical doctor.

Contraceptive use has increased in many parts of the developed world, but continues to be low in Latin America, India and sub-Saharan Africa. Globally, the proportion of childbearing women's use of a modern contraceptive method has risen only minimally. The use of contraception by men makes up a very small portion of the above calculation. The modern contraceptive methods for men have been basically limited to male condoms and sterilization. Both of these choices are generally ignored by most men in almost all cultures. This unmet need for contraception and education remains way too high and is fueled by both a growing population, and a continuing shortage of family planning services.

What can you as an individual do? For starters, make a determined effort to support groups, organizations, and proposals that promote birth control and family planning. This means doing things such as contributing money, doing volunteer work, fundraising, and spreading information to the public. However, the most important thing you as an individual can do ... is practicing what you are preaching.

"Consider the problem of over-population. Rapidly mounting human numbers are pressing ever more heavily on natural resources. What is to be done? ... The annual increase in numbers should be reduced. But how? We are given two choices -- famine, pestilence, and war, on the one hand, birth control on the other. Most of us choose birth control."

Alex Huxley

Fundamental Law #1 (Elucidation)

Let's start with a deliberation on the issue of abortion. Neoteric Humanism acknowledges the difficult conflict arising from the First Fundamental Law which states that "you will not commit or contribute to murder" and the disagreement and discord this creates in the Pro-Choice vs. Pro-Life debate.

There is one principal reason why there has been no common ground or harmony between pro-life and pro-choice supporters. That cause is the absolute lack of agreement as to the precise arrival of human "identity". In other words, at what point does newly conceived life become a human being with full civil rights, the most important of which is ... the right to life. The opinions of people, as a rule, typically fall into one of the two categories listed below.

Human "Identity" begins:

(A) at the moment of conception or (B) at some point after conception but before birth.

If an individual believes in the second proposition (B) above, this then leads to the following dilemma. After life has begun ... yet before birth, under what conditions is an abortion ... a personal choice ... or murder? The positions held by most people of (A) or (B) above, generally fall into one or a mixture of the following camps:

- Abortion is never a personal choice and should always be considered murder, even if performed to save the life of the mother.

- It should be limited to cases where the mother's life is at risk or the possibility of permanent disability to the mother is high.
- It should be allowable after rape or an incestuous relationship.
- Women have the right to an abortion for any reason up to as much as 24 weeks of pregnancy.
- The mother has the right to terminate a pregnancy at any time.

Abortion is among the most divisive and hotly debated topics of our time. At its core, however, is still the key question "when does human identity begin". So what does make a human being ... a human being? It is the considered opinion of Neoteric Humanism that the question has already been answered and has been answered by science. Each human being has a unique genetic code. The fertilized egg will only produce a human being ... not a Spotted Dolphin, Golden Eagle, Redwood Tree, or a beautiful Monarch Butterfly. Your DNA is what makes you a human being and your DNA is created the moment the genetic material from your father unites with the genetic material from your mother. In short, science has already proved that "human identity" begins at conception.

Therefore ... with this clear-cut conclusion as to when "human Identity" begins, under what circumstances should abortion fall under this philosophy's Fundamental Law #1 as "murder", even if "lawfully legal." This being the question, the expressed position of this philosophy is ... that since abortion is ultimately the taking of a human life ... and given the choice of choosing between life or death ... if one is to error ... it should be on the side of life. Consequently, as concerns Fundamental Law #1 ... an abortion, with the exception of serious health issues or risk to the mother's life, cases of rape or incest, being an underage child (under the age of 21) or mentally incompetent ... shall be considered infanticide, and ruled as murder. This sets a philosophy guideline that an abortion done under the special exceptions noted above, <u>would not</u> be considered murder, as long as it was performed in a safe manner and was rare.

This may raise a question as to why an underage child should be included in the exceptions to the rule. Is not it still preferable to save the baby? Yes, it is preferable to save the child and one would hope that would be the choice made by the mother. However, we as a society, have over time concluded that children should be treated differently from adults as they have not yet matured enough to be responsible for many of their choices and actions. Especially at a time of life when young human hormones are ragging and sex is such a strong driving force. This is why we need to include the passion, obliviousness, and ignorance of youth under the exceptions.

It is the position of this philosophy that even though no woman should go to prison or be held liable for murder under the law. It is especially abhorrent and objectionable when an abortion is utilized as a callus form of birth control and will be considered murder under the fundamental laws, even if done legally. ... If this is the ultimate decision, one that will end a human life, than it should be made only after a review of all other options. All concerned should have a full grasp of the physical and psychological consequences of such an action ... both now and far into the future.

So, is there any hope of finding common ground and agreement between the Pro-Life and Pro-Choice factions? ... The answer is yes! I believe the majority on both sides of this issue will agree that <u>prevention is the key</u> to reducing this dilemma. Preventing an unplanned pregnancy would resolve this divisive issue and the undesirable choices it forces on mother, father, doctor, and others involved. Neoteric Humanist's will consequently make it one of their highest priorities to promote contraceptive use while at the same time encouraging sex abstinence as a way to avoid an unplanned pregnancy. Young people in our society, in particular, need information on the risks and consequences of sexual activity. This should be taught in the home and in high school and various contraceptive options should be readily available in convenient and confidential locations.

Resuming this issue ... clarifying Fundamental Law #1 as it relates to War, Self-Defense, the Death Penalty, and Euthanasia. The first two of these, war and self-defense, for the most part, are viewed by nearly all of the civilized world and this philosophy as clear-cut issues. In this discussion, it makes sense to first review the generally accepted definition of the word Murder. Most civilized societies, from ancient times to modern-day, have considered murder an appallingly severe crime deserving of very harsh punishment. Murder is considered wrong by society because it violates the most basic of human rights ... the right to life. Murder is the killing of or the inflicting of grievous bodily harm towards an individual, in most cases, with malice and premeditation without justification or valid excuse. This may take the form of revenge, a crime of passion, reckless indifference, a hired killer, or those crimes committed during war to mention a few. This distinguishes murder from killings that are done within the boundaries of the law, justified self-defense, or the killing of enemy combatants by other lawful combatants. There are of course some exceptions, for example, those cases considered as war crimes or if the killer was suffering from a condition that affected their judgment at the time ... depression, medication or those that had a serious mental illness, disease or defect. These are conditions that should be taken into account when assessing responsibility or punishment. ... Of course, when considering the Death Penalty as the sentence for murder, this raises positions both pro and con.

A few of the asserted Pros:

1. That taxpayer dollars would not be going to support and care for these appalling individuals.
2. That a death penalty would serve as a deterrent for future murders that might be committed by others.
3. That some type of closure can be brought to those families shattered by these offenders, knowing that these people have no possibility of killing again.
4. That with contemporary technology we can be even more certain that the one who perpetrated the crime will be the one put to death.

A few of the asserted Cons:

1. That in most cases, the cost of the execution process and the appeals given the defendant is far greater than the cost of a life prison sentence.
2. That the "deterrent" belief is questionable. That a future serial killer rarely considers their possible death via Capital Punishment prior to committing a murder. A murderer typically operates with the belief they will not be caught.
3. That the death penalty will not bring the victim or victims back to life.
4. That a death penalty is a barbaric form of punishment.

While both positions have legitimate arguments, this philosophy will favor an anti-death penalty platform. The reasoning goes beyond those noted above. Consider the fact that death penalty convictions have been overturned on appeal because of prosecutorial misconduct, as well as serious errors by inept court-appointed defense attorneys. Also, take into account the lack of equal justice under the law when inadequate representation is given to the poor when their very life hangs in the balance? The current system does have faults and unfairly favors the rich and famous. ... With our existing U. S. death penalty program, there have been people on death row where it has later been shown that there are serious questions about their guilt. When the outcomes are life and death, we need to understand that it is preferable that those assumed guilty end up behind bars rather than risk that an innocent dies. ... Here again, this philosophy believes that when it comes to life and death it is better to err on the side of life. Not a single innocent person should ever be put to death and this should not be too much to ask of a fair and civilized society.

Euthanasia is another difficult dilemma that requires open examination. Should Euthanasia or Physician-Assisted Suicide be considered murder? ... The dictionary provides this as the definition of euthanasia: "The means of bringing about a gentle and easy death. The view that the law should sanction the putting painlessly to death of those suffering from incurable and extremely painful diseases". The term "euthanasia" in general refers to a situation in which one party adopts a course of action with the intention of causing the death of a second party in order to alleviate suffering. This practice falls under two categories "non-voluntary "and "voluntary". Voluntary Euthanasia is a term used in those instances of euthanasia in which a clearly competent person makes a voluntary and persistent request to be helped to die. Where-as in Non-Voluntary Euthanasia the person is unable to make a decision or cannot make their wishes known. This includes cases where the person is in a brain dead coma, the person is too young (e.g. a baby), the person is totally senile, the person is very severely mentally retarded, or the person is so mentally disturbed or brain-damaged that they cannot make a decision for themselves.

Proponents of euthanasia and physician-assisted suicide assert that terminally ill people should have the right to end their suffering with a quick, dignified, and compassionate death. Opponents of euthanasia and physician-assisted suicide contend that doctors have a moral responsibility to keep their patients alive as directed by the Hippocratic Oath. They argue there may be a "slippery slope" from euthanasia to murder, and that legalizing euthanasia will unfairly target the poor and disabled.

At the center of the distinction between killing and allowing one to die is the difference between physical causality and moral culpability. On the one hand, to actively bring the life of another to an end … is to directly kill the other, the action is the physical cause of death. On the other hand, to passively allow someone to die from a disease that one cannot cure is to permit the disease to act as the cause of death.

Is there a moral difference between passive and active euthanasia? The distinction between killing "active euthanasia" and allowing one to die "passive euthanasia" is still the fact that lives can come to an end as the result of the direct action of another who becomes the cause of death, or as the result of natural forces where no human agent has acted. However, if one withholds action, it may take the person longer to die, and so they may suffer more than they would if more direct action were taken and a lethal option implemented. This reality provides a strong argument for concluding that, once the decision not to prolong a person's agony has been made active euthanasia is actually preferable to passive euthanasia. The point being here that the process of being "allowed to die" can be relatively slow and painful, whereas being given a lethal alternative is relatively quick and painless.

Reflecting on the above considerations, this philosophy shall deem that voluntary euthanasia shall not be considered murder should it be performed in an active manner if so requested by a fully cognitive and rational patient. Though these decisions regarding life and death would normally fall in favor of preserving life, if it is to be a life of unbearable pain, then an individual's requests shall have priority. This decision should never be taken lightly and should always embrace options for life. Non-voluntary euthanasia shall also not be considered murder. However, in this case, it must meet with the approval and support of a qualified doctor and family member(s) if this has not previously been expressed in a legal document, such as a living will.

With this possible occurrence lurking in the future for each of us, it is highly recommended that all Neoteric Humanist adherents submit a living will. A living will is a legal written expression of how one wishes to be treated under specific medical conditions. This document allows one to express whether or not they want to be given life-sustaining treatments in the event of a terminal illness or critical injury. Members should make sure that family and friends are made aware of their choices and that the document is kept in a place where it is easily accessible.

The Inner Circle:

This association welcomes and encourages the community to visit and learn more about the practice of Neoteric Humanism and to share in many of its scheduled lessons, programs, and events. It is a fundamental obligation of this philosophy's mission to educate, participate, and be of service to the public. However, visitors and guests who wish to receive the most important and significant benefits, which are reserved for those of the Inner Circle, must be both qualified and worthy.

To meet the above two requirements, it is first necessary to substantiate that those who desire to be part of the Inner Circle are eligible. The Candidates for the Inner Circle are "qualified" by these eight requirements: They will be qualified if they abide by all the provisions found in **SUITABLE:** These individuals have …

- Synergized mind and body with the methodology of Neoteric Humanism.
- Undertaken all but the last two stages of the eight-step guide.
- Incurred no violations of the Four Fundamental Laws.
- Totally committed themselves to the Desirable Traits.
- Adhered to its mission, participate in this philosophy's endeavors, and are genuinely committed to its objectives.
- Built on and are questing toward the goals stated in the Pursuits A-P.
- Lead an ethical livelihood and are acting with sound moral conduct.
- Engaged and dedicated themselves to not only pursue their own personal growth and aspirations … but for those of others as well.

Of equal, if not of greater importance, is the second pre-requisite of being "worthy". If the Inner Circle is to completely embrace a new candidate, they must first determine if the individual is absolutely trustworthy, reliable, and of good and honorable character. This is vital for two reasons. To begin with, the new member will have 24 /7 access to all but a few private facets of the assembly's facilities. The Inner Circle must have total confidence that this full admittance privilege will not be misused. Furthermore, and of more import, is that one day an Inner Circle member may depend on this person to provide assistance to them in a time of genuine necessity. Those in the Inner Circle need to be assured that this new initiate will fulfill their sworn obligation to provide shelter, sustenance, support, and protection in times of hardship. This is a pledge that the prospective new member needs to be fully committed to. It is the central obligation and a key responsibility of every participant in the Inner Circle. Those permitted to join must be people of steadfast and unfailing trust. Those with whom you would, if need be, leave your children and have total confidence in their safekeeping. They must be completely dependable and reliable individuals, that when times are at their darkest, will bring hope and assistance into another member's life. For those permitted to join the Inner Circle, the privilege is a great honor and a testimonial both within the membership and throughout the community. Your admittance declares to the world your ideals, virtue, and character. It affirms that you are a person who may be completely trusted and one who has impeccable ethics, fidelity, and integrity. A person to be valued, respected, and appreciated.

The candidate(s) for the Inner Circle is "worthy" if they meet these four basic stipulations. If the Inner Circle is to completely embrace a new person as a true affiliate, they must first agree that the individual will be steadfast in their obligations to the values found in **TEAM:** That they are ...

- **T**rustworthy and responsible.
- **E**thical and honorable.
- **A**uthentic and sincere. And of ...
- **M**oral and steadfast character.

So you see ... joining the Inner Circle should not be taken lightly. It is only for those willing to take on a life of commitment, dedication, and personal responsibility. It is for those who truly wish to forge a better world and are willing to do more than just provide lip service. It is for those who, at the conclusion of their days will be able to look back and say "Yes ... my life was valuable, it made a positive impact on the world, and had genuine meaning."

"Inner Circle "Initiation

Becoming a member of the "Inner Circle" is a necessary step if one is to attain all the advantages of Neoteric Humanism. It is at this stage where one is embraced by the very core of the organization and becomes much more than just a simple participant within the association's gatherings. The candidate, after initiation, ceases to be an emerging adherent and becomes a full member of the "Inner Circle". It is at this moment that they are bestowed with all the rights and privileges of this special group and the HUB itself (See the HUB on page #167 for more details). For the candidate to be granted these rights, access, and privileges it is necessary for them to make confirmations, commitments, and vows and to take on specific obligations and responsibilities. While they are doing so, they will, in turn, be receiving similar promises and vows from those in the Inner Circle as they take on obligations and responsibilities to the candidate. The elements of this will become self-evident as you read through the detailed ceremony that follows. This occasion in of itself is not considered a spiritual, mystic, or religious experience. It is treated, however, as a very serious and formal affair. It is an event consisting of affirmations that contain specific symbols, terms, and actions that are designed to illustrate or illuminate an important theme or concept. Try to maintain an inward-looking awareness and comprehension of these as you begin reading about this rite of passage.

One might ask ... why have a formal initiation ritual? To be perfectly clear, it is not compulsory and if the Senior Director (La Kompaso) determines that all entrance conditions have been met and all commitments have been fulfilled, than the candidate may receive full membership. ... However, having a comprehensive ceremony like this serves as an important social binder to the rest of the membership. The detailed themes and actions create a communal atmosphere that brings members closer to each other and instills in them a distinctive identity. The ritual itself also reminds everybody of what is truly important and inspires individual motivation as they go about their lives.

A secondary function is that this ceremony also transforms an otherwise ordinary event into something that has an impact ... an impact that goes beyond what a less formalized affair would add up to. In other words, there is a combined effect because the totality of impressions produced in this ritual stimulates emotions and adds to self-identification, thus making the event both special and memorable. The activities performed in this ceremony likewise promote beneficial values and ideals. These values and ideals, whether they may be traditional or new, can then be vividly and openly conveyed to all participants. ... For all of us, life brings changes. ... This observance signifies a change in a person's life ...

a transition from their former self to a superior individual. This transition provides a purpose and function at both the individual and the group level by revealing this conversion and bringing it into the light. This initiation into the "Inner Circle" is especially significant because it not only provides support and security for the individual and the group ... but it also produces a direct positive value to those who live in their community.

The Formal Initiation Ceremony

The participants of this procedure: (Their designations in Esperanto)

La Kompaso: The Senior Director of this particular Neoteric Humanist Association. *La Kompaso* shepherds all members and helps keep them moving in the right direction. *La Kompaso* will assist and guide them if they get off course or lose their way. *La Kompaso* wears a white stole with the TIME, BING, QUEST WHEEL, DESIRABLE TRAITS, TRANSFORMAION, COMPASS, KUPP, EIGHT STEPS, FOUR LAWS and AFFINITY SYMBOL imprinted on the front. *La Kompaso*, holds a White and Red Staff in their right hand, designed as a Compass Needle in likeness, and a KUPP in the left hand. See the section on "Visual Symbols" to use as a reference. Review their individual declarations for their purpose and significance.

La Suno: The local Apprentice Director appointed by *La Kompaso*. *La Suno* will lead the Applicant(s) out of the darkness and into the light. *La Suno* will assist the Applicant(s) in practicing and preparing them for the entire ceremonial process. *La Suno* will wear a white stole with the shinning SUN over their heart and the four main parts of the day: SUNRISE, NOON, SUNSET, and NIGHT symbols below on the front.

La Luno: The Youth Director and Deputy appointed by *La Kompaso*. *La Luno* is the skeptic and antagonist of the Applicant(s). *La Luno* asks the hard questions and pursues any issues of character, reputation, and integrity regarding the Applicant(s). *La Luno* investigates the individual's background for any negative or questionable actions or activities. *La Luno* wears a white stole with the NIGHT MOON over the heart and the four seasons: SPRING, SUMMER, FALL and WINTER symbols below on the front.

La Partnero(j) Spica and Arcturus: These are the two or more individuals, pledging their personal support and allegiance to the new Applicant(s) and the ones who will attest to the positive qualities and moral fiber of the Applicant(s). One will wear the SPICA STAR and the other the ARCTURUS STAR symbols over their heart. In their left hand, they will hold a short and narrow 6" tree branch or wooden rod.

La Kandidato(j): The individual(s) wishing to become part of the "Inner Circle". La Kandidato(j) shall wear a plain white stole over their clothing with their novice Quest Wheel emblem pinned over their heart and an Ascender emblem on the right shoulder. In their left hand, they will also hold a short and narrow 6" tree branch or wooden rod.

1. Begin with a full gathering of the "Inner Circle" ... all standing in a circle but positioned evenly in either the Southern or Northern arch of the ring. This area is than divided in two by an approximate 4 foot wide by 12-foot long entry carpet or pathway inside it running from East to West.
2. *La Kompaso* will be seated on the West end of the carpet or pathway, soon to be holding a KUPP of purified

water in the left hand and the Compass Needle designed Staff in the right. On a table to the right sits a
HUB Key with neck chain, Yea and Nay Stones, Gold
tinted Quest Wheel, and a Wedge of Clay.

3. At the agreed-upon time, *La Kompaso* stands, raps loudly on the floor with the staff while announcing: "It is
time, it is time, it is time, it is time". This signals everyone to be in their proper positions and to be silent.

4. *La Kompaso* calls out, *"La Suno* is rising in the East and
is approaching." *La Kompaso* starts clapping loudly and
together so do the members of the Inner Circle.

5. *La Suno*, at the sound of clapping, retrieves *La
Kandidato(j)*, who is holding a short 6" branch/rod,
from a dimly lit area of seclusion and then proceeding
from the East, enters into the light and stops at the beginning of the carpet or pathway.

6. *La Luno* comes forward, closely examines *La
Kandidato(j)*, and then questions *La Suno*, "Who is this
… that approaches our "Inner Circle?"

7. *La Suno* replies, "I bring forth, an Ascender (*La
Kandidato(j) Name(s)*), who is emerging from the darkness, and is seeking deeper meaning, purpose, fellowship and fulfilment by joining with us."

8. *La Luno* walks half-way down the pathway, stops, and
then turns around facing *La Suno*.

9. *La Kompaso* asks, "Are you (*La Kandidato(j) Name(s)*),
prepared to leave the darkness behind you and live
your life completely and fully in the light?"

10. *La Kandidto(j)* replies, "I am."

11. *La Suno begins* escorting *La Kandidato(j)* along the
pathway.

12. *La Luno*, still at the half-way point puts foreword a
hand and states "Halt!" Then continues, "Perhaps *La*

Kandidato(j) is corrupt or enters with malicious intentions? Perhaps (he/she) is part of a vile or contemptible occupation or has exhibited shameful unethical or unacceptable behavior?

13. *La Kompaso* asks of the Inner Circle ... "If there is anyone here, who objects to this individual or can give any valid reason why we should not accept them, speak now so we may know your mind and consider your grounds. (Assuming no issues arise ... continue. If a statement of trepidation is made, the ceremony must stop until such time as it can be resolved by those concerned.)

14. *La Kompaso* "Very well, there being no objection or knowledge of ill will or grievous behavior. Do you, (*La Kandidato(j) Name(s)*), promise and swear, that you enter this "Inner Circle" in good faith and with no wicked, mischievous or harmful intent. That you will never purposely mislead, deceive or take advantage of anyone in our membership, their families, or their friends."

15. *La Kandidato(j)* "Yes I do so swear and promise. May I be cut off from all ties to this Inner Circle and this association, from my family and my friends and may my tongue be excised and my forehead branded as a deceiver, should I ever break this solemn bond and vow that I now make."

16. *La Kompaso* states, "*La Luno* ... you may let the candidate(s) proceed."

17. *La Luno* walks three-quarters of the way along the path ... trailed by *La Suno* and *La Kandidato(j)*.

18. *La Luno*, turns around and halts them, then states "Who shall be partners and shield *La Kandidato(j)* ... and agrees to act as their *La Partnero(j)*? Tell us what you know about this individual(s) and why you find them

worthy not only of your partnership, support, and protection, but that of this "Inner Circle". Is *La Kandidato(j)* truly worthy of the Stars of Spica and Arcturus who advocate and champion *La Kandidato(j)* efforts in completing the eight steps of the guide, its principles and the mission we all observe and abide by?"

19. *La Partnero(j) Spica (SPI-kah: The star of Harvest and Good Fortune: portraying Health, Prosperity, Opportunity, Success, Know-how, Regeneration and Security,)* steps forward from Southern Arch and gives a brief account of *La Kandidato(j)*, how they known them, their character, honesty, etc. *Spica* presents a tiny offering of food to *La Kandidato(j)* and then says "I freely promise to give comfort, support and protection to *(La Kandidato(j) Name(s).* Spica presents a 6" long thin tree branch/rod to *La Suno* and stands in the back of *La Suno* and *La Kandidato(j).*

20. *La Partnero(j) Arcturus (ark-TOO-rus: The star of Joy and Navigation: portraying Love, Family, Jubilation, Knowledge, Wisdom, and Generosity.)* next steps forward from the Northern Arch and relays their personal knowledge of the applicant's character and then places a small piece of cloth on the back of *La Kandidato(j)* while stating, "I freely promise to give comfort, support, and protection to *(La Kandidato(j) Name(s)."* Arcturus presents a 6" long thin branch/rod to *La Suno* and then proceeds to stand in the back of *La Suno* and the *La Kandidato(j).*

21. *Both Spica and Arcturus La Partnero(j)* then pronounce together … "We find and pledge that *(La Kandidato(j) Name(s))* is deserving, honorable and worthy to become a member of our "Inner Circle".

22. *La Kompaso* asks, "Should misfortune transpire, who else will raise their right hand and agree to provide sanctuary and sustenance for this *La Kandidato(j)*".

23. *All Members* in the North and South Arches raise their right hand and respond "we will".

24. *La Kompaso* states to *La Kandidato(j) and La Partnero(j) ...* "Come Forward then and let us witness your allegiance to each other and our association". *La Kandidato(j) and La Partnero(j)* move in front of *La Kompaso.*

25. *La Kompaso* asks "Do you take these obligations freely"?

26. *La Kandidato(j) and La Partnero(j)* say, "We do".

27. *La Kompaso* asks the candidate "Have you read, understood, and agree with the terms and usage of the HUB and all our facilities?"

28. *La Kandidato(j)* says, "I do"

29. *La Kompaso* says "*La Kandidato(j)* ... drink of this **KUPP** and then tell us the Four Key Aspirations you aspire to attain?"

30. *La Kandidato(j)* Drinks and says, "To **K**now and improve myself. To **U**nderstand and be of service to others. To **P**ractice kindness, truth, fairness, and **P**roduce a positive impact with my life choices."

31. *La Kompaso* says "*La Kandidato(j)* tell us ... what four factors do you believe will lead to an individual's completeness, safety, contentment and well-being?"

32. *La Kandidato(j)* says "The Quest Wheel and its Four Quads ... **W**isdom, **I**ntegration, **S**ecurity, and **H**armony?"

33. *La Kompaso* says" *La Kandidato(j)* will you support and work to advance the "Inner Circle's" Goals, Ambitions, Principles, and Mission?"

34. *La Kandidato(j)* says, "I will"

35. *La Kompaso* says *"La Kandidato(j)* To the best of your ability, have you adhered to all the steps of the guide but this and the last level?"

36. *La Kandidato(j)* says, "I have"

37. *La Kompaso* says *"La Kandidato(j)* are you actively living by The Desirable Traits and are undertaking the Pursuits A through P to become a better individual … and you have not broken any of the Four Fundamental Laws?"

38. *La Kandidato(j)* says, "I am and have not"

39. *La Kompaso* says *"La Kandidato(j)* Do you fully understand that if you break any of these 4 laws that you will be cast out of this "Inner Circle" and our association? That you shall remain outside, having lost all privileges, vows, obligations and the security promised therein. That your name will be deleted from our membership and that all your affiliation components will be repossessed.

40. *La Kandidato(j)* says "I do".

41. *La Kompaso and then La Kandidato(j)* "Very well … Recite with me this oath … I (*La Kandidato(j) Name(s)* _____, … promise before all those now present … That I will when needed … provide sanctuary, comfort, and sustenance … to any who belong in the "Inner Circle. … Furthermore … I give my solemn promise to never abuse this privilege … and will voluntarily agree to give up my membership … should I fail in this vow I have now made … should that be the judgment of the association's Director." *La Kompaso* says "Now please pass your branches/wooden rods to *La Suno* and prepare to sign the oath you have just committed to in the "Inner Circle's" membership book."

42. *La Kompaso* says, "All members please witness that *La Kandidato(j) and La Partnero(j)* have given *La Suno* their branches/rods of mutual support, and the membership book is now to be signed. (*La Suno*, takes the branches received and proceeds to bind them. *La Suno* then presents a pen for *La Kandidato(j) and La Partnero(j)* to sign their names in the membership book. When the book is signed *La Suno* advises them to then step back to their original positions standing in front of *La Kompaso*.)

43. *La Suno* now hands the bound branches to *La Kompaso*.

44. *La Kompaso* states ..."Very well done! (Holding up the branches/rods high) ... Just as the sun rises on earth in the East and sets in the West, so have you, (*La Kandidato(j) Name*) journeyed and so you will continue your quest. But from this point on, you may rest assured that your well-being is now also protected by the strength of this "Inner Circle", just as the union of these branches/rods is strengthened by being bound one to another. As a worthy initiated member, you are now entitled to the following benefits"

   A. *La Kompaso* says "The Key to our sanctuary and amenities (*La Luno* holds high for all to see and then presents the Key, attached to a neck chain over new members head) where all of the facilities, for you, will always be open and available."

   B. "Your official Yea and Nay stones so that you may exercise your right to vote and have a voice on important issues of this association". (*La Luno* holds a box of stones high for all to see and then offers box to new member(s).

   C. "Now we will replace your Quest Wheel with one tinted in Gold, one that will show your dedication and one which will keep central in your mind our purpose, principles and mission." (*La Luno* holds high for all to see then removes the novice Pin and attaches the Inner Circle Pin of admittance to the new member's white stole.)

D. "And lastly a formless Wedge of Clay so you remember that it's up to you to shape your future. (*La Suno* holds up and hands the Wedge of Clay to new member(s).

45. *La Kompaso* … "Let all of us now here recite our mantra … **BING**."

46. *All Membership* "It is my belief that … As I **B**etter myself I will I **I**mprove my family and my community, as I improve my family and community, a **N**ew vision for people will evolve, as a new vision for people evolves, I **G**ive hope and optimism to the future."

47. *La Kompaso* says "Now, I reveal our Affinity Greeting, its usage and why Four Fingers are important. It is signified thus … Thumb down and four fingers of the right hand raised or formed before shaking hands. This hand signal, is used when greeting other members or family and friends and is followed by saying in English or Esperanto … **P**eace, **H**ealth, **H**appiness, and **P**rosperity or **P**aco, **S**ano, **F**elico kaj **P**rospero … an active Inner Circle member's response should be … **T**o **y**ou **a**s **w**ell or **A**l **v**i **a**nkau. … The number four is noteworthy and is repeated throughout this philosophy because of what it represents to us. It reminds us of the Quest Wheel: **W**isdom, **I**ntegration, **S**ecurity, and **H**armony that leads us to our completeness, safety, contentment and well-being. The numeral aids our focus on the 4 cardinal virtues of **J**ustice, **P**rudence, **F**ortitude, and **T**emperance. It speaks to us, of the 4 major bearings: **N**orth, **S**outh, **E**ast, and **W**est and thus

the importance to continue in the right direction and on the right path making a constructive and positive impact in all things that we do. It causes us to reflect on the 4 parts of the day: **S**unrise, **N**oon, **S**unset, and **N**ight and that we must strive to make the very most of each day for our family and our community. We think of the 4 seasons: **S**pring, **S**ummer, **F**all, and **W**inter and this teaches us that it takes time and patient dedication if we want to shape a better future. The number 4 causes us to consider the natural elements: **E**arth, **W**ater, **A**ir and **F**ire and to recognize that each of these contribute to change, just as it is up to each one of us to play an active and involved role in transforming society for the betterment of ourselves, our families, our communities and our world. ... Finally, we contemplate the 4 parts of life itself: **B**irth, **Y**outh, **A**dulthood, and **D**eath. ... Through this we understand our mortality and that all things are integrated into one great wheel, a wheel in continuous motion and modification without a beginning and without an end. That it's up to us to impact and advance our world, understanding we are here for only a limited amount of time!"

48. *La Kompaso* states: "Now ... As we join together at this time and this place. We ask for peace, health, happiness, and prosperity. May our association continue to grow with every new member, marriage, and birth of a child. May every hardship make this "Inner Circle" stronger. May it always be that whenever we reach out in need, that our hands will find our family, associates, and friends. At all times, we will share with others, so they may grow in strength and spirit. At all times we will remember those who need and most depend on us. We are family, we are *La Partnero(j)* we are friends

and ... we are one united community. ... Therefore, by the authority bestowed upon me by this association ... I pronounce you (*La Kandidato(j) Name(s)*) (*La Kompaso* taps twice on each shoulder with the staff) a fully vested member of our Inner Circle ... congratulations!! ... Before we break to begin enjoying our meal together, let each of us come forward and greet and welcome our new brother(s) and/or sister(s)."

** *Concerning an act of Redemption: An individual who has broken any of the Fundamental Laws requires a review by the Director and Inner Circle Members as to whether they may be reformed and redeemed.*

1) *All requests for redemption must be formally written and submitted to the Director of the association by the expelled individual(s).*

2) *If the Director decides redemption may be possible. He or she will layout the terms and conditions which must be met before re-admission would be theoretically possible.*

3) *The Inner Circle Membership then must be offered a blind container for Yea or Nay counting on this potential re-admission. The vote taken must be **80% YES** or greater to be granted.*

4) *If YES ... All terms and conditions must be met before re-admittance will be allowed.*

At this point, it is necessary that we will build an Inner Circle membership profile. Why is this important? If one is to develop a healthy and close relationship with others, it is crucial to understand that these relationships don't just happen; they're built. In order to build these healthy personal connections, we have to be open enough to communicate our history, needs, wants and desires so that members can understand each other and then are more able to champion each other in the way each needs to be supported.

"Inner Circle" Member Profile Date:_____

All questions below "are optional". Please complete only to your degree of comfort. This material will be kept for internal use only and will not be made available to anyone outside of the "Inner Circle". The purpose is to provide contact information for meetings or emergencies. To help celebrate with your family, new births, birthdays, anniversaries, honors, awards, and events. This data will also let us know what is important to you and will allow us to assist or help you in those areas.

With the exception of the "Inner Circle", this will be kept confidential in a safe area and will be available for you to completely remove, change or update.

Please PRINT clearly.

1. Your Full Name / Nickname:_____

2. Marital Status:_____

3. Professional or Vocation title:_____

4. Home Address:_____

5. Home / Cell Telephone / E-mail:_____

6. Same Work Information:_____

7. Important Co-Worker's Names:_____

8. Birth Date and Place:_____

9. Town (s) you were raised in:_____

10. College / Professional / OtherDegrees:_____

11. Skills / Talents / Special Abilities:_____

12. Clubs & Associations / Honors:_____

13. Children / Grand Kids:_____

14. Siblings:_____

15. Sports and hobbies you have or are participating in:

_____

16. Military / Based Where / Rank / Awards:_____

17. Things I enjoy: _____

18. Something you should know about me: _____

19. An important goal for me:_____

20. Something I could use help with:_____

(Duplicate same information for Spouse / Companion profile)

The Emblem of Neoteric Humanism

The image above will appear numerous times trough out this Philosophy's text, functions and activities. Earlier in this book, it was used to characterize Neoteric Humanism's "Quest Wheel". The Quest Wheel and its separate components, as we discussed earlier, denoted either an important aspiration of this Philosophy or to explain one's relationship within the association. Each section or quad of this wheel included a spoke traveling inwards, the ultimate purpose being, to connect and join with the Inner Circle. ... Now is a good time to point out that in addition to being this philosophy's "Quest Wheel", this insignia, simultaneously functions as the official symbol of Neoteric Humanism. It proclaims to all a commitment to the betterment of the individual as well as the world community. Displayed by an evolving novice or Inner Circle Member, it marks one's ongoing dedication to and within the Neoteric Humanist Association. The following provides an overall explanation.

Begin by looking closer at the wheel itself. Inquisitive guests and novices are viewed as those who occupy the "outer rim" of this image. They are welcome to attend most gatherings and are invited to listen and learn about Neoteric Humanism. They may participate in many of the classes, activities, and events that are offered by the association. As non-members, however, they are not yet eligible to enjoy the exclusive advantages and privileges available to those who are part of the "Inner Circle".

Practicing novices are encouraged to wear the small copper replica of the emblem and are those who are actively striving to move from the rim of the wheel to its innermost center. They begin this trek by first adhering to the aspirations of its four quads which will direct them towards Wisdom, Integration, Security, and Harmony. These individuals will seek counseling and guidance from the association's La Kompaso (Director) and other members as needed while being fully committed to abiding by the eight-step process of the guide. They engage in this effort to better themselves, enrich their families, improve their community, and provide hope and optimism to the future. It is their intention, to become both qualified and worthy so that they may be admitted into the "Inner Circle". However … until such time as they are fully initiated … there will still be meetings, voting, actions, access, and special events where only those of the "Inner Circle" will be allowed to enter and participate.

The central hub of the Quest Wheel (The "Inner Circle") represents those people who have fully transcended their past lifestyle and have begun living one with greater meaning and purpose. At this point, the "new you" has arrived, has been initiated into the "Inner Circle", and has been bestowed with its most sought after rights, access, and privileges. Your emblematic Gold Quest Wheel no longer that of a novice, but now that of a full-fledged member declares to the world … your integrity, virtue, and character. Your obtaining of this brightly polished pin is a great honor both within the association as well as in the community. It proclaims to all that you are a person in whom the "Inner Circle" has complete faith, trust, and confidence. Those who achieve access to the "Inner Circle" are permitted to enter at all times the association HUB, participate

in all activities, vote and have a voice regarding important issues of the membership. This is the ultimate aim of all those
who desire to attain completeness, safety, contentment, and
well-being through Neoteric Humanism. This is your path to
Peace, Health, Happiness, and Prosperity.

So why not go ahead and commit yourself joining the
"Inner Circle"? We are all in this life and universe together
and what-ever we chose to do, one day our individual clock
will run out of time. This is the case for all of us, so you may as
well make this the most wonderful and fulfilling life you can.
Chose the Neoteric Humanist methodology to become the
best you can be … and then put your heart and mind into pursuing it. You have much more "will power" than you know.
One determined individual has always and will always be the
spark plug that can make our world a better place.

"All men are caught in an inescapable network of
mutuality, tied in a single garment of
destiny. Whatever affects one directly affects all indirectly.
I can never be what I ought
to be until you are what you ought to be, and you can never
be what you ought to be
until I am what I ought to be."

Martin Luther King, Jr.

The Humanist Union Bastion (the HUB)

The Humanist Union Bastion, aka The HUB, is the gathering place where the Inner Circle Members, novices and inquisitive guests will meet, work, plan, retreat to, learn, and play while promoting the goals, mission, and ideology of Neoteric Humanism. Its purpose being to provide a convenient, suitable, solidly built and safe facility for its members and those in the local community to gather and utilize. Its primary function will be to facilitate the safety, personal growth, education, and communal activities of its practicing participants and others within the community.

Should there be an opportunity to build a HUB complex from the ground up, there are many features it would be desirable to have included. Beginning from the initial blueprints to the laying of the foundation, to its completion, it is intended to be very sturdy in its construction. This is a crucial factor as a key role of the HUB is to provide a safe retreat for its members and the community in times of imminent peril or in the event of a man-made or natural disaster. Preferably, the main central building will have two levels, one robust section above ground and a strong and durable supporting basement underneath. Both levels should be built with exceptional strength and protection in mind. The optimum site for the HUB construction would be on a sizeable tract of stable land, preferably erected near its highest point. If possible, this site would be located near a good water source and yet situated well above any potential floodplain. Within this primary building, there could be set aside specific areas for an independent power supply, storage containers of fuel and fresh water, a septic tank, and a recycling / waste disposal system.

In addition to being a very sturdy structure it would also be constructed in such a way as to be highly resistant to not only hurricane force winds, but also tornados, fires or floods. Internally, it would be ideal to install easily adaptable divider walls which would allow for a variety of diverse activities and functions. These being: ... meetings, education, ceremonies, meditation, sports, exercise, skill-building, multi-media, performing arts, social dances, and similar programs. This upper-level layout preferably would allow for a large great room, with high ceilings and a raised stage to one side. Specific areas could be set aside for storage, dressing rooms, toilets, showers, and multiple well-designated emergency exits. The exterior windows should be installed not only to let in light but also should be of a robust and heavy-duty nature. These windows having heavy shutters mounted which could be easily and securely closed and sealed during extremely unsafe or threatening outdoor conditions.

Finally, once safety, structural soundness, and function have been addressed, the exterior design of this upper level could then be considered. This would be an opportunity to make an artistic and visual statement in its overall appearance. One approach that would help accomplish this would be crafting the overall building to resemble the "Quest Wheel" symbol itself. The main round HUB structure would thus be located at its center and from this inner core; four spoke-like corridors would lead outward toward four auxiliary buildings. These secondary facilities, by their rectangular, elongated and arched design would then form the outer rim of the wheel. The exterior walls of this wheel would provide ideal locations for an assortment of works of art relating to the desires, pursuits and principles of Neoteric Humanism.

As regards the lower level of The HUB, assuming it is feasible and attainable ... it should be constructed in a similar manner as regards strength and safety as well. In this basement location it could provide not only protection, but also special areas for general service equipment, utility functions, meeting rooms, and additional storage. An ideal composition of this level would include these:

- both backup wood and propane heating systems for comfort, hot water, showering, washing, cleaning, food preparation, and cooking.
- a standby generator, solar panels, fuel, and batteries for cold storage, heating, lighting, and general electrical needs and services.
- storage units for holding a variety of emergency food stocks, water, basic domestic supplies, bed kits, blankets, and a variety of assorted utensils, cooking, food preparation, and cleaning supplies.
- lockers containing heavy-duty clothing, hard hats, work gloves, rubber boots, rain ponchos, and general work tools and equipment.
- an equipped wood, metal, electrical, and plumbing workshop.
- a HAM Radio/communications /computer and internet center.
- a medical station stocked with emergency supplies and equipment.
- Food and supplies for animals and pets.

Having advance preparations and ongoing training in place will provide members and the community with the necessary expertise, equipment, and supplies should a natural disaster or manmade calamity occur. In dire circumstances, having a localized rapid response capacity could save numerous lives and provide calm and hope in an otherwise grave and uncertain situation. Imagine how many could have been helped or saved in tragedies such as 2005's Hurricane Katrina, the 1974 thirteen state Super Tornado Outbreak, the 1993 Storm of the Century, or the earthquake such as was experienced in the small country of Haiti. Rather than waiting and relying on the government or special relief organizations, well supplied and medically competent citizens could immediately spring into action.

A separate purpose, to be considered, for this level would be to provide sections restricted just to those who belong within the Inner Circle. It would allow for private rooms where such members could gather, have meetings, read, relax, or work on special projects. No others would be permitted into these areas of the facility, and access would require special keys or codes for admission. Access and being allowed as being one of the rewards of belonging to the Inner Circle.

In addition to these uses, a supplemental function for this level could be to provide temporary living quarters for families in times of hardship or difficulty. For example, it could serve as a short-term refuge should someone experience a personal situation or disaster that leaves them without a home. These living quarters could be made available to anyone in times of genuine need at the discretion of association's Director. If this should involve an Inner Circle Member, than all those in the association would do all they could to provide help and assistance to that particular individual and / or their family by opening their homes and hearts to what-ever their needs may be.

As time allows, additional HUB expansion could be established by building and utilizing the before mentioned auxiliary buildings for various purposes. Moreover, the open ground to the East and West sides of these structures could be developed as activity fields, play parks, and exercise stations. They may also be used as platforms for various sports, outdoor games, music presentations, and similar events. During the year families, friends, and visitors would be encouraged to participate in a multitude of outdoor competitions, concerts, the arts, and community events. The overall emphasis and purpose being family and friend's enjoyment and entertainment. Furthermore, on the Southern side of these buildings might be constructed a small operational farm and a variety of utility workshops for training and educational purposes. These areas containing storage bins for stock feed as well as various holding enclosures for poultry and livestock. This site could then be used to instruct guests, novices and members on how to grow, harvest, and preserve grains, vegetables, and meats. It might also offer "Hands-On" opportunities for teaching such things as how to operate a grist mill or instructions for metal, wood, electrical, and plumbing expertise. These facilities would also service well as tutoring and experimentation stations and would provide outlets to practice newly acquired abilities and skills.

Once these outer rim facilities and workshops are established and functioning, than an even greater effort should be made to involve the general public. Each of these visiting individuals or groups would be warmly welcomed and encouraged to learn more about Neoteric Humanism, its goals, ideals and mission.

This complex would provide many advantages and everyone would **GAIN:**

Growing food and livestock on a community farm reconnects the link between the food we eat and the land it was raised on. It also reminds us that human beings actually worked to grow and process the food you eat, not just some large national company.

Advocating and supporting neighborhood farmer's markets creates more local jobs and helps lower pollution from vehicles commuting to and fro to obtain food and supplies.

Incorporating a farmer's market into communities offers a wider variety of fresh edible food into our everyday lives. In addition, these agricultural systems tend to be more durable as they would have a greater diversity of species. If a disease strikes crops or animals, there is a greater chance that there will be some variations that would endure.

Nourishing seasonal fruits and vegetables produced by small community farms serve as a healthier alternative to the over-processed commercial use of corn and wheat currently marketed in stores. Not only that, meats would be less likely to have preservatives, antibiotics, and other chemicals that are added by commercial production companies making them more natural and safer choices.

A "Typical Weekly" Calendar of Action

It is only natural that there would be some curiosity about what will take place during the scheduled gatherings of this association. What types of subject matter will be covered and what topics and issues will be discussed? What are the anticipated activities and programs to be? How much time will it oblige of a person and will it conflict with their other obligations? Finally and most importantly, is it worth the time and effort required to pursue this philosophy? Is there truly a worthwhile and meaningful dividend to be had by attending and becoming a member?

To these questions, I submit a "Typical Weekly" Calendar of Action. After evaluating this, it will be up to the individual to decide if this would be time well spent. Whereas members and novices are expected to actively participate in as many topics and activities as possible, guests may pick and choose those elements or subjects they find most interesting and those they would like to engage in. All topics or events will be diverse in subject matter and are intended to be either educational, health-related, inspirational, practical, and where ever possible fun and entertaining.

The "Typical Weekly" schedule presented on the following pages is designed to be flexible and is most definitely not set in stone. It can be modified and updated on a "usage desired" basis and be adaptable to meet the needs of the membership and the community. This simulated outline is primarily offered to give one a feel for what they might expect when they partake in a session as a visitor or become a full-time member.

As you will see later in this text, the basic objective for each Core Session is to generate greater competence in both the modern world, as well as to re-learn those abilities and talents lost to the past. Members, novices, and guests will learn to sharpen their proficiency in both new abilities and old disciplines. The aim is to be prepared not only for unexpected difficulties as they arise today, but also to be ready and able to take advantage of possible personal or career opportunities tomorrow. To start, let's look at some optional possibilities for the days Monday through Saturday.

Optional Activities Monday – Saturday

Monday through Thursday The HUB might set aside regular hours for voluntary exercise, training, and recreation. Fridays and Saturdays The HUB could offer specific time periods for Arts and Crafts, Outdoor Projects, Youth Programs, Family Functions, Specialty Venue Occasions, Adult and Youth Events for those who want to participate.

Monday: 6:30 PM Stretch & Flex Training / 7:15 PM
           Cardio Training
           8:00 PM Youth and/or Adult Volleyball Games
Tuesday: 6:30 PM Stretch & Flex Training / 7:15 PM
           Cardio Training
           8:00 PM Personal Self-Defense Training &
           Discussion (How to avoid conflict and what to
           do when you cannot)
Wednesday: 6:30 PM Stretch & Flex Training / 7:15 PM
           Cardio Training
           8:00 PM Youth and Adult Badminton Games
Thursday: 6:30 PM Stretch & Flex Training / 7:15 PM
           Cardio Training
           8:00 PM Youth Kickball and Adult Pickle Ball
           Games
Friday: 7:00 PM Adult Cards, and /or Board Game
           Night

>9:30 -12:00 PM Community Teen or Young Adult Dance
>
>Saturday: 1:00 – 3:00 PM Adults Core Session
>
>1:00 – 2:00 PM Youth Grades 9-12 Practical Living Lessons
>
>2:00 – 3:00 PM Youth Grades 9-12 Arts, Crafts and Games
>
>7:30 - 9:00 PM Adult Dance, Music or alternative event
>
>9:30 -12:00 PM Community Teen or Young Adult Dance
>
>7:30 – 9:00 PM alternative events:
>
>a) Water Balloon Family Feud
>
>b) Talent Night or Open Microphone
>
>c) Theatrical Production or Guest
>
>d) Father/Daughter Dance ... etc.

To gain competence or skill in something new, it is best for people to imitate and learn from an expert or authority. Therefore, The HUB will provide weekly lessons, topics, and activities to help its members and guests participate in this notion of eyes, ears, and mind ... before engaging action. All attendees will be encouraged to participate in instructional workshops lead by well-informed, talented, and experienced guests. There may be some who will dismiss the necessity or value of these lessons. It is true that most people like to feel self-sufficient and would rather learn from their own mistakes than be taught from someone else. We try to convince ourselves that we are surely intelligent enough to "figure it out" as we go along. Life, however, is too short for this kind of attitude. We all make mistakes, even the brightest of us with the best of forethought and planning. So why add to these mistakes when they could be prevented or avoided? As the maxim goes:

> *"A fool learns from his own mistakes, a wise person learns from the mistakes of others."*
>
> Unknown Author

> *"By three methods we may learn wisdom: First, by reflection, which is noblest; Second, by imitation, which is easiest; and third by experience, which is the bitterest".*

> *"I hear and I forget. I see and I remember. I do and I understand."*
>
> Confucius

As much as we may hate to admit it, the fact is, we actually do need the help, skills, and expertise of others. Learn from those who already know and are willing to share their proficiency and abilities.

A Typical Model Core Schedule:
(Times are to be flexible to meet the activity)

(1) 1:00 - 1:10 PM Adults: Goals and Objectives Statement and Visitor Invitation.
1:00 – 2:00 PM Youth Grades 9-12: Practical Living Lessons/Younger Ones Games.
(2) 1:10 – 1:20 PM Adults Announcements, Information, and Volunteer Requests.
(3) 1:20 PM Adult: Guest Speaker on Topic and/or Proceed to an Activity/Class.
(4) 1:30 - 2:30 PM Adult Designated Activity, Topic or Lesson for the day begins.

2:00 – 3:00 PM Youth Options: Arts, Crafts, and Games
(5) 2:30 – 3:00 PM Adult Language Lesson and Practice. A combination study of basic greetings, phrases, and understanding of Esperanto, Spanish, Latin, and Greek.
(6) 3:00 PM Adult Free time after for social with healthy snacks & drinks. Member, novice, or guest music, art or poetry.
(7) 7:30 - 9:00 PM Adult Dance / or alternative event
9:30 -12:00 PM Community Teen Dance or Young Adult Dance or alternative event

Adult Event Alternatives:
a) Creating Healthy, Fun & Tasty Snacks
b) Zany Cloths and Hat Gala
c) Weird Chili Challenge Cook-Off
d) Pumpkin Decoration Competition

<u>Read or Review at home:</u>
• Pick a language(s) along with study guides
<u>Homework:</u> Practice above at home with spouse, siblings, or friends.

The New Year, beginning with the following are examples of the first 4 weeks, starting of course, with January.

Week 1) <u>Selected Topic, Activities, and Events:</u> (Assuming it's a New Year's Saturday.)
11:00 AM This day is set aside for the Formal Initiation Ceremony of new Inner Circle candidates if this is the decision of the Director.
12:00 PM Initiated Inner Circle candidates are welcomed by the membership and is concluded with a New Year's luncheon buffet and social gathering.

Read or Review as you can at home:
- "A History of Knowledge, Past, Present, & Future" by Charles Van Doren.
Homework: Begin or continue work on a family history album. Discuss with children.

Week 2) Selected Topic, Activities, and Events:
1:30 PM Proper diet, exercise routines, and good health.
The rest of the day same as the model core session.

Read or Review as you can at home:
- "Eat, Drink and Be Healthy" by M.D. Walter C. Willett.
Home Work: Start or review an exercise program. Practice good nutrition adding plenty of fruits and vegetables.

Week 3) Selected Topic, Activities, and Events:
1:30 PM Preparation of a 4-month emergency stock of family essentials.
The rest of the day same as the model core session.

Read or Review as you can at home:
- "The Prepper's Pocket Guide" by Bernie Carr
Home Work: Emergency Preparedness. Replace & Replenish Stocks including replacement of batteries.

Week 4) Selected Topic, Activities, and Events:
1:30 PM Home first aid, CPR and medical emergency training.
The rest of the day same as the model core session.

Read or Review as you can at home:
- "Handbook of First Aid and Emergency Care" by The American Medical Association.
  Homework: Update home and mobile medical kits and supplies.

Other Typical Topics, Activities, or Events:

Below are examples of selected subjects, issues, or actions that may be the main topic, activity, or event. For instance:

- Home fire prevention and establishing multiple escape routes.
- Rational problem solving, creativity techniques and free-thinking.
- Why a common world language is valuable and desirable.
- Home defense: Security, safety, and protection.
- Computer skills, upgrades, and problem-solving.
- No meeting August 19th, World Humanitarian Day (Individual Engagement)
- A study of American traditions and cultural variations.
- Tax preparation and financial planning.
- Understanding the legal system and your rights.
- Learning to use maps, a compass, and navigation skills.
- Beautification, conservation, or community project.
- Jobs, careers, and developing multiple steams of income.
- Honoring Mother's Day! Discussion of marriage and family life.
- How to identify and use important plants and minerals.

- Small scale farming, processing and preserving techniques.
- Summer vacations, water safety, and swimming lessons.
- Honoring Father's Day! Discussion of marriage and family life.
- Examining human population growth, nature, and the environment.
- Training and practice of wilderness survival skills.
- Discussion on gratitude and forgiveness.
- Neoteric Humanist Wallet and Target Prompters.
- Creating a personal will, taxes, the law, and practical estate planning.
- Avoiding scams and racketeers. Where and whom to report or contact.
- Forming legal contracts and documents.
- New technologies, their practical uses now and in the future.
- Your livelihood, principles, and ethics.
- Kids Fun Day … special games and activities just for them.
- Reviewing your progress towards the "Pursuits A-P"?
- A discussion of intoxicants and personal responsibility.
- Family & Friends festival, cookout, sporting event, and fun.
- Open forum for all political candidates to speak and meet.
- The Declaration of Independence, Constitution, and Bill of Rights.
- Electricity, alcohol stills, and various types of fuels.
- Astronomy, space, and constellations. Our future habitat?

- A study of world religions and philosophies.
- Assisted living, nursing homes, death, and final rites.
- The Arts. Local artists invited to come and show or discuss their projects.
- New Year Resolutions: Setting good habits rather than goals.

Several of the previously stated examples will require more than one scheduled session during the year. For instance: language practice, beautification projects, financial planning, swimming lessons, and self-defense instruction. In addition to these multi-session activities, there are also some topics that are simply too complex and will involve more time to complete. What's more, the above projected themes will need to be adaptable and flexible enough to allow for unexpected events or opportunities that may suddenly arise.

Read or Review at Home:

The books suggested below may be found useful when used in conjunction with Core Sessions. These should not be considered required or mandatory reading, however, they will provide more information on those topics you may have a special interest in or wish to learn more about. These books are:

- "A Rule Book for Arguments" by Anthony Weston
- "A Republic If You Can Keep It" by Neil Gorsuch
- "Cracking Creativity, Secrets of Creative Genius" by Michael Michalko
- "Home Security, Your Guide to Protecting Your Family" by James Hufnagel

- "Ten Talks Parents Must Have with Their Children" by Pepper Schwartz
- "How to win friends and influence people" by Dale Carnegie
- "The Seven Principles for Making Marriage Work" by John M. Gottman
- "Wills, Trusts and Estates, Examples and Explanations" by Gerry Beyer
- "What color is your parachute?" by Richard Nelson Bolles
- "Identifying and Harvesting Edible and Medical Plants" by Steve Brill
- "The Family First Workbook" by Dr. Phil McGraw
- "How Many People Can the Earth Support?" by Joel E. Cohen
- "Country Wisdom and Know-How" by Storey Publishing
- "How Good People Make Tough Choices" by Rushworth M. kidder
- "Everybody Wins" by Gary Chapman
- "Buzzed … Drugs from Alcohol to Ecstasy" by Cynthia Kuhn
- "Our Cosmic Future, Humanity's Fate in the Universe" by Nikos Prantzos
- "The World of Philosophy: an Introductory Read" by Steven Cahn
- "The Creativity Challenge" by Tanner Christenson
- "Create A Life That Tickles Your Soul" by Suzanne Soglio

Reading books is vital because it helps improve one's mind. The mind is very much like a muscle and it needs exercise to stay healthy. Reading is one of the most effective ways to do this and is the primary way how we discover new things and expand our imagination. Books allow an individual to educate themselves or learn a new skill in just about any area of life they have an interest in. It also improves the creative and innovative part of our brain … most of the time for the better … but also sometimes for the worse. We need to read and research with a critical eye to promote good ideas as well as expose the flawed or evil ones. The power of written ideas dispensed through reading is the primary reason why some authoritarian governments oppose free and unrestricted forms of communication. Illiterate and ignorant people are easier to oppress, persuade, and control. They are not allowed to do selective reading and research. They are forced to rely on what they have been told and learn from the regulated information provided by those who hold the reins of power.

Reading books is also very important because words vocalized and written down are principally how we come into being as individuals. You are, right now, prominently the result of words that you have heard, written, read, and thought which clarified and solidified in your mind who you are as a person. What kind of person you become in the future will depend on what you believe about yourself from this day forward. Read and then read some more … choose to be a more well-read and better- informed person tomorrow than you are today!

Please consider these Four Thoughts about reading:

* The reading of great books will offer you a breather from your everyday life. It will infuse serenity within you, make you more at ease, and will expand your mind. There is much more to living than meaningless daily routines … turn off your T.V., cell-phone, computer and game console and rediscover

your personal potential. Reading will assist you in developing this awareness of your innermost beliefs and will make your views and feelings much more well-defined. It will help you understand who you are and will give your life more direction. Reading will make your thinking clearer, your actions more sound, and you a better person.

* Making time to read great books, by itself, is not sufficient. How you focus and think about your reading is even more important. When you encounter a new idea or a different viewpoint, take some time, and consider it with an open mind. Try to understand the writer's position and the point that is being asserted. As you continue on with your reading and reflection … your beliefs, customs, and traditions will be tested. It will be up to you to come to a conclusion on what is false, what is true, what reasoning you discard and that which you keep.

* Build a personal library of your favorite books so that you will be able to refer to them often or as needed. They will broaden your perception of the world by providing an extensive panorama of the entirety of human knowledge and experience. You will be exposed to a full view of history, science, culture, ideas, and shared experience from many perspectives. Envision getting to know people such as Socrates, Cleopatra, Joan of Arc or Ramses II. You can learn all about them and many more. Great thinkers, spiritual leaders, world conquers, famous scientists, creative artists, and countless others invite you to discover who they were and how they impacted our civilization. You will find that books and their valuable contents are the true equalizers in our society. They give to all, regardless of their background … knowledge, understanding and wisdom.

* Keep in mind that it's easy to become so involved in a reading routine that you miss the main purpose. The key

objective of reading is to make you into a better person and this can only happen through a personal transformation. Simply finishing one text after another without any real-life change won't advance you. What kind of person you aspire to be and what you eventually become depends greatly not just upon the type of subject matter that you've read and the knowledge acquired but how much you've integrated it into your mindset, deeds and behavior.

Pre-K/Boys & Girls Day Care/Event Venue

In addition to providing a secure and comfortable center for gatherings, exercising, self-defense, education, dances, and games The HUB should also attempt to make available a much-needed service for local families. This sought-after service ... is a safe, convenient, and affordable 7AM to 6PM child care facility. The HUB should dedicate itself to providing this valuable family support at least five days a week. This welcome assistance would be one more avenue for the association to express their commitment to help the community and carry out a worthy public service.

The Director and Assistant Director of the association's HUB, with the support of pre-screened assistants, would provide pre-school and elementary children (over 12 months) with practical and supervised daily activities. These planned activities would be designed to be both fun and educational. All children would be provided safe and secure play areas or classrooms with two or more assistants present at all times. Under no circumstances would children be allowed to come in contact with any other activities of The HUB unless one of their parents is present, or has previously agreed to it. Any caretakers of these children would be required to pass a comprehensive background check, would be fingerprinted, satisfy a personal good health exam, become Red Cross CPR and First Aid Certified as well as pass all state-required licensing courses.

While the Day Care would provide a needed community facility, in the beginning, it would also help offset some of the construction costs and initial operating expenses of The HUB. The HUB is, in spite of everything else, intended to be a self-supporting unit. The association's membership would be expected to make up the balance of any expenses by a combination of fund-raisers, donations, government subsides, and / or monthly dues. Once the facility is on a solid financial footing and operating expenses are covered, any positive cash flow will go back to a general fund. These excess funds could then be used to help lower the weekly child care cost for the betterment of our community's families or other appropriate projects and services.

It would be the association's aim to offer affordable, reliable, quality child care for all phases of early childhood. It would exist to offer a low cost, fun-loving and educational experience while also incorporating family values of love, moral character, self-discipline, team-work, and compassion for others. Its mission would be to nurture and educate infants, preschool and school-age children in a variety of wholesome family orientated programs. This would help the children in the association's care to develop positive social skills and values and learn about our world through age-appropriate play and learning activities. All would be provided a safe, stable, and secure environment that would promote a future of peace, health, happiness, and prosperity.

An additional service and fund raiser for this facility would be to include opportunities for hosting special events. This means a detailed and meticulous effort should be applied in the design, layout and construction of some buildings or rooms to accommodate various venue uses. These events might be weddings, receptions, birthdays, award ceremonies, sweet 16 parties, business meetings, etc. Other uses might include headquarters or meeting amenities to support local Girl and Boys Scout clubs, 4 H, Lions, Moose, Elk and other community groups.

When planning any of the above undertakings, it must be kept in mind, how easily the facility is accessible for all, in good weather and bad, with plenty of parking, and with a well-staffed and accommodating team to make it successful.

Part II

NEOTERIC HUMANIST PARABLES

Creativity complements knowledge.
Legend satisfies when history fails.
Colorful stories give life to facts.
Tales enlighten us … if we listen.

Bob Poor

The Question

As the sun's rays filtered through the towering pines, the winding dirt trail finally came to an end. The weary lad then paused and sat himself down upon a weather-worn and decaying stump. Tossing his head back, he took several leisurely drinks from his nearly drained canteen as his eyes began to focus on the nearby hillside dwelling. The cottage itself sat nestled on top of a slight rise near a freshly hoed garden of mixed vegetables and rows of sweet yellow corn. There, rocking in a wicker chair on her front porch was a silver-haired woman knitting, smiling, and humming a cheerful tune. As he drew near, he respectfully removed his cap and inquired "Pardon me … would you be Ms. Minerva?" She gave him a quick glance and countered "If you're here for the sweater, I'm not quite finished yet". "No, I'm not here for the sweater ma'am", he replied. "I'm a student at the university where you used to teach Life Lessons, Skills & Choices. My name is Chase Sage and I'm here on a personal quest to hopefully learn from your experience and wisdom. The last two hours I have traveled many miles just for the possibility of finding you here. You see … Mr. Magister, an instructor in one of my favorite classes, spoke often and very highly of you. He told me you had taught at the university for 25 years and were the most scholarly and learned person he had ever had the pleasure of working with. In fact, he counseled me that if I ever had a troublesome question for which he could not provide a satisfactory answer that I should find and talk with you." To this, the elderly woman put down her needles, looked at him intently, and gave a short "Umm humm". After taking a moment to review her work she queried him in a direct and dry manner, "What is this question that seems to be bothering you so much young man?" Clearly encouraged, Chase continued "Ma'am, in all my academic studies at college I've never found a satisfactory answer to the most basic of all my questions. ... If you wouldn't mind, please tell me ... in your view ... is there a true purpose to our life and a model standard or guide we should live by?" The woman smiled back and seemly amused declared "Is that all?" After lifting and brushing some loose threads from the sweater, she looked at Chase and asked "If you wouldn't mind, would you do an old lady a great favor? Go and bring me two cuttings, one from my garden, and then pick another from that wild field down below." Putting his hat back on Chase promptly hurried over to the garden, looked around, and picked out a bright red pepper. Turning to his right, he stumbled slightly and then bounded down to the lower field. There he selected a tall and wispy dandelion, now puffy and full of white seeds.

Clutching them both he climbed, as gracefully as he could, back up the grassy slope. There he found her, still rocking steadily on the porch as before, just finishing the last stitch in the crumpled but now completed sweater. Acknowledging his return she invited him to bring the two chosen specimens up near to her so she could see them distinctly. Examining them closely, she challenged him to explain how each one was dissimilar from the other. To this request, Chase proceeded to go into great detail about the differences between the pepper and the dandelion; their texture, color, shape, and smell. When he had finished the old woman spoke, "Yes indeed quite unalike they are from each other, but also very much the same ... as with all living things. Consider, if you will, the life cycle of these two plants. They sprout, struggle for existence and grow until they mature, and then spread their seeds in the soil. There the seeds go to sleep and wait to return the following season. ... In this cycle of life, there are many opinions about how it began, its purpose and where it may lead one day." She slowly rose up, set aside the sweater, and then continued, "But, to answer your question, is there a true purpose for life and a model standard or guide to live by, the answer is quite simple. Understand that when life by one means or another happens it puts this cycle of physical existence into action! Life happens and it can be very difficult, hard and demanding in what-ever form it takes. You must acknowledge this fact and yet be joyful in your heart to be part of such a rare and wonderful event. Yes, joyful in your heart, even knowing the tests, let downs, and sorrows we will all certainly face. We did not come into this existence by our own determination. We had no vote or voice in the matter. We had no options as to whom our parents would be, their financial situation, their education, their morality, how they would choose to raise us, or whether or not they would even remain together as a couple. We may or may not have been wanted, we may or may not have been born entirely mentally or physically whole or healthy. But, what we do have is extremely valuable and it is inside each and every one of us. As human beings, we have the power of individual choice. This power of choice allows each of us to decide how we will live our lives. Be happy with this wonderful gift, for it is how you engage and respond to the challenges of life that makes all the difference."

Chase, with a sudden flash of insight, interjected, "So what you're saying is … the truly relevant question should be, that since this cycle of life exists and we are part of it … it's the meaning and purpose, we choose to give it that truly matters. … Correct?" To this, the old woman clapped her hands together and laughed out loud "Exactly …we all have a choice young man. We can choose to park ourselves in a pile of negativity, apathy, and discontent … or we can get up, clean up, and give our existence a positive and worthy direction! We are extremely fortunate beings, as we have within ourselves, the ultimate freedom of choice in both the best and worst of any of our given situations. We had no control over our arrival in this place and time and perhaps very little influence on how we make our exit. The only thing we can attempt to shape and control ... is how we choose to live in the here and now."

"Yes, I completely understand that." said Chase, "But how does one attempt to best shape and control their life?" ... "Well" she answered him, "If you want the opinion of an old woman ... please lift up your hand and show me your four fingers."

Pointing at his fingers she continued, "These four fingers, young man, will provide a reliable road map that you can refer to for the rest of your life. Your first finger encourages you to seek Peace, for without Peace there is only misery and suffering. The second finger reminds you to maintain good Health in both mind and body so you may experience all that life has to offer. The third finger is there to inspire you to pursue what brings you Happiness and to share that joy with others. Lastly, the fourth finger is for you to seek Prosperity, value and contentment in your work and in your life."

Looking intently at Chase she then raised her own finger and said, "Of greater importance, however, is this question I now have for you. Since you now recognize this, will you put this reality into action? Your answer will determine if what you have gained here today is merely knowledge, or knowledge and the wisdom to put it into practice. As has been said ... If knowledge is not put into practice, it does not benefit one."

"One ship sails East, And another West,
By the same winds that blow, Tis the set of the sails
And not the gales, That tells the way we go"
                                        Ella Wheeler Wilcox

"If a man knows not to which port he sails, no wind is
favorable"
                                        Seneca

A Young Soul

Early dawn was steadily erasing the shadows of the night and a lazy cloud still clung to nearby mountain peaks. As the sun broke over a distant ridge, a young soul emerged from the morning mist and approached the pedestal of the lofty pass. Nearing this long and ageless entry point, the child carefully approached the luminous and glowing eternal bridge that allowed access to the land of the living. Just as the young soul was about to cross, a tall brawny creature stepped forward from a dark moss-covered hut and into the light. Grasping a large wooden club bristling with several sharp menacing spikes, the giant swaggered over to the entry and barricaded the way. Not understanding, the young soul inquired "Why do you impede my way into the land of the living?" The stoic and burly giant slowly raised his arm and pointed to a thick stone table with a delicate glass goblet resting at its center. The hefty guardian growled, "Take that goblet and go up to the clean and unsullied meadows of this mountain. Fill the glass from the pure and cool stream flowing there and bring it to me. If you hurry and I find the drink and its fresh cold taste to my satisfaction, perhaps then I will let you pass." Having no choice, the child agreed and slowly edged toward the mysterious table. At the center, next to the finely crafted chalice, were eight words etched deeply into its hard surface ... "*At all times, act with Love and Kindness*". ... The young soul contemplated this for a moment and then in a low thoughtful voice inquired "What is the meaning of this?" The large creature simply stared at the child and continued to point at the cup and then back to a path that led up a rocky incline. Unhappy and frustrated, the young soul took hold of the cup and climbed the steep and uneven route that led upwards toward the meadow and stream. After scaling several fallen trees and working around some hefty boulders met along the trail, the young soul finally reached the meadow and banks of the shimmering stream. Drawing close to the gentle flow of the tranquil brook the child dipped the goblet deep into its depths. At that same moment, a small, podgy, and elderly gnome emerged into the clearing from a grove of apple trees nearby. The shoeless little man seemed to be cursing and was limping as he steadily approached. "Young one," he pleaded "please help a tired and hungry old sprite. I'm desperate for a little bit of food to eat and I simply must have a cool drink for my parched throat." Surprised at the abrupt arrival, the young soul replied; "I would like to help you sir, but I'm on an urgent mission and in a terrible hurry." But the gnome persisted "Oh please, share some kindness. I am so very weary, my hands feel numb, and my feet are cracked and callused. While trudging up the footpath from my village I took a very nasty fall and twisted my one good leg … and I too am running late for a most important engagement. In fact, I just know that if I don't have some nourishment soon, I won't have the strength to make it there at all." The child, feeling sympathy and pity said "Alright, I will help mend your leg and then I'll fetch you some apples and a cool drink from the stream. But please, don't move from this small clearing or wander off somewhere … the day is getting late!" The young soul returned within a few minutes and put a sturdy splint on the old gnome's leg. After securing the last knot the child gathered some ripe apples and proceeded to fill the glass chalice with the streams cool and refreshing liquid. The dusty and famished gnome thanked the youth and accepted both food and drink in heartfelt gratitude. The odd little fellow then eagerly began to eat the crisp red apples and lifting the cup of water to his lips drank it all down in one long draw. Unfortunately, in his thirst and haste, the glass slipped from his numbed hands and fell to the ground shattering into

a hundred small pieces. The young soul stood there in disbe-
lief then dropped to the ground and began sobbing in despair.
"The goblet is destroyed and now there's no way, I can complete my task." "Oh … I am so very sorry," said the gnome …
"I'm just a clumsy and poor old fool. I wish I could repay you
for the damage I've caused … but I have no silver or gold. I am
truly sorry and very much in your debt. Perhaps one day I can
do something to make it up to you." The child answered back,
"Do not worry or trouble yourself, I understand that it was an
accident. It was just the luck of my day … I will find another
means to resolve my problem." The old man thanked the child
and apologized once again. He then pushed himself to his feet
and little by little wobbled his way past a bog filled pond and
disappeared in the distance.

Thoroughly disheartened the young soul sat by the river,
fully immersed in thought, until the sun began to set. At long
last, having come to no plausible solution the child decided to
return to the lower plateau and try to cross the bridge again
hoping that perhaps the burly creature would not be there.
Gathering up a few of the glass shards for the return trip the
young soul, sadly and quietly, ambled down the mountain. By
late that evening the child arrived once again at the stone table
and the ancient bridge. Only this time, it was the old gnome,
standing watch at the entry. "What happened to the giant
guardian that was here this morning?" questioned the child.
"Oh, that was my son-in-law." replied the forest creature. "I
am here fulfilling that important engagement I mentioned to
you back up in the meadow. You see … I am to safeguard the
pass while he takes an opportunity to eat a meal and rest. I
am again truly sorry for dropping your handsome cup … if
ever I can repay you … I am in your debt." The youth smiled
broadly and then politely asked for permission to cross the
bridge. The gnome thought for a moment, put his hand to

his chin, and then stepped to one side saying, "I've seen by your kindness that you are truly a good and worthy soul, so yes … you may enter the land of the living. … However, It's important to remember young one, that once you arrive … your purpose will be to find … true love. As you cross, keep this thought in mind … one can live without true love … but life without true love is not worth living." The child set off on the crossing but at the halfway point stopped and looked back. "What's wrong?" asked the smiling sprite. "How will I find … true love?" questioned the young soul. The gnome straightened himself up and said, "True love comes to those who offer true love, it comes to those who find their joy in others' joy, their tears in others' tears. The secret to finding true love is simple … act with abundant love, generosity, and kindness." The child then waved goodbye and wished the gnome a long and happy life. The old sprite leaned forward and called, "Don't worry, you will know true love when it …. finds you. It will lift you like a leaf on the wind and your spirit will rise to the moon and stars high above. True love will warm your heart like a hot drink on a cold and brisk winter day. It will be the joy of your life … and the smile of your morning."

"There is only one happiness in life, to love and be loved"
George Sand

"If you were all alone in the universe with no one to talk to, no one with which to share the beauty of the stars, to laugh with, to touch, what would be your purpose in life? … it is love, which gives your life meaning."
Mitsugi Saotome

Ancient Egyptians believed that upon death they would be asked two questions and their answers would determine whether they could continue their journey in the afterlife.

The first question was, "Did you bring joy?" The second was, "Did you find joy?"

Leo Buscaglia

"When we love, we always strive to become better than we are. When we strive to become better than we are, everything around us becomes better too."

Paulo Coelho

Sophia's Floral Acumen

It was the evening before what was to be one of the happiest days in Davina's life. She and her grandmother Sophia were sitting at the kitchen table which now was overflowing with coiled strips of ribbon, pieces of green foliage, rolls of a soft pink fabric and an collection of various flowers. Neither Davina nor her soon to be husband could afford an elaborate and expensive wedding, so she was determined that everything they could have would look as beautiful and lovely as possible.

To save money, her grandmother agreed to help her create flower arrangements for each of the guest tables and one especially eye-catching composition just for the bride and groom. The two had been sitting, clipping stems, and chatting for some time when Davina suddenly became quiet and seemed lost in thought. "What's the matter sweetheart?" questioned her grandmother. "I guess I'm a little scared about this whole business of getting married." the bride to be confessed. "Oh, there's nothing to fret about pumpkin, people get married all the time." assured her grandmother. "It's a wonderful thing when you finally find your soul mate and fall in love. By tomorrow, the party will be over, the guests will be gone, and you two youngsters will begin your lives together as Mr. and Mrs. Beatus." "Yes … I know." agreed Davina "I'm not as concerned about the party and festivities so much as to how this merger of Booker and myself is going to work. Life will be totally different and entirely unpredictable. What if we have kids … or what if we can't have children. Suppose Booker's newly formed company or his division should get transferred to a new city or they downsize people in the accounting department again. Most of the time Booker and I seem to be heading along the same path and other times we manage to get sidetracked … or worse yet, some days we just feel adrift for any direction. …. Gram, how have you managed to keep things straight and sorted out in your life?" Her grandmother smiled, put away her scissors, thought for a second, then began to admire and adjust the flowers lying in front of her. "Davina" she replied, "While you and I have been sitting here together, have you by chance noticed how we've been organizing and placing the flowers in each of these vases? Look at our finished arrangements on the dining room counter. See how simple each is yet how wonderful and lovely they all turned out. I would like you to take a moment and try to pretend that this last empty vase, sitting here in front of us, is your future. Think of the large red roses you will be placing in its center as the key things that are most important to you; things such as your future husband, the children you will certainly have, your parents, and your good friends. These full and beautiful roses represent the important things in your life that matter most to you. Now consider the smaller pink carnations that you will be positioning around and below those roses. These carnations you might want to think of as symbolizing the other significant concerns in your life, but ones that are of lesser consequence. These might be your job, your home, or maybe if you're quite successful … perhaps a nice boat or fancy car. Nice rewards … yes, yet not as essential as the roses. Finally, there are the tiny white baby's breath and green ferns that you will spread around the roses and carnations. These might represent everything else, the little everyday matters." Taking a deep breath and picking up the empty glass container, her grandmother continued …"So, let's assume you are now going to create your future as if it were a flower arrangement. If you yearn to have a balanced and complete life, you should start with the roses first, followed by the carnations and finally filling in what's left with the baby's breath and ferns. ... Think about this and how we've prepared these vases of flowers whenever you start to feel troubled. Just remember; always begin with what's most precious ... the roses. You see, keeping your life on track is actually about managing what you and Booker's priorities are and then taking enough time to make well thought out choices. If you compose these priorities in an appropriate way, each part will complement and enhance the others ... and your life will have direction, balance, and joy." ... Setting the glass vase back on the table her grandmother offered Davina one last piece of advice, "Don't wait too long to balance, organize and rank the grouping of your family's flowers. Keep in mind, that even though this flower composition is beautiful now because it is fresh and new ... if you wait too long sometimes the flowers may wilt and then it becomes challenging to save and realign them. ... As it's been said before, even though Booker and you have sailed on different ships, you're both in the same boat now." Slowly standing up, her grandmother stretched, smiled again, and then submitted ... "I see nothing but smooth sailing ahead for you two ... now time for bed and rest young lady, Booker and you have a big day tomorrow!"

"Your life is the sum result of all the choices you make, both consciously and unconsciously. If you can control the process of choosing, you can take control of all aspects of your life. You can find the freedom that comes from being in charge of yourself."

Robert F. Bennett

"You are the person who has to decide. Whether you'll do it or toss it aside; You are the person who makes up your mind. Whether you'll lead or will linger behind. Whether you'll try for the goal that's afar. Or just be contented to stay where you are."

Edgar A. Guest

"Organize your life around your dreams and watch them come true."

Unknown

The Cheerful Stranger

For the humble farmer, the rough road and weekly routine to the nearby village had been an uphill battle for him all day. He was resentful that his rickety cart was old and that his exhausted mule was older still. What made matters worse he knew if he didn't reach the settlement by nightfall, he would likely miss his best customers in the market the next morning. Disaster loomed, as his harvest was fresh and would surely spoil if he couldn't sell it to those that dwelled on the far side of the hill. He pushed onward, the erratic rain continuing to drench his clothes, and he cursed as he slipped in one of the many mud filled potholes that further delayed his task.

Rounding the following bend, the farmer came upon a tall lanky man, who was gleefully whistling while carrying a wet and swollen brown sack over his left shoulder. Protruding from the top of this sack were the young tips and green foliage of two dozen or so red raspberry shoots. The stranger was methodically working his way up the same trail as the farmer but was stopping here and there to gaze out over the countryside. His muddy boots, well-worn trousers, and twisted walking stick somehow seemed out of place when compared to his otherwise clean-cut appearance. A few hundred feet beyond and in front of the stranger strode a finely dressed and stately looking fellow. This dignified gentleman was balancing a large impressive umbrella in one hand fending off the rain and the leather straps of a powerful black stallion in the other as he also marched onward on the irregular and rising grade.

It wasn't long before the simple farmer reached the stranger and inquired of him, "My fellow traveler, are you, on this miserable day, also on your way to the village market?" "Well … good day to you." The man responded cheerfully, "Unfortunately sir … I am not. I am on my spring outing to the crest of this wonderful hill." "Good day … indeed" the farmer sneered, "this would hardly qualify as a good day. I'm a poor man, my shoes are almost worn through, my cart is falling apart and my old mule will probably collapse and die before I reach the upper pass. If it weren't for my miserable problems … I'd have practically nothing at all. If only I was like that rich gentleman in front of us, then my life would be perfect and free of troubles."

The stranger appeared to quietly laugh to himself and then spoke. "Life is a series of problems, my friend, whether you are rich or poor. Either you are just coming out of one, or you're about to go into another." "Perhaps so" the farmer lamented, "but I'm sure I'd be much, much happier." To this, the stranger smiled and replied, "Yes, that's my belief as well … you may certainly be happier with wealth and riches. However, I believe a more fulfilling happiness can be found if one focuses on reciprocal harmony and tries to leave this world a more beautiful and joyful place. You see," he continued …" if you concentrate solely on achieving a personal fortune and think merely of your own problems … your life could end up being one of loneliness, sadness, and misery. From my own experience, I've discovered that I've become more content, satisfied, and cheerful once I moved my thinking away from just myself and onto the welfare and well-being of others." "Perhaps so" agreed the farmer. "But if you're rich and famous, just think of all the things you could buy and everyone would certainly want to be your friend." To this, the stranger answered "What if you did something today that made you instantly very wealthy and also brought to you great fame and notoriety? Would you now consider your life complete and live each day just for yourself? Perhaps it is better to ask yourself … am I going to live solely for possessions or popularity? Am I going to be obsessed with personal gain, a rich man's distractions and indulgences? Or am I going to be motivated by a greater end and a set of higher principles for my life? Trust me on this we are not born just to acquire wealth or prestige. Who you are on the inside, your intimate bond with family and friends, and what you do for the benefit of others, is what's truly important."

"Are you honestly telling me that you wouldn't change places with that man in front of us!" declared the farmer. "You could drop that bulky bag of plants and be riding that fine black horse." "Perhaps so," uttered the stranger, "but I've been carrying sacks like this to the top of this hill for years. I've hand cultivated many fruit bearing trees and tasty berry bushes for the people of this village to harvest and enjoy. Soon those same trees and bushes will again bud and flower and their sweet fragrance will fill the mountain air. You will hear buzzing bees as they race to and fro collecting packets of nectar to feed their young. During summer and fall the local villagers will go into these hills and gather the fruit and honey to make jelly, sweets, and pies. Later, when I and my kinfolk visit, they offer warm beds for my family and me and invite us to share a meal of fresh milk, home baked bread, and sweet jam. We talk late into the night by a friendly fire, tell stories, and share many pleasant memories together." The stranger stopped for a moment and scanned the lush green valley below. He then went on to say, "The view is beautiful, isn't it? … Just speaking for myself, of course, I've found that, in both good and difficult times … one should sometimes stop, take a moment, and just be thankful to be alive in this marvelous world. I remember what my grandfather once told me. He said to always be grateful for what we had, for there was always someone else who had even less. He said we should always try help and show kindness to our neighbors. For if you do, that kindness will be reflected back at us four-fold."

Considering these words, the simple farmer began to grin and said; "Please throw your bag upon my cart so that I may lighten your load, my new friend." The stranger answered back "Thank you sir, my name is Cato ... and now let me lighten your burden as well, my friend, by having my servant ahead attach my strong black horse to your cart so that you will indeed make it to the village before nightfall."

"Life is mostly froth and bubble,
Two things stand like stone,
Kindness in another's trouble,
Courage in your own."

Adam Lindsay Gordon

Judgment On Crow's Knob

In days past there lived Uku, a Cherokee Indian elder, who had four exceedingly impatient sons Chasse, Moytoy, Gaagii, and Wohali. These four would, in a few short years, attain an age when they would begin taking over powerful council seats within their flourishing and expanding tribe. In these high-ranking positions they would be responsible for resolving conflicts, determining verdicts, and if deemed necessary, the possibility of making of life or death decisions. He wanted to instill in the young men a valuable lesson about reaching fair, impartial, and just conclusions in such situations. So one day he gathered them all together and spoke of a journey for each to take to the top of a sacred peak known as Crow's Knob. The purpose of this outing would be to record what they experienced along the way and what they thought of a tall and mature fruit tree that could be found at its very summit.

Uku's instructions were the same to each; "Take a dried animal skin and sketch pictures about your adventure and the age old tree you find there. When you return, speak to no one about what you have seen or what you encountered until I ask you." He told his sons that he could spare only one of them at a time, so the oldest, Chasse, would go in the winter, Moytoy in the spring, Gaagii in the summer, and the youngest, Wohali, in the fall.

When one year had come and gone and all had completed their father's task, he called them together to sit by his evening fire. He told each to bring their animal pelts and to be prepared to describe their journey and what they had seen and experienced.

The oldest son, Chasse, spoke up first. "It was a miserable winter day and a very dispiriting chore" he exclaimed. He held his animal skin upright showing how it had been

numbingly cold, had snowed each day, and how he had frequently slipped and fallen while climbing to the cap of Crow's
Knob. Finally, upon reaching the top, he was disappointed to
find that the fruit tree he sought looked dead, was bent to one
side, and was twisted in its trunk. It was an ugly tree and of no
doubt to him one of little value.

"Ha," said Moytoy as he interrupted Chasse, "that's not
what I experienced, mine was an extremely wet trip." He
raised his drawing, showing how he was forced to use a make-
shift shelter during a thunderstorm, how he had to swim a
swollen river, and then climbed over muddy ravines before
reaching Crow's Knob. "The tree I found wasn't ugly at all.
It seemed to be just awakening from a deep sleep and it was
loaded with young buds, it was alive, yet had no fruit to eat so
it was a tree of little worth."

Gaagii arose and laughed … "You both must have gotten lost and climbed the wrong mountain!" He displayed his
journey showing himself enjoying the sunshine, easily wad-
ing across the river, and effortlessly scaling Crow's Knob. The
tree he discovered was laden with both beautiful pink blos-
soms and a few small apples and looked absolutely beautiful.
"I tried some of the green fruit hanging there but it tasted sour
so I found the tree to be bitter and probably one best avoided."

At long last, Wohali spoke up in a soft voice "My journey
was much better. It was a very pleasant, vibrant and colorful mountain path that gently rose upward. The leaves I saw
were of every band in the rainbow and they fell at my feet as
I climbed to Crow's Knob. The tree I found there was magnificent, drooping heavily with ripe abundance. The fruit was
utterly delicious. I ate my fill and even brought back a full sack
to share with others. It was a good and nourishing tree and
well worth the trip."

Uku poked at the fires glowing embers and then explained to his sons that each of their stories and the tree that they found there were exactly what he had expected. Though each of their stories and conclusions about the tree were different they were made based on what you had seen for that time of year. "You were all partially right ... because each of you had each seen just one season in the tree's life." The father continued, "My sons, I want you to think long and hard about what I am going to say. ... You cannot evaluate a tree ... or a person for that matter, by one season alone. The essence of who they are, the joy, the love, the misfortunes and the sorrow that result from that life can only be measured when all the seasons have been considered. If you come to a conclusion when it's winter, you will miss the possibilities of spring, in spring the beauty of summer, and in summer the yield of fall. ... As you are called upon to be leaders in our tribe, keep this journey to Crow's Knob you have completed close to your hearts. It is my hope that it will remind you to be open-minded, fair and consider all the details in both your reasoning and in your final judgments."

> *"We should learn to be patient with ourselves. Recognizing our strengths and our weaknesses, we should strive to use good judgment in all of our choices and decisions."*
> Joseph B. Wirthlin

Precious Gems

As the intense heat of the day subsided, the weary travelers began folding their tents and packing their belongings. The time had come to continue their night time passage through the outer reaches of the Gobi Desert to their destination, the town of Bayankhongor. Their intent was to reach the settlement quickly as they wished to see their good friend Conrad before his severe illness claimed him. Cancer had recently appeared in Conrad's left lung and had been spreading rapidly throughout his whole body. Now his days were numbered and his time was running short. Traveling with heavy hearts they did their best to keep their spirits up even though they knew he was slipping away from them. Conrad had been their mentor and had aided them all to become the exceptionally successful people they were. He was much more than just an advisor, Conrad had always been there to either help celebrate good times or provide a shoulder to cry on in bad. However, over time, because of their busy schedules the group had fallen out of touch with both Conrad and each other. Now, as they were loading their camels for this last stretch of the trip, their desert guide Arvio called them together. He wanted to extend a few warnings about traversing this more dangerous part of the Gobi desert. Arvio had crossed this section numerous times before and would always consult the local mystical shaman for good luck. He would share with this wise and spiritual man, the motive for their travels and then would ask for his blessings and words of wisdom. Arvio wanted the group of travelers to listen to this man's words but thought they might sound somewhat strange to this collection of well-educated professionals. The shaman more often than not tended to act a little odd and typically spoke in short riddles, rather than speaking clearly and outright. However, Arvio asked the group to spare a few moments to hear him out, as his advice had proven to be worthwhile many times in the past.

Fortunately, all in the group agreed to sit down with the shaman and Arvio proceeded to ask for his counsel and advise as they prepared for this final leg of the journey. The old mystic closed his wrinkled eyes and little by little drifted into a profound trance. As his head moved from side to side … he slowly began to speak. "Choices … choices and a quandary I foresee … confuse not your purpose … as the grains of time run short. When your passage abruptly becomes dark, listen for the West Winds warning siren, for you shall be touched by fate four times … for each one, I deeply urge you to stop and gather some small pebbles before proceeding on. From this vision I have, I see that at the end of your crossing that you will find yourselves both happy … and sad." The shaman promptly opened his eyes, rose to his feet, and left without a further explanation. Needless to say, everyone felt a little perplexed, although Arvio assured them there was always an underlying and sometimes misunderstood meaning to his words and that it might cause them bad luck to ignore or take them lightly.

"What do you suppose he was trying to tell us one woman inquired? I don't know responded another, but let's talk about it as we travel, as we really need to be on our way." They mounted their camels and their guide Arvio led them out of the camp at a brisk pace. Before too long the sky grew murky and became blurred by thick heavy clouds. Immediately, a blinding wind picked up from the West, and indeed it began to sound like a warning siren. The companions halted and spoke about this strange coincidence of what the old mystic had just foretold. It was at that moment, that Thomas, the most superstitious of the party, remembered the shaman's counsel to stop and gather stones. He quickly dismounted and began engaging in what he believed was the shaman's spiritual directives.

"Just to avoid bad luck" he murmured to the others. Not hav-ing a container to put the pebbles in, he emptied his nap sack and proceeded to pat around on the ground to search for any small stones he could find. It was difficult to see with the blow-ing sand, but eventually, he was able to fill the side pouches of his bag. Rejoining the band, Thomas and his companions, once again started off, most of the troupe grumbling about lis-tening to a crazy old man and the time they had lost. Within an hour the wild wind rose from the West like a siren once more and the travelers again came to a standstill. On this oc-casion, there was even more debate as they argued not only about the shaman, but also valuable time again wasted. After a heated squabble, they decided they would forgo the advice of the shaman and proceed directly to the village without any further delays. As they continued, they could not help but no-tice the hard-wearing and curious wind rising and falling two more times, the last time, just a few miles before they entered the community of Bayankhongor.

Over the next few days, they would go visit Conrad as of-ten as they could. However, being the successful individuals they were, they were also communicating with their offices and conducting business as their high-status and demanding careers required. The telephone lines were often knocked out of service as the high winds continued to rise from the West, creating, again and again, a loud wailing sound. Some in the group resorted to cable messages and others sent memos by mail. However, on the third day, this all came to a stop as they learned that their friend Conrad had passed away. The cancer was even more advanced than anyone at the small local hos-pital had believed and he would never wake from his sleep that night.

Later that same morning, the travelers gathered at a small cantina for one last meal together before the cremation of their friend. As they sat at the table, Arvio entered carrying the nap sack that Thomas had partially filled with pebbles several nights earlier. "You all should see this," he said as he approached them. Lifting the bag over the table, he spilled the contents onto its center. Instead of pebbles pouring out, small bright and beautiful gems formed a glimmering pile right before their eyes. "There must be thousands of dollars in precious stones here", one of them proclaimed. They all became excited … and then one by one fell silent again. They were all thinking back on what the shaman had told them. "I know what you are thinking," said Arvio "but I believe you are wrong. You are both happy and sad as the shaman predicted … yes. Happy with your new riches but at the same time sad that you did not stop and take the time to collect more. I think I understand now, and I say to you that I believe the shaman was not speaking of material wealth, but in reality, was talking about a personal treasure regarding your friend Conrad. He was counseling that you spend more time with Conrad over his last days, the collecting of stones signifying the gathering and sharing of memories before he passed away. The shaman understood that those memories would soon become for each of you like rare jewels and that you would be both happy and sad. Cheerfulness for the times you spent with Conrad and yet sadness in knowing that those precious days will never come again."

"Ordinary riches can be stolen, real riches cannot. In your soul are infinitely precious things that cannot be taken from you."

"When we honestly ask ourselves which person in our lives means the most to us, we often find that it is those who, instead of giving much advice, solutions, or cures, have chosen rather to share our pain and touch our wounds with

a gentle and tender hand. The friend who can be silent with us in a moment of despair or confusion, who can stay with us in an hour of grief and bereavement, who can tolerate not knowing, not curing, not healing and face with us the reality of our powerlessness, that is a friend."

Oscar Wilde

Life Preservers

Four female naval officers were sitting outside a local café each enjoying a tall glass of ice tea and a thin slice of lemon cake. They were taking pleasure in the warmth of the morning sun and were reminiscing of their military service, current married lifestyles, and the arrival of children. One, a lieutenant, was telling the story of her nephew, a naval gunner during the 1st Gulf War. His ship had been attacked near the Strait of Hormuz by an Iraqi Cruiser. During the assault, a missile launched by the enemy ship ripped into the starboard side of the front deck near where he was standing. The huge explosion not only knocked him unconscious but tossed his limp body far up in the air and dropped it into the chaotic ocean. Fortunately, he was wearing a recently developed strap-on flotation device that saved his hide. One that was designed by the manufacturer to open automatically on impact with the water. … "You know", she said, "I wonder if he ever called the company who came up with that idea and thanked them for making a lifesaving invention that popped open and inflated just when he needed it?" The woman on her right took a sip of her drink, thought for a moment, and then spoke. "You know, all these young sailors are just like our own kids, I guess it's our duty to be like mini-life preservers and always be on the lookout for them." After a few more minutes of silence, the 3rd woman in the group added her view. "Have you ever considered, how well we as parents are preparing our own children's life preservers? What I mean is, have we done our very best to include all the many types they may need … a life preserver for their physical needs, one for their educational needs and also one for their emotional needs? We all know there will be days ahead when they will need to call on one or all of these resources to help them get past life's challenges." To this, all four women smiled and agreed. The lieutenant then raised her glass in a toast and said, "To the women and mothers in this world ... our work is tough and never done. Please give us the strength, the wisdom, and the will ... to see our mission and battles won".

"Children are not casual guests in our home. They have been loaned to us temporarily for the purpose of loving them and instilling a foundation of values on which their future lives will be built."

Dr. James C. Dobson

"There are only two lasting bequests we can hope to give our children.

One is roots, the other, wings."

Hodding Carter

"And don't all children deserve to be protected? To be loved and nurtured so that they may grow and shape the world to make it a better place?"

T. J. Klune

We Journey Together

"Living is a voyage upon the sea that we find
Some steer with a vision while some steer blind.
One must choose values which are noble and good
If one is to awaken and the rewards understood.
To be a better man or woman learn to be kind
Learn to calm one's tongue as well as one's mind.
Look for the goodness in others and unveil your own
Then goodness you will find and yours will be known.
Be the one who offers help in sad, grim or hard times.
It will be joyfully repaid and your spirit will shine.
We are one on life's journey and the choices that we make.
We must learn to love each other for each other's sake"

Bob Poor

"We must learn to live together as brothers or perish
together as fools."

Martin Luther King, Jr.

The Choice

(It's some future day and there is a newly formed shanty town just to the North of the city, it's early, all is quiet, and a middle-aged man is about to waken.)

Stultus shuddered as a jolt of pain raced through his neck and along the muscles of his back. His clothes smelled of diesel oil and were still damp as rain began to fall through the leafless branches of nearby trees. Rubbing his bloodshot eyes he gradually moved toward the corner of his crudely erected tent where the entry skirt was now thrashing in the strong pre-morning wind. He knew he needed to get up but his pain and aching body fought every effort he made to do so. The faint light indicated it must be approaching sunrise and he knew he needed to go check his traps before someone else got there first. Was it two days ago or three when he last had enough to eat? … He couldn't be sure. It used to be so easy, in the beginning, before the stores were all looted of food and useful supplies. He couldn't believe that in just a few weeks everything of value had disappeared from the racks and shelves. Remembering those bewildering times filled Stultus with rage and anger and he cursed as he slammed his fist into the soggy dirt. Just thinking of how he'd been forced out of that warm cabin by a cop with a 12 gauge shotgun. Why had he un-barricaded his door just because of a man with a uniform and badge? Now he found himself homeless, freezing, and worrying about potential starvation.

Life had changed dramatically in a very short period of time. No one surviving the event could clearly identify what happened that day almost four months ago. There was a brilliant flash of light along with a transformation in the color of the sky from a deep blue to a combination of red mixed with billowing brown clouds. It was then that people began to notice that all electronics or machinery that generated power no longer functioned. Computers, telephones, and televisions … cars and trucks … lights and elevators … anything that required electricity abruptly stopped. It didn't take long for panic to set in as people began to realize that this was not only a local … but rather a countrywide event. Therefore, no help would be coming, winter weather seemed to be arriving early, and for everyone, it was becoming very, very cold.

Those who were once considered the civilized and sophisticated inhabitants of this nation suddenly became aware of a terrible and dreadful truth. The technology they depended on so completely had just collapsed before their very eyes. There were no functioning buses, subways, or private vehicles to get them back to their homes or anywhere else, for that matter. Children had been left stranded in schools and families were separated. No usual means of communication existed. No news could be found except for hastily posted signs or messages painted on the sides of buildings and walls. Someone walking would no doubt notice scattered candle lights in windows here and there, and for some lucky groups, a wood-burning fireplace gushed smoke from the chimney. Money lost its value almost immediately and bartering of one item for another ruled the day. That was until food, medicine, and fuel started running in truly short supply. From one day to the next, it turned into an ugly scene of mass fear and confusion. It became a society ruled by the gun and whichever gang of the day was toughest and strongest.

The elderly, the ill, and the very young were the first to suffer and the earliest to depart this world. Some courageous good Samaritans did what they could but eventually had to consider their own family's welfare. In roughly eight to ten weeks desperate people began stealing from each other, even killing if need be. The large overcrowded cities were by far the worst. There the tall buildings echoed of gun and rifle fire and screams could be heard through the day and into the night. The dead and dying began filling the allies, the streets, and buildings. It was impossible to escape the odor of both decay and desperation that filled the air. No one had any idea of what to do or how to endure, but most would now do anything to survive. In scarcely 90 days what was once a great civilization and powerful country had become a nation of wild and panic-stricken animals.

As Stultus inched upward and managed to stand, he staggered, fell against a tree, and began to laugh hysterically. What fools we were, he thought, to depend so entirely on so many things we didn't understand. Now it was time to come face to face with this reality and it was truly a repulsive sight. In this upside-down world, everything that was important to him was lost. His seven-year-old son and nine-year-old daughter were missing and were nowhere to be found. The wife he'd had for 15 years had been beaten and murdered by a mob of young kids when she refused to hand over a can of peaches, she'd found. The next day, his brother-in-law suffered a fatal heart attack from the unrelenting stress. His sister had lost her mind and run off somewhere unknown. As the day began that morning, Stultus had no family, no friends, no country, and little hope as the freezing weather slowly changed the raindrops into a torrent of sleet and snow.

Twenty miles to the Southeast a different situation was unfolding. Prudence was with her family and friends who had gathered together at a strong and sturdy shelter. Her children, wrapped from stored wool blankets, were sitting near a wood-burning stove enjoying the warmth and the aroma of rice and beef stew simmering on top. In contrast to the terror and chaos of those up North, the individuals here were moving about and acting on a long-established plan of action.

They had prepared themselves beforehand just in case an emergency situation might occur. The families here were safe, secure, and had reason to hope. There were supplies of food, drink, tools, and yes ... also items for self-defense. Those with injuries or sickness were being treated from cases of supplies that had been arranged well in advance. The medical and first aid training that many had received earlier, now kicked in as if by second nature. ... Yes, times would be difficult and hard but they had their family, friends, a strategy, and ample supplies of stock to see them through the obstacles in the months ahead. Once their local area was deemed to be safe they would begin fanning out into the remains of civilization and would provide assistance and a beacon of hope for those left in their community. They would survive, they would teach, they would train, they would plant, they would harvest ... and they would rebuild!

One might now ask ... if given a choice, which of the above circumstances would you rather find yourself ... with Stultus or Prudence? Or perhaps an even more important thought to consider ... If you choose to do nothing ... you know with whom you'd find yourself.

"There are only nine meals between mankind and anarchy."
Alfred Henry Lewis

"Despair is most often the offspring of ill-preparedness"
Don Williams, Jr.

"Another way to be prepared is to think negatively. Yes, I'm a great optimist. but, when trying to make a decision, I often think of the worst-case scenario. I call it 'the eaten by wolves' factor.' If I do something, what's the most terrible thing that could happen?

Would I be eaten by wolves? One thing that makes it possible to be an optimist, is if you have a contingency plan for when all hell breaks loose. There are a lot of things I don't worry about, because I have a plan in place if they do."

Randy Pausch

Nysa's Incubus

Nysa would be 29 years old next week and she felt in top form. Jogging along at a brisk pace she could feel a cool sweat just beginning to break on her forehead and the back of her neck. Her feet felt light and nimble as they hit the pavement with an eager and steady rhythm. As she rounded the final bend of the city's 5K annual race, she noticed the road was beginning to bear upward at a much steeper slant. Far in the distance, at the top of this rise, she could see the finish line with people smiling, laughing, holding banners, and waving small flags. Nysa pushed herself to go faster but found that the slope of the hill began rising even higher than before and for the first time noticed that other runners were beginning to catch up with her. It struck her as odd that all of these people overtaking her looked somehow familiar. It was then she recognized her sister with her husband and their two children who quickly rushed by her without so much as a word. She yelled to them, "Wait! …Victoria …. Preston, wait for me!" Her legs were growing heavy and several other people were now speeding past her as well … former classmates, old friends, the postman, and now a co-worker. All dashing ahead and reaching the cheering crowds at the end, while for Nysa the finish line seemed to be getting further away and the hill itself was becoming almost impossible to scale. In front of her strange obstacles began appearing out of nowhere and she was forced to jump over all types of gates and barriers. Suddenly, it felt as if something was grabbing at her shirt pulling her down. She fell to her knees, crawling and fighting with great effort just to keep moving forward. What was going on … and why was this becoming so crazy? The road at that moment abruptly became almost vertical and transformed itself into a jagged rocky cliff with Nysa hanging on for dear life. Books, chairs, a computer, pens, and folders all were falling toward her, as if determined to knock her loose. Her fingers began losing their grip and the cliff itself began to crumble on top of her ... now just holding on by only one hand ... and then she slipped and fell backward screaming as she fell.

Aldo, her father, entered the room and switched on the lights as Nysa, sitting upright in her bed, was still grasping at the air. She opened her eyes and finding herself drenched in sweat breathed deeply ... "My God ... it was only a dream." "What happened? ... Are you ok?" asked her father. He sat next to Nysa on her bed and gave her a big hug. "It's alright honey ... you're awake now. You were just having another one of those weird nightmares." Nysa wiped her forehead with her hand and did her best to regain her composure. "I just don't understand why I keep having these dreams. They seem so real and they always end in the same bizarre way." Her dad looked at her and said, "Was this that race again? Did you find yourself falling behind ... and on that cliff once more?" Nysa nodded her head yes and asked, "What does it mean? Am I losing my mind? I've had this same nightmare for almost two weeks in a row ... when are they going to stop?" Aldo stood up and while looking out the window whispered, "It's still dark ... I'd guess it's about 5:30 in the morning. How about I go downstairs and make us some coffee and we can sit and talk a while?" Nysa agreed and got up out of bed looking around the room for her slippers and bathrobe.

In the kitchen, Aldo was already working on his second cup when Nysa came and sat at the round breakfast table. She smiled at her dad and said, "Ok, mister know it all, what is it that's making your daughter go bonkers?" Aldo smiled back as he opened a packet of sugar and dropped its contents into his special blend of coffee. "Do you remember

Sig Olson? He's a pretty smart fella, well-educated and all. He and I used to have some long conversations while bass fishing. We would talk about the kind of clients he had and many of their issues. He never brought up any names as I guess being a psychiatrist you have to keep those things confidential and private. But anyway, Sig had all types of clients, but one comes to mind in particular, who like you, had a problem with constant nightmares. In his client's dream, the man was in his office and all those around him seemed to have it easy. His co-workers got promotions, bonuses, and recognition for jobs well done while all he got was more and more paperwork piled on his desk. When he got home at night, his friends would show up to boast about their new car, brag about recent family vacations, or how great their kids were doing in their private schools. All the while, back at work, the papers on his desk would get taller and taller as he struggled with new bills and deeper debt. His wife would appear hovering above him unhappy and constantly complain about the old fashioned clothes and shoes she had to wear. His two kids seemed miserable as they boarded the buses bound for their inner city public school. The dream would always conclude with a great tower of paper, files, and bills falling in on him as he fought to avoid drowning as this whirlpool swirled around him. What Sig said to me that afternoon was that this man was so wound up with negative thoughts, feelings of failure, and lack of hope that it was affecting his sleep and that was why he was having nightmares." Nysa said, "So what did he do to get rid of the bad dreams?" Aldo thought for a moment and then continued ... "Well, that's the intriguing part. He sat the man down, looked him square in the face and said ... my granddad always told me that whenever life makes me feel defeated ... it's never too late to find success and optimism. I repeat ... it's never too late ... to find success and optimism. To find it, my granddad said, you need to do five things."

#1 **M**ake a list on a sheet of paper of what is positive and what is negative in your life.

#2 **Y**ou must then resolve as to what you're willing to do to have more of the positive things and less of the negative.

#3 **D**ecide ... daily what can be done to help you reach those goals.

#4 **A**nalyze, adjust and continue your progress.

#5 **D**oggedly keep to a daily routine. If you mess up, go to bed and try again tomorrow!

Sig then continued, "The first thing you will come to realize is that you'll find success and optimism in just planning your goals. Just the act of putting them on a piece of paper has moved you a little closer to achieving them. You will also notice that having a plan of action also creates contentment simply by knowing there is a possible way to accomplish these goals. The pursuit gives you hope and hope gives you peace of mind. Peace of mind leads to serenity and serenity will put an end to your bad dreams. Whether or not you reach all of your goals does not matter. It is the planning and the journey that will bring you tranquility, cheerfulness, and hope."

Aldo got up, walked to the kitchen counter, and opened a cabinet drawer. There he retrieved a yellow note pad and a short red pencil. He proceeded to write the five things Sig had laid out for his client. Once finished, he slid the pad over to Nysa. "I can only start this for you, but you will have to finish it yourself. If you start sleeping better, you know who to thank ..." Nysa laughed as she saw that the bold letters of the five steps spelled out ... MY DAD and joked, "Yea ... mister know it all!"

"Life is not having and getting, but being and becoming."
Mathew Arnold

"Two keys to happiness: ONE: being able to tolerate the things that make you unhappy, or TWO: Being able to change the things to make you happy."
Albert Einstein

The Sultan's Competition

It was the year 1611 and Sultan Fahim III's health was failing fast. In his gilded Arabian Palace, he found himself profoundly worried and deeply distressed. The time he had left was short and he had no heir to entrust his kingdom. Being a good and wise sovereign, he and his Royal Council of Four, concluded that they should hold a contest to reveal an honest and well-suited successor to avoid potential discord and conflicts after the sultan's demise.

The Crowned heads decided, after much debate, to send this regal proclamation into to all of the sultan's vast lands and holdings: "Our much loved and esteemed monarch is gravely ill and will soon be joining his ancestors in the Gardens of Peace and Joy. Before departing this world it is the sultan's wish to find and retain a worthy and honorable successor who will be just, govern wisely, and look after his people's welfare. Therefore, it has been decreed, that a competition shall be held to discover the best-qualified individual to rule after our exalted and gracious sultan has passed on to his everlasting reward. All who desire to compete for this honor must appear here on the palace grounds, at sunrise, three mornings hence. Once within this magnificent estate, contestants shall proceed to the Imperial Peafowl stockyards where each will be presented with an extremely special and important egg. You shall take this egg and protect it, keeping it warm and safe. Once the chick emerges from the shell you will keep the hatchling healthy and strong, nurturing its every need for 12 months. At that time, all candidates shall return with these young birds to the palace and present them to the sultan. The owner of the hatchling, which our most exalted sultan determines to be the fittest, healthiest and most exemplary, will then, be acknowledged as his legal heir and successor … the next ruler of our great land."

At a nearby settlement a hard-working lad, named Aadeel, overheard this proclamation and decided he would enter the contest. Learning of this, the local village folk and many of his neighbors scoffed and mocked him for having such lofty ambitions. He was, after all, just a simple breeder and shepherd of sheep and goats. Aadeel, however, was not discouraged by this, as he believed he knew more than most people about raising animals and how to care for them. He didn't know a thing about birds, particularly peafowl, but he was sure he could figure it out. This being his resolve, three days later he joined all the other participants in the growing line within the Royal Stockyard. Aadeel immediately began having second thoughts as his competitors consisted of well-to-do ladies and gentlemen as well as many nobles from the imperial court. Upon seeing Aadeel they all seemed either annoyed or humored at his being there and cast insults his way for being arrogant enough to try and compete with them. He felt his spirits falter and was just about to turn and hurry away when he caught sight of a young girl from the sultan's court, just a few steps ahead. She, also seeing him, flashed a gentle smile, gave a nod and motioned for him to come forward. Aadeel approached and was instantly struck by her loveliness and grace. He watched dumbstruck as she reached down into her wicker basket and retrieved for him an egg. "Don't let these self-centered painted face phonies try to bully you," she said. "They think that their fancy titles make them the obvious choice, but most couldn't even get dressed in the morning without their servants." Aadeel, feeling his face flush, took the egg, slowly bowed … and looking back said, "For you, I will bring back the most magnificent and dazzling peafowl you have ever seen … if only to see your charming and delightful face, once again." He bowed again quickly, smiled, and winked at the young lady. Holding onto his precious cargo he walked with both great excitement and great care back to his village.

It was barely two days later when Aadeel's egg confirmed the first signs of life. He had kept it warm and sheltered in a mound of hay and now it was beginning to move and show a jagged crack. It was just as the full moon of the night was rising that the hatchling burst through its shell. Aadeel was so ecstatic that he began to sing and dance in a ring around his new arrival. Being very impressed by the young chick's determination and strength to break into this new world, he felt his peafowl was surely a male and he decided to call him … Samson. At long last, after finally collecting together his wits, he lifted and placed the chick into his satchel. As the chick had emerged exceedingly hungry, he at once began to search for grubs, insects, and discarded seeds of grain. He cared for this precious ball of feathers for weeks on end, not showing it to anyone in the village for fear they may harm or try to make a meal of him. However, after three months of continuous tending and attention, Aadeel was getting a little concerned about his little companion. Though Samson was very healthy and strong, he was rather small, sort of plump and showed no signs of growing the long and colorful feathers Aadeel had expected. Eventually, at the end of the 4th month, and with still no beautiful feathers in sight, Aadeel decided to visit the village healer and ask for her advice on what might be wrong. The healer, though busy with her charms and tonics, took Samson to a table and gave him a thorough exam from top to bottom. She felt for broken bones, for disease, or any irregularity she could find. Giving Samson back to Aadeel she declared that he was the healthiest, strongest, and finest Jake Turkey she had ever seen. "Jake Turkey?" exclaimed Aadeel! "You are very much mistaken madam; Samson … is a Royal

Peacock!" "My son", the healer said, "I know you very well. You have spent your entire life up in the low hills as a breeder and shepherd of sheep and goats … but I have seen many of these birds in my travels in the high mountains to the West … and this is a definitely a Jake Turkey … not a Royal Peacock!" Aadeel was shocked and then felt extremely embarrassed. He kicked at the ground, left Samson on the table, and departed the healer's hut. Humiliated, he turned and started to trudge his way back up into the hills. He hadn't gone but a short distance when he noticed, that his very healthy turkey Samson … was loyally tagging along behind him. He cursed at the bird and threw stones his way, but Samson always returned unscathed and continued to shadow him although now many yards behind. Time moved on and Aadeel soon forgave and renewed his affection for his non-peacock feathered friend. He concluded that an error had obviously been made and somehow a turkey egg got mixed in with the others. This certainly was not Samson's fault it was just a foolish sheep and goat herder's bad luck. He continued to care for and look after Samson just as before and waited as the contest deadline steadily approached. It was the morning after the fall harvest when the big day at last arrived. Aadeel gathered up Samson and went back to the palace to see which peafowl would be chosen. On his arrival to the stately stockyards, he found many pens each filled with the most stunning and impressive peacocks he had ever seen. Their tail feathers were massive and the colors seemed every shade imaginable. Though not a single peahen could be found, the male peacocks there began calling to each other as if to say "Take a glance at me if you dare and see how incredibly wonderful and exquisite I am!" Aadeel held Samson close to his chest and tried to push his way near to where his kind and helpful egg supplying young maiden might be sitting. He thought to himself, "This will no doubt be the last time I will see her ... if I can just get close enough, maybe I can catch her eye and see her beautiful lovely smile once again."

With the sounding of brass trumpets, Sultan Fahim III entered the crowd to cheers and applause from all sides. He walked to the various holding pens and closely inspected all the impressive peacocks he found there. At one point, he appeared to have found a likely winner, but then he seemed to reconsider and moved on again. After much scrutiny and energetic sales pitches from the proud owners, the sultan suddenly and unexpectedly took notice of Aadeel. The sultan grinned broadly and then steadily, step-by-step walked over to him, inquired of his name, and what he was doing at the competition. Aadeel, surprised by the attention of the great ruler, bowed deeply ... rose up ... and then began to answer the sultan by telling his sad story of how he had tried his best to be a worthy contestant. Holding up Samson to the sultan, he proceeded to explain that due to an unfortunate mistake he had somehow gotten an ordinary Jake Turkey egg instead of a peafowl. The sultan responded, "Well ... it looks as though you have taken excellent care of your fine bird." Aadeel replied, "Well ... not all birds can be Royal Peacocks or Royal Peahens, your highness, even this ordinary turkey deserved care and kindness." The sultan let out a roar of laughter and said, "You are so right my young man. Not all birds can be Royal Peacocks or Peahens, especially when every one of those eggs my good-natured lady courtier handed out ... were all from the nests of turkey hens!! You are the only one, out of all these competitors, who was truthful enough to admit it. ... What's more, even after learning you could not possibly win you continued to look after and care for your young hatchling. ... Because of your honesty, compassion and dedication ... I, Sultan Fahim III, bestow on you my warm congratulations as the winner of this competition and as my future heir! ... Also, let me introduce you to my lovely egg courtier Amira. She is not only beautiful but is very wise in the ways of governing. Perhaps you two should spend some time getting to know each other. I'm very confident my people will live, be happy and prosper exceedingly well in both your hands!"

"I hope I shall always possess firmness and virtue enough to maintain what I consider the most enviable of all titles, the character of an honest man."

George Washington

The Savvy Staff

Life had been harsh for those of the great migration. It had been a trek that lasted the entire summer season and the expanse they covered was tedious and unkind. Many hard and brutal lessons had been taught to the Wolf Clan and its leader Tyee. Their progress had been marked by injuries, misfortune, and most regrettably, the loss of a number of their young children. There was Yonaguska, who drowned while trying to traverse a rushing river. Adahii, who while foraging, was bitten and who later died from a venomous viper. Kangee, who had unknowingly wandered off from the group and was never seen again. Payta, Tyee's son, was severely burned when a fire he had relit one morning got out of control. Others had sickness, broken limbs or various wounds from a slip or misstep during the troublesome relocation of the tribe.

Now, as they finally entered a much more forgiving and plentiful land, the people halted to determine if this is where they should stop and re-settle. That evening the family elders sat and argued amongst themselves making the critical judgement if this is what they should do. Finally, after a much discussion, it was agreed, that yes, this would become the new home of the Wolf Clan. When Tyee was informed of this decision by the family elders he at once mustered the rest of the tribe and said, "Let all the people now come together and join us." … With this call, all the various families and individuals gathered up, pulled in close, and opened their ears to what their chief was about to say. Tyee rose and held up his well-worn and battered staff and bellowed, "My brothers and sisters, we have traveled many sunrises and sunsets together. We have endured tremendous hardships and tragedies in our search for a new home. At long last, we have found clear water, dark soil, and plenty of game. This land holds great promise and potential for our people. Our wise elders have made the determination that we should now stop and dwell in this new territory. Be happy for tomorrow we celebrate our new beginning!" This announcement brought about joyous jubilation from all the people and it took several moments for them to become quiet before he could proceed. "... However, as we celebrate, let us not forget the severe and terrible lessons we have learned along the way. To keep these lessons fresh in our minds, from this day onward, the head of each household will craft what I will call ... a Savvy Staff. To these special staffs, I will bless and give magical powers. The head of each family shall display this staff with respect in a place of honor within your family's dwelling. When your children see and ask about your families Savvy Staff and why you keep it where you do ... speak to them of our lengthy journey and the adversities we suffered to reach this region. This will be your opportunity to pass onto them our hard learned knowledge and experience. Teach them the lessons we have so dearly paid for in our quest for a new home. Instruct them on how to make their own staff which I will also bless and endow with magic. I will give our clan symbols and signs to be etched into their staffs so they will remember our words of wisdom. Make it clear to them, that if they listen to and abide by our advice and warnings and revere their staff as they are told, it will help them avoid trouble and live a better life. By respecting our bitterly gained encounters, it will aid them in evading danger and will help their families stay healthy, prosper and flourish. Finally, and most importantly, we will give each child serious and firm words of caution ... that should they not live in accordance with this knowledge; they may suffer misfortune and bad luck as the Savvy Staff will have lost its special powers to assist them along life's uncertain pathway.

Savvy Staff Symbols & Signs: (Una salus Victus)

 "Water – For thirst but it must be approached and consumed with caution."

 "Fire – For cooking and warmth but it always must be under your control."

 "Shelter – For refuge, comfort and safety during heavy rains and winter flurries."

 "Be Wary – Hunt for food but beware of the danger that always surrounds you"

 "Stock – Prepare 4 moons of smoked and salted food before the first snowfall."

 "Tend – Maintain and care for stock, weapons and tools on a daily basis."

 "Medicine and Song– For sickness, poison, sorrow, impurity and evil spirits."

 "The Tribe – For love, protection, education, training and happiness."

"I have but one lamp by which my feet are guided, and that is the lamp of experience. I know no way of judging of the future but by the past."

Edward Gibbon

Walk With Me

Victus rolled over on his back and studied the warped fan slowly rotating above his head. It's few remaining blades beat out an uneven yet steady rhythm … tap, tap, ra-tap … tap, tap, ra-tap … that echoed off his bedroom walls. Abruptly, there was a loud click and his clock radio came alive blaring out a familiar blues tune from the early '60s. It was an old B. B. King rendition, a song about a man who was down on his luck and his woman had just left him. Victus couldn't bear the music and put a pillow over his head attempting as best he could to block it out. Lying there, he couldn't be sure, but judging from the angle of the light coming through his window he guessed that it must be close to noon. … Damn he hurt! His body ached from head to toe as he steadily inched toward the edge of the bed. He forced himself to sit upright and began searching the cluttered nightstand for his cigarettes. He knew he had a few smokes left, but where were they? Pushing aside two empty bottles of whiskey he found a pack next to a zip lock bag, now nearly void of his dealer's favorite blend … cocaine mixed with crushed horse tranquilizers. Victus and a hooker he'd picked up off the street had gotten wasted on it and she had left after he'd passed out stealing most of his stash with her. Striking a match, he lit up one of his two last remaining Marlboros and took a deep long drag, letting the smoke fill his lungs then slowly and steadily allowing it to escape from his nose. Groaning, he stood, walked to the bathroom, and looked at the person staring back at him from the mirror. Who was that pale, scrawny, and shoddy loser? He threw water on his face and pulled back his unkempt black hair gathering it together with the help of a small rubber band. Taking a closer look at himself, he noted that his shoulder was still black and blue but that the wound on his brow had stopped bleeding.

The last thing he had expected last night when he tried robbing that gas station was that an old lady would wallop him in the forehead. Man, he had thought she was just a homeless and harmless old bag lady. Where did she pick up that hefty rod and how did she manage to sneak up so close to him? Victus was lucky to have gathered his wits so quickly and shove her into the pastry rack before she could wind up and swing again. Even though she had delivered only a glancing blow, it still hurt like hell as if someone had dumped a bottle of iodine onto his fresh wound.

"How did I get myself into this mess?" He said to himself. As he again looked at the mirror, he recalled how he had lost the only decent job he'd ever had because his night-time partying always made him late for work. His ex-wife Soteria couldn't stand the constant drugs and drinking and had taken their two kids and moved back in with her parents. Rent money was owed for the past three months and the city had just threatened to turn off his electricity. To top it all off, if he didn't come up with the $500 he owed to his dealer, Dominic, the dude promised to realign his face and crush both his knee caps. It was because of that horrific thought that he had attempted to rob the Quick Mart Store in the first place. He had been unsuccessful in that plan and now his options had turned from slim to none. ... When someone started yelling and began banging outside on his door Victus panicked. He raced to the open window and jumped out onto the fractured and sagging fire escape ladder. As he did so, the cuff of his blue jeans got snagged on an old nail in the window seal. Struggling to get free, he lost his balance and fell backward off the metal stairs, dropping down the four stories below him. A few seconds passed in silence and then he crashed onto a pile of plastic garbage bags and wooden pallets stacked next to his apartment's dumpster. Knocked unconscious, he laid motionless on top of the rubble.

Ten to fifteen minutes passed and Victus sluggishly began to open his eyes. Foggy and disoriented at first, he finally focused on a man's face looking at him. "Are you alright?" the passerby asked. Glancing upwards he continued, "That was quite a spill you took. Do you feel like you broke anything? … That bump on your forehead is bleeding pretty badly. Here … cover it with my handkerchief and put pressure with your hand right here." Victus did as he was told and then suddenly broke down and began to weep. He had somehow survived a plunge that should have broken his neck … but now he could see no reason why he should go on living. The stranger with a gray beard somehow seemed to understand and sat next to him, putting his hand on Victus's back. "Ya know" said the old man "I think I've been exactly where you find yourself now. When I was a young man like you my life was in shambles too. Yea, I was one big mess. I was depressed and drowning myself in alcohol. If you could wrap it … I'd smoke it. If you could put it into a syringe … I'd shoot it. I borrowed and stole money from my family and friends until I had neither. I had spent my life running down a dead-end street and finally had nowhere else to go." The stranger fell silent and turned his face toward the warmth of the mid-day sun. "So what did you do?" asked Victus. The man looked at him and said "Who me … oh … I died." He smiled and then continued, "Yep … I died. If it hadn't been for Mr. Custos, I wouldn't be sitting here with you today. Mr. Custos knew a lot about everything and fortunately for me, he also knew C. P. R. and a little first aid. He saved me from an overdose … and much more … he saved me from myself." The stranger stood up, took in a deep breath of fresh air, stretched and continued. "Once he revived my worthless soul in that cold back alley, he offered me his hand and said … come walk with me. I stood up and we walked to a nearby café where he bought me a warm meal, we drank coffee and we talked for hours. I told him my story and he listened without judging me. Then he spoke and said that if I was ready to make a change he would show me a new direction. A direction with meaning, purpose, and a means to become a better person. That if I was willing to make the effort, then he was willing to give me a hand." The man looked upward and his eyes teared up somewhat, "I asked if it was possible for me to try and start over?" and he said, "New beginnings happen all the time. … There would be no new music if not for a fresh note, there would be no new trees if not for the seed, and there could be no new beginnings if there were no endings. You are at the perfect place and time … the end of one chapter … and at the beginning of the next!" Looking down at Victus, the man leaned over, extended his hand, and said … "Come! … Walk with me!"

"Do not wait for leaders, do it alone, person to person"
Mother Teresa

A Special Chair

Kord took note of the pending darkness just as a timeworn clock chimed 6:30 PM on the wall of his work shed. Soon his wife would be calling him into the house for their usual family dinner together. He looked at his work and continued rubbing the legs of the special wooden chair he had just finished. It would be a special gift for his oldest son, Alexander, who would be celebrating his 16th birthday that evening. Kord had assembled this chair for a specific purpose and he hoped it would create the impact he wanted on his son, whom at this age, was about to enter adulthood. "Abendessen Zeit" (dinner time) called his wife through the rear screen door. "Ja Ja" Kord answered back as he cradled the chair, turned out a dangling light bulb, and sauntered his way out and over toward the kitchen door. As he entered the house he could smell the rising aroma of sauerkraut and sausages filling the air. How he loved that fragrant bouquet that reminded him of the old country their family had left behind.

Kord reached the dinner table just as Alexander entered the room and his son beamed as he saw the adult sized chair he was carrying. He knew his father had been working on a surprise for his birthday and this had to be it. Kord smiled in response and boomed loudly "Happy Birthday Son!" Alexander reached out for the chair but his father held it back. "Alexander, my boy ... tonight you are about to enter adulthood and as such I want to pass on some important principles you now should always keep in mind. You will notice that this chair has 4 strong legs made to support you. To keep them strong so they can sustain you all your life; you must heed the important meaning that each leg represents". Alexander said, "... and what are they, father?" To that Kord replied "The four legs found on this chair are a guide for a good life ...

they represent Peace, Health, Happiness, and Prosperity. The first leg, Peace, signifies balancing your emotions with other people and learning how to handle stressful situations. Keep in mind the Golden Rule and seek harmony and serenity in all things that you do. Doing this will help you achieve inner calmness and adopt a positive attitude. ... The second leg of this chair symbolizes health. Good health is extremely important as without it you will find it difficult to live the life you want. So take care of your body, eat healthy foods, exercise, and minimize risks. Stay healthy so you may enjoy all this world has to offer. ... The third leg is for happiness. Happiness is having a good family and good friends. Knowing that someone cares for you and is always there for you no matter what is priceless. The giving of love and the receiving of love is one of the most enjoyable and unmatched experiences you can have. ... Lastly, the fourth leg, which denotes prosperity. Prosperity, in this case, means working to improve your lot in life not just for you, your family, and your community but the rest of the world as well. In the end, we must always strive to leave our earth and life on it a little better off than we found it." Extending the chair out to his son, Kord said "Now sit and eat the delicious dinner your mother has prepared and later on some tasty cake ... for tonight we celebrate! your erwach-senenalter!!" (Adulthood)

The Tradesman's Gold Coin

Cooper, a young man in his early twenties, was laboring hard to finish his wooden-bladed shovels and rakes. For him, 1807 had been a tough year as more and more of these work tools, mostly made of iron, were now being made and sold by a local mill. Cooper's job tended to be a very time-consuming trade as each tool would start with a seasoned oak tree and then had to be split into smaller manageable pieces. The pieces, if shaped correctly, would fit together snuggly so he could more easily assemble the particular tool he was joining together. If lucky, some days he would get a lucrative commission to construct a butter churn or whiskey barrel but those days were now far and few between. Cooper had spent years as a boy being an apprentice to learn his trade, however, his business had dropped off substantially as the new stronger and more durable metal equipment began arriving. He found life so discouraging in his hometown that he decided to try his craft elsewhere so he packed a small satchel with cheese and bread and headed off towards a promising nearby settlement. As he reached the crest of a small hill he found a tradesman, his horse, and mercantile wagon on the side of the road. The tradesman was seated on a stool with a red and black cane in one hand and an ornate ceramic mug in the other. "Good day to you young man" greeted the tradesman. "Would you like some coffee … and perhaps afterward you can take a few moments to consider some of my fine wares and rare treasures?" Cooper frowned and replied, "Thank you sir, but I have not a penny to spare and I am so miserable I would likely make poor company." "Why so?" queried the tradesman. To this, the lad tossed his bag to the ground and complained aloud about how things were so difficult for him. He could not see how he was going to make it in his hometown and hoped his trade would fare better in a new village. The difficulty to complete each wooden shovel or rake being so demanding and only profiting so very little for the effort. The tradesman said "My name is Alger" and motioned for the lad to have a seat offering him a cup of coffee. "Life can be hard, no doubt about it," he said. "I myself have to spend days on end traveling from one town to the next if I hope to sell my stocks and foodstuffs." Then he leaned back, grinned, and said, "But I am a happy man." Cooper looked puzzled and asked, "How can you be happy having no home, no family, and no guarantees about the future? Tomorrow your wagon could break down or your horse die ... what then?" Without saying a word, Alger stood up and reached into his front pocket where he pulled out a small solid gold coin and placed it onto a stool next to his cane. He then reached for his mug and set it alongside his colorful cane and the shiny gold coin. Turning to the young man he queried; "Besides their obvious differences do you know what separates these three things from each other?" The young man shrugged his shoulders and asked; "What do you mean?" The tradesman, being the eternal salesman, put on his top hat and then picked up his cane in one hand and the mug in the other. "This beautiful cane" he declared "will one day get old and frail and in time it may easily break in two and I will toss it away and look for an even better one. The same can be said for this fancy and delicate mug. In time it may chip or shatter and I will also simply toss it away as it will have lost all use and value and I will find an even nicer one." He then smiled, reached and picked up the gold coin, and declared "Ahhh ... but this gold coin ... it can be hammered, it can be cut in two ... it may be put in a tooth ... it may even be melted and reformed into something totally new. It adapts to its latest use and to the world around it. It never gets old and has eternal value because of its strength, its flexibility, and the way it can remodel itself and change depending on its new circumstances." Taking off his hat and sitting down again the man looked over at the boy and said "Ya know … life is a series of peaks and valleys … sometimes in this world, you're up … sometimes you're down. I'm a firm believer that it's how you respond in those moments when you're miserable that genuinely defines the kind of person you are. When you learn the ability to adapt and transform yourself to navigate the difficult times, you will not only live a happier life but will also discover your value as a person." Then Alger asked, "Before you continue on your journey my young lad, answer me this, when you next face difficult times … as you surely will … are you going to be like this old staff … this fragile coffee mug … or this malleable and adaptable gold coin?"

"The difference between stumbling blocks and stepping stones is how you use them."

Unknown

YOLO … So … Carpe Diem!

As she walked to her bathroom, Anstace thought to herself "What a boring and soul crunching couple of months it's been". Her life after finishing school had been much more a bowl full of pits than an enjoyable dish of sweet cherries. Her days were filled with just three things … work, late-night TV, and finally sleep. There was no joy, no love, no pets, and no hobbies … just a monotonous and disheartening routine. Standing at her over-crowded and slow draining sink, she mumbled to herself "It's time to change things up." Anstace raised her fists high, looked in the mirror, and declared outloud "Enough is enough … you only live once … tomorrow I will take control of my day … and my life! Tomorrow I will do things differently!" Moving into her bedroom and sitting on a comfortable bean bag there, she took a pen and composed a list of all the changes she wanted to make in her life and then committed herself to begin going to bed and waking up one hour earlier each day. Setting her alarm clock for 6 A.M. she snuggled into her bed with her Teddy Bear and a big fluffy quilt. When the alarm clock began chiming the next morning, Anstace got up immediately, stretched, and slipped on her comfy slippers. She avoided the temptation to stay a few more minutes in bed by thinking of all the new things she had planned for the rest of the day. First … getting up and taking a long relaxing shower, washing her hair, and then jumping into her nice black slacks and a brand new blouse her mom had shipped to her the day before. Waking up an hour earlier had given her more time in the morning, so she figured … why not partake in a warm, nutritious, and tasty breakfast? Anstace found that by leaving the T.V. and radio off it allowed fewer distractions and less negative news … and that her healthy breakfast made her feel even more alive … and a happy grin unexpectedly appeared on her face. Feeling good she chose to sit on her front porch, enjoy a 2nd cup of coffee, and there determined that today she was going to convey an upbeat and optimistic attitude no matter what. Opening up and reading from the bedtime list that she had titled "My new life" she declared, "Today is my day," and then she whispered to herself. "Today … I will …

* smile more and pass my smile onto anyone I see!
* do the best I can do and be the best I can be!
* be patient and generous toward all others.
* handle my issues in an optimistic and decisive manner!
* spend time with my family and friends!
* offer help to a friend, co-worker, or neighbor!
* do something I enjoy; like jogging, singing or writing!
* become better at something today than I was yesterday!

Anstace stood up, grabbed her jacket off the kitchen chair, and trotted down the steps to her car. Putting the keys in the ignition and adjusting her mirror she felt fresh and at ease. She realized that the extra hour made her happier and more relaxed. As she pulled out and slowly headed along the road she waved and smiled to all the people she saw and noticed they smiled and waved in return. When she got to work she greeted everyone with a heartfelt "Good Morning" and noted that they responded back to her with a sincere "Good Morning "as well. Being rested and alert she performed better at her job and her boss praised her for tasks that were well done. Her co-workers seemed inspired by her sunny outlook and they, in turn, acted friendlier and were also more productive. As the shift was about to end an attractive staff-worker approached Anstace and asked if she would be available later for dinner. Apparently Anstace's new welcoming manner made her more open and warm to a shy manager who had been uncertain how to approach her. ... The day had been wonderful and now the prospects for that evening were definitely looking up. Anstace accepted the dinner offer and thought to herself "Wow ... This has turned out to be my most enjoyable and sunny day ever! From now on I will begin every day like this ... for the rest of my life!"

YOLO ... so ... Carpe Diem! (You Only Live Once ... so ... Seize The Day!)

"Your life isn't behind you; your memories are behind you. Your life is ALWAYS ahead of you. Today is a new day – seize it!"

Steve Maraboli

"Each morning we are born again. What we do today is what matters most."

Buddha

Part III

MEDITATIONS, MANTRAS, AND PROMPTERS

Quiet your mind, focus on breathing,
and you will hear your inner voice.
It is in listening to this voice, that you
will know your path and your purpose.

Performing a Neoteric Humanist Meditation

Below is a typical routine that will allow you to review, study or practice Neoteric Humanism and its individual components. The best time to establish a habit for this activity would be either early in the morning or just before retiring at night.

Prepare: In loose-fitting clothes and in pleasant surroundings settle into a comfortable position. This may be done either by yourself or with others. Arrange before you a three-ring binder with paper, this book opened to the page (s) you wish to revisit or perform, pocket notebook, pencil/pen, and your circlet of meditation beads.

Meditation Beads: This is a circular string of identifiable beads that are grouped by number, size, shape, and /or color, and are assembled in a precise meaningful order. It is used as an aid in memorizing, reviewing and contemplating the methodology of Neoteric Humanism as well as focusing one's thoughts and feelings. The "Key" to understanding the meditation bead symbols are revealed as follows:

0 is used as the beginning of the cord, as a spacing bead or the end of the strand. Four beads may be added at the beginning and the end for Peace, Health, Happiness and Prosperity as well as the Four P's.

The ------ represents the filament that these are strung onto. All other bead symbols:

⃠ ☒ ☑ ☒ ☐ ⊙ ☐ ⓪ O ☐ △ ③ are of various types and colors and are used to aid the individual in their meditation routine. "Letter" beads may be substituted if you find them easier to use.

Notice how each group of beads, shown in the diagram below, corresponds to Neoteric Humanism's Ideals, Mission, Desires and Pursuits. Each individual bead helps the participant recall a word, concept, or ambition.

0--O-O-O-O-**0**-⊠-⊠-⊠-⊠ **0**-⊘-⊘-⊘-⊘-**0**-
  B I N G K U P P   W I S H
⊙-⊙-⊙-⊙-⊙-⊙-⊙-⊙-**0**-☐-☐-☐-☐-**0**-
A E C O M A I M   F A W N
☑-☑-☑-☑-**0**-☐-☐-☐-☐-**0**-◎-◎-◎-◎-**0**-
Q U I L   M E D S   T O P C
⊠-⊠-⊠-⊠-**0**-△-△-△-△-△-△-△-△-△-△-△-△-△-△-△-△-**0**-
M I D T   A B C D E F G H I J K L M N O P
③-③-③-③-**0**-☐-☐-☐-☐-
T I M E   P O G S

A more condensed tool would be the use of a <u>Meditation Wrist Prompter:</u> 4 beads for Peace, Health, Happiness and Prosperity as a Wish or Hope for humanity and as a Greeting, 12 beads for reciting each Mantra, 16 beads used exclusively for reciting the Pursuits A-P, and 4 beads for the Four P's (See page #290 = 4 P's)

<u>To begin:</u> Open this book to the section you wish to examine or enact. Hold your meditation beads in your hands and lightly close your eyes. Slowly and deeply draw in air, hold and exhale four times. Continue with this breathing while leisurely, from the top of your head down to the tips of your toes, relax your muscles, and progressively allow yourself to unwind. Imagine yourself relaxing on a quiet, warm and sunny beach far away. Feel the sun's warmth on your body. Now envision that sensation

growing and moving through your entire essence until it reaches the very center of your being. ... Now breathe deeply and fully ... Open and close your eyes ... using the meditation beads as needed ... to memorize as well as to contemplate how abiding by these Mantras will elevate and enrich your life.

(**BING**) <u>The first bead / or group of beads.</u> In a low voice ... repeat: *It is my belief that*

As I **B**etter myself ... I will **I**mprove my family and my community.

As I improve my family and my community ... a **N**ew vision for people will evolve.

As a new vision for people evolves ... I **G**ive hope and optimism to the future.

(**KUPP**) <u>The second bead / or group of beads.</u> Repeat: *It is my purpose and goal to:*

Know and improve myself.

Understand and be of service to others.

Practice kindness, truth, fairness and

Produce a positive impact with my life choices.

(**WISH**) <u>The third bead / or group of beads.</u> Repeat: *The Quest Wheel WISH and its Four Quads:*

Wisdom, **I**ntegration, **S**ecurity, and **H**armony
will lead to my completeness, safety, contentment and well-being.

(AE/COM/AIM) The fourth bead / or group of beads. Repeat:
The Eight Steps:

<u>A</u>cknowledgment, <u>E</u>ducation, <u>C</u>haracter, <u>O</u>ccupation,
<u>M</u>editation, <u>A</u>ssimilation, <u>I</u>nitiation, and <u>M</u>otivation
will show me the way.

The fifth bead / or group of beads.
Repeat: *I will live by the Desirable Traits ... I will be*

(FAWN)   *<u>F</u>aithful and dependable,*
           <u>A</u>ccountable and ethical,
           <u>W</u>ell-groomed and mannered,
           <u>N</u>ovel and free-thinking.

The sixth bead / or group of beads. Repeat: *I will be ...*
(QUIL)   *<u>Q</u>uality focused and guided,*
           <u>U</u>nderstanding and tolerant,
           <u>I</u>nclusive and charitable,
           <u>L</u>oyal and trusted friend.

The seventh bead / or group of beads. Repeat: *I will be ...*
(MEDS)   *<u>M</u>indful of behavior and deeds,*
           <u>E</u>ducator and student,
           <u>D</u>iscerning and judicious,
           <u>S</u>eeking of truth and wisdom.

The eighth bead / or group of beads. Repeat: *I will be ...*
(TOPC)   *<u>T</u>ruthful yet kindhearted,*
           <u>O</u>ptimistic and cheerful,
           <u>P</u>unctual and prepared,
           <u>C</u>lean in mind and body.

(MIDT) <u>The ninth bead / or group of beads.</u> Repeat: *I will not violate the Four Fundamental Laws … I will not commit or contribute to **M**urder. I will not commit or contribute to unjustified **I**njury. I will not commit or contribute to foul **D**eeds. I will under oath tell the absolute and complete **T**ruth.*

(The Pursuits A-P) <u>The tenth bead / or group of beads.</u> Repeat: *I will undertake the Pursuits A-P … I will …*

A = <u>Act</u> *with abundant love and kindness. I will transform my inner nature into a benevolent and copious spirit.*

B = <u>Bring</u> *the earth's natural beauty into this world and maintain and care for all things of value. Where Nature and Industry must co-exist, preservation, protection and reclamation will be my focal point.*

C = <u>Create</u> *a home and mobile emergency kit and keep a 4 month supply of food and provisions within my abode.*

D = <u>Develop</u> *intimate ties with good family and friends.*

E = <u>Educate</u> *myself and support the best schooling possible for future generations. I will first Generalize my skills and knowledge then I will Specialize and perfect my expertise in an innocuous occupation. I will promote Meritocracy.*

F = <u>Follow</u> *an active and prudent lifestyle and a healthy diet. In healthcare, I will stress personal choice in my medical services yet will also espouse a government sponsored public safety net for those less fortunate.*

G = <u>Greet</u> *failure with a renewed dedication to succeed.*

H = *Honor* and protect my family and teach my children to be good, fair, and kind as well as to exhibit gratitude and forgiveness. I will educate them on the greatness of a Constitutional Republic and the value of Life, Liberty and Justice for all.

I = *Inwardly* purify and cleanse both my mind and body of toxins, addictive substances, and negativity.

J = *Join* with others in resolving the needs and goals of our community, our country, and our world. I will cultivate and encourage new Neoteric Humanist Membership.

K = *Keep* a stable budget, invest wisely and live modestly.

L = *Learn* and practice multiple pragmatic languages.

M = *Maintain* and practice restraint yet be proficient in personal self-defense.

N = *Nurture* Creativity, Innovation and Adaptability. I will champion research, exploration, fresh discoveries and newfound potential life endowing habitats.

O = *Openly* advocate inspiring art, stimulating music, competitive games, and sports. I will employ reason, logic, strategy and the freedom of ideas and thought to solve problems.

P = *Practice* family planning by using contraceptives or abstinence to prevent an unplanned pregnancy. I will advance the ideal of a balanced world population based more on the quality of life than quantity.

(TIME) <u>The eleventh bead</u> / <u>or group of beads</u>. Repeat: *I will master …*

Time … as once spent it is departed forever. Inner nature … as it determines my character and my behavior. My body … as it impacts and governs my health. Effort … as it will shape my life and the world we all live in.

Next prepare yourself for the POGS strategy that follows below.

I devote myself to **POGS.**
(POGS) <u>The twelfth bead</u> / <u>or group of beads</u>. … Clap your hands lightly together four times, take four deep breaths … refocus and think on the POGS statements below. Complete or change as you find necessary. (Your GOAL – Your PLAN – Your ACTION – Your REVIEW)

People I wish to be closer to are:

_____

One thing I will do to accomplish this is:

_____

Goals Short Term and Long Term I have are:

_____

So that I may attain my goals I will:

_____

Finish by saying: "Let me act each day of my life to accomplish these!!"

Write your thoughts, impressions, and POGS statements and place in your 3 ring binder. Note all remaining tasks to be completed in your pocket notebook. When finished collect your things and make a point to review your binder on a regular basis. Carry your pocket notebook with you and check off daily tasks as you accomplish them. Your objective is to learn most of this meditation by heart so you will not need to refer to this book or the beads as your memory will be sufficient. This is to be followed up by putting into practice what you have just committed yourself to do. ... Becoming that better person! ... Practiced Purpose Perfects Proficiency!

<u>Target Agendas</u>

To create a Target Agenda, first, complete your meditation routine as described at the beginning of this section "The Neoteric Humanist Meditation". Once you have concluded this self-examination and you have finished writing your thoughts, impressions, and notes in your binder, put away your pencil or pen. Take a few minutes, to calmly re-adjust yourself and then prepare to clear your mind once again.

Now, review the next few pages and you will find an example of a Target Agenda and additional notions to consider. Begin by pondering and answering in your mind the questions below. Once you have clarified your response, write each one in the spaces provided on the Target Agenda you will discover on the following pages. All answers should be written in a short and concise manner. ... Think seriously about ... what are your:

Long Term Goals?

Short Term Goals?

Monthly/Weekly/Daily Goals?

Plans and Deadlines for achieving them?

<u>Before</u> moving on and completing your personal Target Agenda ... take a moment and reflect on some scholarly age-old Greek wisdom:

- Improve yourself with each passing day.
- Use empathy and reason to resolve your problems.
- Avoid extremes and instead practice moderation in all things.
- Understand your assets, strengths, and weaknesses.
- Seek and abide by what is accurate and true.
- Address things as they truly are, not what they seem to be.
- Without the freedom of choice ... you cannot find joy or fulfillment.
- Show respect for others as well as who you are as an individual.

A "Personal" Target Agenda: _____ Target Agenda
                                    (Your Name)

Long Term Goals and Plan to achieve them:

_____

Short Term Goals and Plan to achieve them:

_____

Monthly / Weekly / Daily Goals and Plan to achieve them:

_____

Current Status:

_____

Take a few minutes once again, to bodily re-adjust yourself and then prepare to clear your mind for an additional task. It is time to go deeper and further with your goals and become even more inclusive in your overall efforts. Now is the time to make additional Target Agendas, beyond your personal one, which will identify the aspirations of your family, friends, and associates. Thinking of other's hopes and dreams is not only the right thing to do but helping others fulfill their ambitions and desires will make them more inclined to help you in satisfying yours.

(Duplicate the form above for "Family or Friend" Target Agendas)

Over the next few weeks, as you create additional Target Agendas for family, friends, and associates, you will notice on those Agendas that there is an area for you to list how you have helped that person move closer to their goals and when you did so. Keep this up to date as it will show your progress and where you may need to put in some extra work. Review all of your Target Agendas often. This will not only aid you to stay on track with your dreams but will keep you mindful of opportunities to assist others. Stay in touch with these people and confirm occasionally that their hopes and desires haven't changed. Lend them a hand in implementing their endeavors and offer to support them in achieving the necessary steps to get there.

From now on, as part of your meditation session, begin by opening your three- ring binder to your Target Agendas. Examine your progress and how you have aided the advancement of others. Reaffirm your personal ambitions and commitments as well as the objectives of family and friends. Let your imagination see yourself and others taking great pleasure in the fulfillment of each their hopes and dreams. ... Take time to review and evaluate your Target Agendas frequently, but above all ... take action!

> "**LOST** ... *yesterday somewhere between sunrise and sunset ... golden hours, each set with golden minutes ... no reward is offered for they are gone forever.*"
>
> Horace Mann

Don't be discouraged if you seem to be making slow progress with your goals. Remember that even young toddlers are clumsy in the beginning. They often waver and seem to be on the verge of falling as they push forward. No one is born with all the necessary talents and abilities to walk and run. It requires one step at a time until we master the skills or develop the means we want. Some goals take stages or perhaps there is a need to refine a plan or perfect a technique. It's best to set a target for your next step, not your final step. One must accept that in life we will all face many challenges placed before us and it is our task to muster the drive to overcome them.

Whenever you can, take the focus off your ambitions and place it onto the aspirations of others. Set aside time to encourage a friend or someone you know in the pursuit of their particular interests and well-being. Keep in mind that the focal point in our daily life should be to show kindness and generosity to our fellow human beings. ... Be that beacon of light for someone who may be struggling in darkness. Be their constant cheerleader and staunch supporter with the belief that they will eventually succeed in attaining their dreams. In doing so you will discover the very best in you ... and the enjoyment felt in the victory of another will do wonders for your spirit and happiness. ... When all things are considered, simply finding yourself "being happy" is in the end, being successful in fulfilling a vital slice of your own wants and desires.

"You must be the change you wish to see in the world!"
Gandhi

"There's only one corner of the universe you can be certain of improving, and that's your own self."
Aldous Huxley

A Body & Mind Meditation:

To actively engage in both a body and mind meditation, begin much as you would for a typical meditation routine. Wear comfortable clothing, find pleasant ambiances, and seat yourself into a comfortable position. When possible, include this book, your 3-ring binder, a small pocket notebook, and a pencil or pen.

Begin: Lightly … close your eyes. Draw in air, hold and exhale four times … slowly … and deeply. Continue with shallow breathing while leisurely, from the top of your head to the tips of your toes, relax your muscles, and progressively allow yourself to unwind. Imagine yourself relaxing on a quiet, warm, and sunny beach far far away. Feel the sun's warmth on your face and body. Now envision that sensation growing and moving through your entire essence until it reaches the very center of your being. … Now … breathe deeply and exhale slowly. Repeat these words until you feel in balance and focused: "*Stay the way, Shed the shell, Form the clay, Fill the well.*"

At this moment, having found your focus, engage in the easy exercise below:

(1) Start with both of your hands lying comfortably in your lap, draw in the air slowly … and deeply, hold and then slowly exhale. Repeat this four times.

(2) Leaving your elbows near your lap and hips, straighten the 4 fingers on both hands and point forward (horizontally); bend thumbs inwards and bring your fingertips together. Breathe deeply … hold … and gently bring both hands, now in the shape of a teepee like position, to your forehead … and exhale … saying … *Pursue Goals* … (Let those goals cross your mind.)

(3) Take in a breath and slowly exhale. Remove your hands from your forehead and place them back in your lap in their original finger tips together position. Breathe deeply … hold … and gently bring just the tips of the fingers of both hands to your forehead … and exhale … saying … *Cleanse Soul.*

(4) Take in a breath and slowly exhale. Remove your hands from your forehead and back to their original finger tips together position. … Breathe deeply … hold … and move both hands so that they cross over your chest and exhale … saying … *Make Whole* … then move back to original finger tips together position.

(5) Take in a deep breath … open hands outward, as if releasing a bird, and exhale saying … *Calm Day Be So …* *(Evening: … Calm Night Be So …)*

(6) Begin again as in step #2. Restate this routine four times. After the fourth repetition … repeat: *"I will live by The Desirable Traits and will do my best to fulfill the Sixteen Pursuits and their objectives. I will obey and will not violate The 4 Fundamental Laws."*

(7) Continue with light breathing, and assess your POGS dedications in your mind. Now … review those tasks in your life that you either foresee as coming soon or are matters you are currently acting on.

(8) When doable, immediately write out your urgent tasks in your small pocket notebook and record and date future planned actions in your 3-ring binder. Evaluate your Target Agendas to monitor your progress. Remove the urgent task list from your small notebook and keep it in a wallet or purse for reference during the day. Cross off tasks as you complete them. Smile and think happy thoughts!

Another meditation relating to "Love and Kindness" can be found on page #294.

Reflecting on Life's Choices

When allowing yourself time for deep reflection, let the following enter your mind:

- There are four essential keys to contentment: developing loving relationships, focusing on the positive, managing the negative, and pursuing worthy goals.
- Be flexible and adaptable ... all things will change sooner or later.
- If you want more peace in your life pursue well thought out choices.
- Shifting a negative to a positive creates more peace and harmony.
- Debates don't require a winner, just mutual understanding and respect.
- Circumstances and end results will not always be just and fair.
- Hate and envy are a waste of time and energy.
- Some causes are worth dying for ... but they fill a very shortlist.
- Jubilation can exist for long periods of the time ... but not all the time.
- Humor can cut deep without drawing blood and defends without a shield.
- As a rule of thumb, a good plan now is better than a perfect plan later.
- You only come this way once, provide time to find your joy and bliss.
- The only ones who truly care about you are those who love you.

- To influence or change the world, it is best, to begin with kindness.
- Evil must be extinguished or it will thrive and grow.
- Satisfaction can usually be found in meaningful activity and wise choices.
- Maintaining a healthy body and an active lifestyle contributes to a happy life.
- One channel to personal fulfillment is solving one of life's problems.
- An open mind will more likely find fresh ideas and novel solutions.
- Love is holding hands, sharing, offering to help, and caring for each other.
- To clarify who you are and your goals … allow time for study and meditation.
- Everyone has flaws and faults. Accept theirs and hope they will tolerate yours.
- When you meet repetitive negative results, try new tactics, or change the goal.
- Trust your inner feelings or "gut" … and frequently you will be right.
- A loud demand gains a raised hand, whereas, a soft request receives an open ear.
- Practice, each and every day, what you want to be until you succeed.
- Remember … quick and thoughtless choices can have lifelong consequences.
- Anyone who truly loves cannot escape pain, grief, and sorrow.
- One great pleasure in life is bringing forth the composition that is within you.
- Prune away little issues before they grow into large and weighty problems.

- With the exception of love, it is best to live modestly and in moderation.
- A happy person is not the one with the most, but the one who needs the least.
- The ability to find humor in a bad situation will help you survive it.
- If you feel insignificant, help someone else ... then see how you feel.
- Sometimes your desire is already in your hands but you are too blind to see it.
- Ignorance, intolerance, gluttony, unchecked lust, and revenge all lead to misery.
- Art brings forth both remarkable flowers and delicious fruit on the tree of life.
- Music is like a snowflake in summer, it fills the heavens and then melts away.
- Great art intoxicates your senses and invigorates your body and spirit.
- Personal artistic or creative expression is one of life's greatest pleasures.
- Don't wait too long ... before sharing or helping others.
- Most of the time it is wisest to speak less, keep quiet, and listen.
- Force used on the unwilling seldom produces good results and rarely lasts.
- Vanity, bragging, conceit, and arrogance create an unwelcome fool.
- Being 100% truthful ... leaves no room for kindness.
- When confronted by a growing threat ... think well before you act.
- Always give more than is expected and do it with a smile.

- When you are wrong admit it quickly and apologize sincerely.
- Great accomplishments sometimes require great risk.
- Just because you lost the battle … doesn't mean you can't win the war.
- If you do not give respect … you will not get it in return.
- Not dealing with issues now is hard but postponing them can make them worse.
- It is easier, to tell the truth than remember lies.
- By listing your life goals, you will have a better chance of reaching them.
- To be invigorated, see new places, do new things, and accept new challenges.
- Knowing what is right and doing what is right usually creates the best result.
- Learning and mastering a trade is hard but having no skills is even harder.
- Bear in mind that bad things are more likely to happen when you are tired.
- Every life eventually sets limits; this may be your last chance to _____??
- Balancing Truth with Kindness during your daily interactions will be welcomed.
- You cannot get better in the same place or situation that is mistreating you.
- A Giver must know their limits … as a Taker does not.

Four ways to make Good Choices that best line up with your Life's Goals:

1. Remain true to your Core Values. Your core values form the glue that binds your choices and your life's goals together.
2. Make Mindful Choices. Think before you act. There is a fine line between good choices and both impulsive and irrational decisions.
3. Listen to "Your Gut" ... It will usually give you the best advise.
4. Love yourself and others.

"Decision making is easy when your values are clear."
Roy Disney

"Life is an opportunity, benefit from it. Life is beauty, admire it. Life is bliss, taste it. Life is a dream, realize it. Life is a challenge, meet it. Life is a duty, complete it. Life is a game, play it. Life is a promise, fulfill it. Life is sorrow, overcome it. Life is a song, sing it. Life is a struggle, accept it. Life is a tragedy, confront it. Life is an adventure, dare it. Life is luck, make it. Life is too precious, do not destroy it. Life is life, fight for it."
Mother Teresa

Visual Symbols

For some people, visual symbols can be of great assistance in both understanding and committing something to their memory. For those individuals who are more pictorial orientated, please review the following … as has been said many times before "*a picture is worth a thousand words*". In this case, these illustrations exemplify the mantras, values, positions or concepts relating to Neoteric Humanism. You will notice that the symbols are presented in the same systematic order as that of the Meditation Bead sequence. However, in these examples, the focus is based on visual cues rather than physical touch and interaction. These images are also intended to be used by the members both inside and outside of The HUB. This may involve written literature, messaging, placards, cue cards, artwork, or any other purposes that may prove useful.

The pictograms you will find on the next pages embody the Goals, Principles, Desirable Traits, Laws, and Pursuits of Neoteric Humanism. They should be studied until they can be associated easily with their message and meaning:

BING: *It is my belief that … as I **B**etter myself, I will **I**mprove my family and my community. As I Improve my family and my community, a **N**ew vision for the people will evolve. As a new vision for people evolves, I **G**ive hope and optimism to the future.*

KUPP: *It is my purpose and goal to **K**now and improve myself. To **U**nderstand and be of service to others. To **P**ractice kindness, truth, fairness, and **P**roduce a positive impact with my life choices.*

The Quest Wheel WISH and its Four Quads: *Wisdom, Integration, Security, and Harmony will lead to my completeness, safety, contentment, and well-being.*

The Eight Steps of This Guide: …
Acknowledgment, Education, Character, Occupation, Meditation, Assimilation, Initiation, and Motivation will show me the way.

*I will live by the **Desirable Traits:** I will be …*

(FAWN)

Faithful and dependable, Accountable and ethical, Well-groomed and mannered, Novel and free-thinking.

(QUIL)

Quality focused and guided, Understanding and tolerant, Inclusive and charitable, Loyal and trusted friend.

(MEDS)

Mindful of behavior and deeds, Educator and student, Discerning and judicious, Seeking of truth and wisdom.

(TOPC)

Truthful yet kindhearted, Optimistic and cheerful, Punctual and prepared, Clean in mind and body.

The Fundamental Laws: *I will obey and not violate the four laws.*

I will not commit or contribute to Murder. I will not commit or contribute to unjustified Injury. I will not commit or contribute to foul Deeds. Under oath I will tell the absolute and complete Truth.

Transformation: *Shed the cocoon and become who you wish to be!*

I will undertake the **Pursuits A-P:** *... I will:*

<u>A</u>*ct with abundant love and kindness. I will transform my inner nature into a benevolent and copious spirit.*

<u>B</u>*ring the earth's natural beauty into this world and maintain and care for all things of value. Where Nature and Industry must co-exist, preservation, protection and reclamation will be my focal point.*

<u>C</u>*reate a home and mobile emergency kit and keep a 4-month food and provisions supply within my abode.*

<u>D</u>*evelop intimate ties with good family and friends._*

<u>E</u>*ducate myself and support the best schooling possible for future generations. I will first Generalize my skills and knowledge then I will Specialize and perfect my expertise in an innocuous occupation. I will promote Meritocracy.*

<u>F</u>*ollow both an active and prudent lifestyle as well as a healthy diet. In healthcare, I will stress personal choice in my medical services yet will also espouse a government sponsored public safety net for those less fortunate.*

<u>G</u>*reet failure with a renewed dedication to succeed.*

Honor and protect my family and teach my children to be good, fair, and kind as well as to exhibit gratitude and forgiveness. I will educate them on the greatness of a Constitutional Republic and the value of Life, Liberty and Justice for all.

 Inwardly purify and cleanse both my mind and body of toxins, addictive substances, and negativity.

 Join with others in resolving the needs and goals of our community, our country, and our world. I will cultivate and encourage new Neoteric Humanist Membership.

 Keep a stable budget, invest wisely and live modestly.

 Learn and practice multiple pragmatic languages.

 Maintain and practice restraint yet be proficient in personal self-defense.

 Nurture Creativity, Innovation and Adaptability. I will champion research, exploration, fresh discoveries and newfound potential life endowing habitats.

__O__penly advocate inspiring art, stimulating music, competitive games, and sports. I will employ reason, logic, strategy and the freedom of ideas and thought to solve problems.

__P__ractice family planning by using contraceptives or abstinence to prevent an unplanned pregnancy. I will advance the ideal of a balanced world population based more on the quality of life than quantity.

I will master ... __T__ime ... as once spent it is departed forever.
__I__nner nature ... as it determines my character and my behavior.
__M__y body ... as it impacts and governs my health.
__E__ffort ... as it will shape my life and the world we live in.

I devote myself to POGS.

POGS:

__P__eople I wish to be closer to are:

_____

__O__ne thing I will do to accomplish this:

_____

__G__oals Short Term and Long Term I have:

_____

__S__o that I may attain my various goals: I will:

_____

The Wallet Prompter:

The rationale for the prompter is to assist an individual in learning and then applying the goals, principles, and the mission of this philosophy. It is best carried on one's person for ease of practice. To create one for yourself, simply photo copy page #277, cut out the graphic, fold it and place it in your wallet or purse. An even better idea is to do a screen shot and post it in your telephone, laptop or other device. In today's world this may be the most convenient way to access the prompter as well as the mantras, objectives, meditations, and other sections you may wish to have easily available. Understand, that the essential objective for the person using the wallet prompter is to study and absorb … and then actively engage in its purpose. One way to accomplish this is to do so in stages. Initially, begin with the noted greetings and acronyms and then move on to using the illustrations as your main teaching aid.

Ideally, as with the meditation beads mentioned before, the ultimate aim would be for the individual to discard this prompter altogether once it has served its function. … Keep in mind that memorizing and understanding by itself is not enough, it must be put into action or you will not advance yourself to the individual you aspire to be! After creating your wallet prompter, we will next move on to some Simple Acts or Ritual Adages (page #279). These may be used at various gatherings and are meant to offer additions to or alternatives to social blessings and/or prayers.

The significance of these Simple Acts and Rituals are that they allow times for us to remind ourselves that we are not alone in this world, that we genuinely value our family and friends and that we are truly thankful for the time they spend or have spent with us. It allows time for us to express our gratitude and bring more peace and comfort into our life. It is a practice that allows us to remember all of the good things in our lives, no matter how big or small. It helps us to be humble and compassionate as we realize how fortunate we are in life and how lucky we are to have each other.

Your Wallet Prompter

Wallet Prompter: Paco, Sano, Felico kaj Prospero   Al vi ankau

BING - KUPP - WISH - AE/ COM/ AIM
FAWN - QUIL - MEDS - TOPC
MIDT - PURSUITS - TIME - POGS

This is your personal Wallet Propter that will help you practice and learn the principles, values and mission of Neoteric Humanism. Cut the above illustration out, fold it and carry in your pocketbook, billfold or purse. When you find a quiet moment to sit and reflect, remove the graphic snapshot above and rehearse and commit the above mantras, ideals and concepts to memory.

As mentioned earlier, you may also wish to take a snapshot of the above and carry it in your telephone, laptop or computer as well. Of course, the ultimate goal is to eliminate the Wallet Prompter entirely as you will carry its contents within you.

Things to keep in mind when using the wallet prompter and practicing:

Remember, your success in this process will not be an unwavering line straight to your goal. There will be ups and downs, but if you are moving in the right direction, you will be making progress. Don't compare yourself to others on this journey; compare yourself to who you were yesterday.

Understand that, the butterfly does not look back at the cat-erpillar in shame. Just as you should not look back at your past in shame. Your past was just part of your eventual transformation.

Keep in mind; you start each day with a set amount of time, 24 hours, 1,440 minutes and 86,400 seconds. The choice is yours, you can waste them or use them wisely, but you can never use them again, they are departed forever. ... Use this time to create new habits that will change your life for the bet-ter. Reading and studying just 10 pages a day is like reading 10 to 15 books a year. Walking or running one mile a day is 365 miles per year. Saving or investing $10 a day is $3,600 more in your pocket annually. Your putting in just a little more effort today than yesterday will make you that many times better at year end! What you improve on by this effort ... you keep for your lifetime!! Never underestimate the power of making small habits your reality!

No risk, no change ... no change, no progress ... no prog-ress, no dreams fulfilled... no dreams fulfilled ... no happiness ... and without happiness there is no contentment, serenity or well-being in life. Don't take life for granted as it can change in the blink of an eye. Please ... live your life to the fullest now; as you may never have this chance again.

Simple Acts or Ritual Adages for Gatherings

Simple acts or rituals may be used, if you desire to do so, in addition to or as a replacement for a blessing or a prayer. Here are some appropriate librettos for occasions when you are called upon by others, or when you want, to give an oration.

By oneself at a meal:

I am grateful for this nutritious meal.
I am thankful for my good family and friends.
May I find ways to overcome my flaws and failings.
May I always be at peace with my family, friends, and neighbors.
And … let every new day find me a better person.

With a group at a meal:

We are grateful for this gathering and this meal.
We are thankful for our good family and friends.
May we find ways to overcome our flaws and failings.
May we always be at peace with our family, friends and neighbors.
And … let every new day find each of us a better person.

At a gathering of people:

We are grateful for this gathering and for this time together.
We are thankful for our wonderful family, friends, and neighbors.
May we always find peace, harmony, and good-will with each other.
May we learn from every hardship we face and may it make us stronger.
May we always share with others, so they may feel secure and sheltered.
And may we always come together in friendship, harmony and joy.

For the loss of a loved one:

We are thinking of you _____... for you we mourn.
We think of you in silence ... and our memories are reborn.
These memories we will keep alive... and will always maintain.
We wish you could have stayed longer ... but time would not ordain.
A piece of our heart goes with you ... to a place for us unknown.
Please rest in peace knowing we are here and you did not go alone.
May this be ... only a gateway to new wonders.
New joys, bliss, harmony and happiness.

For a closer relationship with people you care about utilize ... **MORE**:

Meet more often with each other: If logistically possible ... start seeing them at least once a month. If they live far away, use the telephone, e-mail, texting, or written notes to establish and maintain contact. Resolve to know more about them, which of course, requires establishing a regular line of communication. This, however, must be a mutually shared desire by both parties, not one person demanding more time than the other is willing to give.

Openly share more of your life: The more occasions you participate in with others is a huge factor in determining the warmth and fondness of your relationships. Make an effort to include the people you care about in your family's activities by inviting them to special dinners or parties. Perhaps you can initiate opportunities to get together at planned sports, school, or community events. You might want to suggest sharing home improvement projects or shared childcare days to assist each other. This will also give you an opportunity to become involved in the routines of each other's every-day issues and interests.

Regularly encourage more ongoing dialogue: Establish a few minutes every other week to talk to each other about the other's workday, to share political or religious topics or to swap recent activities, outings or trips. You might want to ask for advice. Maybe they are seeking someone with a sympathetic ear for an issue they have. Try to become a supportive, informative and helpful person in their life.

Embrace talking more about problems: Sometimes we tend to disregard little or even large problems. But don't sweep these difficulties under the carpet. Issues dealing with money, family, and children can have important consequences for relationships. Be a polite listener and take care to be sure you understand their position before trying to interject your thoughts. Jointly try to find a suitable or practical option or solution. … If building and maintaining a strong relationship is challenging now, the more time goes by without dialogue … the more difficult it will become.

Self-Discovery

It is important to take time to discover who you truly are … not just what your career, business or trade may be. As you embark on this quest, ask yourself these questions: Are you an honest and ethical person, a loving and supportive spouse, an involved and caring parent, a thoughtful and dependable friend, a good and well-thought-of son or daughter? Do you have a talent to compose rousing music, write inspiring poetry, perform a dramatic role in the theater, or express yourself through interpretive arts? Who and what are you actually? If your life is totally absorbed in only how you earn a living, then you need to re-examine all of life's options and possibilities. While one's work is certainly important … if you are failing at being a loving spouse or involved parent, do you believe money alone will fill these voids in their lives? How will it compare to being there for your son or daughter's first school play or those hand in hand walks with your spouse? The time we set aside and the memories we create for our family will be treasured much longer than the material things we give them. If you want your home life, your friendships, and your talents to thrive and grow, you must make them a priority. As you examine your life now, what do you see? If it is not the picture or life you want or long for … think about what you can do to change it? What can you do now to improve and cultivate the truly important aspects of your life?

Take a moment and expand your deliberations to an even broader vision. What about your activities in your hometown community? Are you involved in local clubs or civic groups? Are you a high school coach, la-cross team referee, or meals on wheels volunteer? Do you know the issues going on in your neighborhood, county, and state? Are you involved in a political faction or have you run for a local office? Do you even know who your state representative(s) and senator(s) are? Most people today are so immersed in watching television, playing video games, or downloading music on their cell phones, that they are utterly oblivious to the outside world. Does any of the above sound like you or those in your family? Is this truly the best use of your time or how you think you should spend your life? If you want to make a difference and make a positive impact, then you must get involved. Read the community section of your area paper and choose one or perhaps two organizations to join and become active in. Get to know your representatives and promote the agendas you agree with. Maybe your child's high school needs someone to help move equipment on Saturday nights. Possibly an elderly or disabled person needs help with their lawn. Perhaps you might offer to help a neighbor or new arrival fix or locate something. This would be assistance given freely ... with no expectation of a reward or an obligation to return the favor. You may, suddenly, find yourself uncovering new friends who will add joy, zeal and gusto to your life. The friendships you make and the contentment you receive for a good deed done, will bring a greater sense of well-being and completeness to your life.

The kindness you pour into the community and the positive influence you provide will make this world we live in ... a better place. Think about the following:

<u>These bring Despondency:</u>
Not having lived the life you wanted to live!
Not having spent more time with family!
Not keeping in touch with friends!
Not having stood up for your true beliefs!
Not choosing to do what makes you happy!
Not finishing or applying yourself in school!

Not being financially or emotionally ready for a baby!
Being greedy, selfish, or decadent!
Marring too soon or not to the right person!
Hurting someone you love!
Not forgiving a grudge!
Not living in moderation!

"Miserable people focus on what they hate about their life.
Happy people focus on what they love about their life."

Zig Ziglar

These bring Happiness:

Finding love and being loved!
Being physically and mentally active!
Seeking out the silver lining!
Listening more and speaking less!
Spending time with family and friends!
Expressing more appreciation!
Being grateful for what you have!
Sobriety, cleanliness and self-control!
Using moderation in most things you do!
Doing what you truly love to do!
Living below your means, saving and investing more!
Continuing to learn and gaining new abilities!
Being financially stable and secure!

Happiness is when what you think, what you say, and what
you do are in harmony.

Mahatma Gandhi

What things are making you unhappy and what steps are you taking to resolve them?

I would advocate that you practice the very basic Mantra "KUPP" found in this philosophy and then ask yourself how you feel. ... *It is my purpose and goal to:*

Know and improve myself.
Understand and be of service to others.
Practice kindness, truth, fairness and
Produce a positive impact with my life choices.

"Thought is the sculptor who can create the person you want to be."

Henry David Thoreau

The "Gift" We Can Give To Others!

I'm sure most of us wouldn't be too surprised to learn that many people we know are extremely hungry for someone to reassure and/or cheer them on. With this in mind, I believe there are several wonderful ways to give our families, friends, and acquaintances more optimism and greater joyfulness in their lives. To accomplish this feat, we should carry all of the following promptings in both our hearts and minds and make a commitment to fulfill these desires at every opportunity! … Each of us should practice and encourage …

GIFT:

1) **G**enerous love and support: The gift of love and support is fulfilled by sincere and generous hugs and kind and thoughtful words. Make a point to tell the significant people in your world that you love and care for them. Make this known to your spouse, family, children, and your friends. Tell them "thank you" for being my better half, a treasured member of our family, or for being such a good friend. Say, "I love and value you, and I'm grateful and happy to have you in my life."   Show your support by urging people to "hang in there" and to keep striving for the goals they want to achieve. Buoy them by sending positive notes, call and compliment them on their progress, take them out for a meal and discuss ways you can help. Express pride and say, "I'm very proud of what you are doing. You are helping to make this world of ours a better place."

2) **I**dentify one's Value: The gift of value is satisfied by communicating gratitude and approval, particularly in recognizing a person's achievements or good deeds.

Most of the time, especially in a work environment, financial rewards are expected for work performed. However, the expressive desire for individual value is found to be largely empty or lacking. Offering gratitude and approval fills this need by building up or affirming a person's singular worth and acknowledging the importance of their contributions. I have witnessed many individuals at award ceremonies break down in tears after receiving a simple small plaque or a warm and openly expressed recognition. Show respect by believing, acting, and treating that person as a valuable and worthy part of your life. Show sincere thoughtfulness to your spouse's opinions. Listen in a nonjudgmental way to your children. Be considerate of people's time and viewpoints. Be kind and understanding of people's feelings and perspectives from different backgrounds, cultures, and beliefs.

3) Focusing and engaging: This gift is achieved by earnest and intent listening and then responding to those individuals who may be in distress with words of support and compassion. Do not say: "If you need anything, please call me." People usually don't know what they want or need, and they won't call you. ... Instead, consider what needs to be done and then do it. Family or friends buy groceries, do the laundry, drop off a meal, cut the grass, take the kids to school, clean the house, drop off notes of encouragement, etc. Any such acts of love and service make life easier for that person. These acts say, "I am thinking about you"; "I am here to help"; "I love and care about you." This need for a personal connection is quenched when you come in contact with someone and give them your complete attention and understanding. Take notice when someone

is experiencing episodes of anxiety and do your best to empathize and comfort them. Recognize that the need for engagement arrives when we decide to participate in another person's reality. Understand how important it is to spend time with that person ... time really listening with compassion and kindheartedness. Know that developing a close and personal relationship with that individual is the greatest way to show your love and humanity.

4) Tactics for safety and peace: The gift of protection, security and peace is realized when we establish relationships that free people from fear or threat of harm. Make sure that those for whom you are responsible are confident that you will provide for and safeguard them if and when called upon. Inform others that could become involved so they will know and understand what to expect from you. Assemble and ready a safety and refuge plan to show that you are not only willing but also well prepared to assist those who may need to rely on you. Once you have prepared a secure sanctuary, establish an oasis of tranquility and serenity in your home for family and friends by providing an environment of positive and optimistic ambiances, calm and quiet. Provide an atmosphere that allows them to unwind, relax, think and reflect. Permit peace and time to gently flow into their life and only provide an understanding ear to listen ... wait and do not offer solutions until they are invited. When conditions are right, encourage them to focus on affirmative, upbeat and constructive options and opportunities. Look for the silver lining and the sun behind the clouds.

We must acknowledge that to advance humanity we must first change ourselves and our actions. In doing so we help others see and comprehend a new vision for a better world. This involves transforming a person's heart and mind and is the best way to achieve progress and improvement not only for the individual ... but for our culture and society as well.

"I am a firm believer that helping others is the quick way to find true happiness. You were making someone's day a little bit brighter will, in turn, make your day that much better. Supporting people who are in need and facing challenges is an excellent service to humanity. No matter how small the good deed seems to be, extending a helping hand is the right thing to do. Life can be challenging for a lot of people. It gives you phases of struggles, challenges, and adversities. But the least you can do is provide them with help, support and a helping hand to sail through it."

Unknown

"It's not enough to have lived. We should be determined to live for something. May I suggest that it be creating joy for others, sharing what we have for the betterment of personkind, bringing hope to the lost and love to the lonely."

Leo Buscaglia

"It's the action, not the fruit of the action, that's important. You have to do the right thing. It may not be in your power, may not be in your time, that there'll be any fruit. But that doesn't mean you stop doing the right thing. You may never know what results come from your action. But if you do nothing, there will be no result."

Mahatma Gandhi

The Four P's

<u>Use The Four P's: Practiced Purpose Perfects Proficiency!!</u>

Practicing the 4 P's means learning this philosophy's methodology in the proper order and in the most efficient manner possible. This means setting daily goals and actively pursuing them. Sometimes those goals can be small – like a specific mantra. Other times it might be a substantial goal such as engaging oneself in the total process. Either way, setting goals and practicing specifically to achieve those goals maximizes your time, efficiency, and ultimately will give you the best chance of achieving them. The more consistent you are with your practice times, the more focused your sessions, the more quickly you'll learn and the faster you'll excel. When it comes to learning this methodology, pursue a commitment to practice more on individual parts rather than racing for the desired result. Once you form this steadfast habit, the goal will eventually follow and you will become that who you wish to be. … The important thing is don't give up … stick with it!

Creating an Ideal Society

When you go about your day reading newspapers, cruising the internet, listening to the radio and watching the television do you feel overwhelmed by the world's problems? Do you wish you had a magic wand that could make them all go away? Do you feel bad for all those hurt by senseless violence and misfortune but feel helpless to do anything about it? We, as a society, seem trapped in our daily routine when it comes to the rest of the world and tend to seek solace in our private personal escapes.

As the world continues on, however, starvation can be seen in all parts of the planet, violence beyond belief appears before us daily, pollution is on the rise, open land and many species are disappearing, our politicians seem unethical or dishonest, lawyers win cases based on those with wealth or fame alone … and yet we continue on with our lives as if nothing is amiss. We have that feeling in the back of our brain that something has gone terribly wrong and we are losing faith in traditional institutions and each other. Every day we are assailed with negative T.V., blogs, newspaper and radio reports. What do these storylines shout at us "Breaking News" somewhere in the world someone has committed murder, been assassinated, was arrested, is dying of, is infected with, stole from, or somehow will be doing one of these things soon in a neighborhood near you. The news is focused around the world on corruption, tragedy, battles, disgrace and any kind of dirty laundry that will create a big headline. This downbeat messaging hits us constantly and we involuntarily begin storing this negativity in our thoughts … this pessimism then sub-consciously affects us and we become discouraged in how we look at and react to the world. When these depressing views become the "new normal", we detach ourselves and withdraw into our apathetic separate lives. We as a society seem to have lost our way and are lacking an approach to guide ourselves back to a brighter future. ... So what can be done? This progression of negativity and hopelessness <u>must be broken</u>. The good news is ... that it can be done by employing these 4 actions:

1) Read and understand this philosophy's vision for improving our world.
2) Analyze and then decide if this philosophy does define what the world's explicit problems and solutions are. If you believe it to be accurate and true ...
3) Develop real-life solutions for those problems and how to best address them.
4) Narrow it down to specific steps, then implement a suitable plan for each step ... and finally ... and most importantly ... put it into action.

It is time to be accountable and make the changes we want to see in our world. The time is right now if we truly want to create superior values and outcomes for ourselves and future generations. We must make a genuine commitment to act with our children's future in mind rather than the pursuit of our own wants and needs. As a community and as individuals we must live by and express a set of exceptional values that will shine a bright light on what is good and virtuous for our society. No culture or nation will survive for long without a moral compass to guide its decision making and advancement. These standards and ideals need to be actively exhibited and brought back into our daily lives. Imagine how our world might look ... a world where peace, improved health, more happiness and prosperity abound and where each person or family has found harmony and security. Each living side by side enjoying close family relationships and true friends. Visualize leaving this kind of world to your children.

Keeping this vision of a better future in your daily meditation will provide you with the inspiration and motivation you will need to constantly work on your transformation and progress as your personal journey develops. Our life is much like the Meditation Beads on the string I described in Part III. Every day we add a new bead ... from what we learn and from what we experience. You are evolving from one day to the next. The old you is passing away and the new you is arriving. Are you becoming a better person? When you look back at the end of your days ... will you be happy with the kind of individual you have become and the legacy you have left behind? Will your life have made a valuable and positive impact in this world? Have you caused humanity and our world to become further troubled, harsher and corrupt or have you helped it to become better, happier and more virtuous? ... It's my genuine hope you choose the latter!

"There are two primary choices in life: to accept conditions as they exist, or accept the responsibility for changing them."

Denis Waitley

A Love and Kindness Meditation

Think of someone you care deeply about and bring them into your mind. While visualizing this person say *"May you reside in Comfort, May you be Happy, May you be Safe, May you be Healthy, May you know Love, May you seek Wisdom, May you share Kindness, and May you live your life in Harmony with others."*

Then, bring to mind, yourself, and say to yourself *"May you reside in Comfort, May you be Happy, May you be Safe, May you be Healthy, May you know Love, May you seek Wisdom, May you share Kindness, and May you live your life in Harmony with others."*

Next, think of someone you don't have good or bad feelings towards and say *"May you reside with Comfort, May you be Happy, May you be Safe, May you be Healthy, May you know Love, May you seek Wisdom, May you share Kindness, and May you live your life in Harmony with others."*

At this point, (and this may be difficult) also bring up someone you have negative feelings towards or someone who has harmed you and say *"May you reside with Comfort, May you be Happy, May you be Safe, May you be Healthy, May you know Love, May you seek Wisdom, May you share Kindness, and May you live your life in Harmony with others."*

Finally, think of all people everywhere and say *"May you reside with Comfort, May you be Happy, May you be Safe, May you be Healthy, May you know Love, May you seek Wisdom, May you share Kindness, and May you live in Harmony with others."*

Here is an interesting challenge for you. Take out a piece of paper and a pen and seat yourself at a table. Now... imagine something terrible has just happened and you are dying and are taking the very last breath you will have in this world. Yes ... your very last breath and now you are surely going to die. While you are in this final state and you think back on your life, what was it you treasured and enjoyed the most? Do you have any missed hopes, longings, guilt or regrets? If given a second chance at life, what would you do differently? ... POW ... lucky for you someone nearby knew CPR and has revived you and you are back and ALIVE! ... The question for your challenge is this ... <u>what are you going to do now?</u>

"In the end, we only regret the chances we didn't take, the relationships we were afraid to have, and the decisions we waited too long to make."

Lewis Carroll

Visual Initiation Symbols:

Affinity Symbol/Compass/Staff/BING/KUPP/Quest Wheel/ Steps/Laws /Desirable Traits/Transformation/TIME/Sun Insignia /Morning/ Noon/ Evening/Night/Moon Insignia /Spring/Summer /Fall/ Winter/Arcturus & Spica and Ascender Insignias. Box of Yea & Nay Stones. Stoles used by La Kompaso, La Suno, La Luno and La Kandidato.

Neoteric Humanism Acronyms:

See list and page number below for their location.

Expanded Reading: A recommended list of books to examine:

The following inventory of books cover various categories including religion, philosophy, science, history, politics, art, health, and literature. You may begin anywhere, but I would suggest you start by selecting the ones that sound most appealing or intriguing to you. How deep you dive into each is entirely up to you. Some volumes you may want to use in conjunction with Saturday core sessions, one or two as simply a reference, others you may want to probe much deeper. This broadened knowledge will, hopefully, expand and open your mind and lead you to greater awareness and wisdom. Reading more is an excellent way to broaden your horizons and will certainly move you along the pathway to living a complete, meaningful, and happy life. … Some people will advise you to avoid talking about religion, politics, and personal problems when visiting someone else's home or perhaps having dinner with family or friends … However, I say that if you genuinely want to get to know someone … speak to them of their religion, politics, and personal problems. Just do so in a non-judgmental way and with an approach of understanding or helpfulness, not one seeking confrontation or in a bid to start a debate or argument. Truly being open-minded to another person's viewpoint usually lessens tensions and conflict and will generally bring harmony and serenity. If not, than you are more aware of what topics to avoid in the future with them.

"Exploring the Religions of our World" – by Nancy Clemmons
"The Secular Outlook" – by Victus Cliteur
"Esperanto (the Universal Language) – by O'Connor, J. C.
"Getting Started with Latin" – by William E. Linney
"Spanish for Gringos" – by William C. Harvey

"Learn Ancient Greek (Greek and Latin Language) – by Peter Jones

"The History of the World" - by J. M. Roberts

"Political Ideologies" – by Andrew Heywood

"The Eight Pillars of Greek Wisdom" – by Stephen Bertman

"Law 101: Everything You Need to Know" - by Jay M. Feinman

"Rational Choices in an Uncertain World" – by Reid Hastie

"Art is Everywhere" - by Lorenzo Servi

"You are the Music" – by Victoria Williamson

"Histories Great Speeches" - by James Daley

"The Organized Mind" – by Daniel Levitin

"The Big Book of Health and Fitness" – by Philip Maffetone

"The Best Guide to Meditation" - by Victor N. Davich

"Self Defense Made Simple" - by Phil Pierce

"Books That Changed The World" - by Taylor Andrew

"The Greatest Minds and Ideas of All Time" - by Will Durant

"Don Quixote" - by Miguel de Cervantes

"The Odyssey" - by Homer

"One Thousand and One Arabian Nights" - by Geraldine McCaughrean

Mini Farming: Self-Sufficiency on ¼ acre - by Brett L. Markham

The Complete Guide to Food Preservation - by Angela Williams Duea

100 Simple Secrets of Happy Families - by Ph.D. Niven David

100 Things Every Homeowner Must Know - by Editors Of Family Handyman

"Blockbuster Bacon" - by Truly Kidding (Just checking if you were paying attention!) ☺

Remember you can use audiobooks, DVD's, CD's, and all library resources.

I hope this selection and those books found in the "Ideal Calendar of Events" section will be the beginning of a life-long, pleasant, and enjoyable reading habit. May new ideas, knowledge, and challenges move you to a higher plateau of understanding. Addressing and engaging in new ideas will keep your mind sharp, your wit strong, and your life more interesting.

"Write to be understood, speak to be heard, read to grow ..."
Lawrence Clark Powell

"Books are the carriers of civilization. Without books, history is silent, literature dumb, science crippled, thought and speculation at a standstill."
Barbara Tuchman

Final Thoughts

If you plant honesty, you will reap trust.
If you plant goodness, you will reap friends.
If you plant humility, you will reap greatness.
If you plant perseverance, you will reap victory.
If you plant consideration, you will reap harmony.
If you plant hard work, you will reap success.
If you plant forgiveness, you will reap reconciliation.
If you plant openness, you will reap intimacy.
If you plant patience, you will reap improvements.
If you plant faith, you will reap miracles.
But
If you plant dishonesty, you will reap distrust.
If you plant selfishness, you will reap loneliness.
If you plant pride, you will reap destruction.
If you plant envy, you will reap trouble.
If you plant laziness, you will reap stagnation.
If you plant bitterness, you will reap isolation.
If you plant greed, you will reap loss.
If you plant gossip, you will reap enemies.
If you plant worries, you will reap wrinkles.
If you plant sin, you will reap guilt.
So be careful what you plant now, It will
determine what you will reap tomorrow,
The seeds you now scatter will make life worse or better,
in your life or the ones who will come after.

(Islamic principle)

"Life is like a journey on a train ...

with its stations, with changes of routes and with accidents! At birth we board the train and met our parents, and we believe they will always travel by our side. However, at some station our parents will step down from the train, leaving us on this journey alone. As time goes by, other people will board the train; and they will be significant i.e. our siblings, friends, children, and even the love of our life. Many will step down and leave a permanent vacuum. Others will go so unnoticed that we don't realize that they have vacated their seats! This train ride will be full of joy, sorrow, fantasy, expectations, hellos, goodbyes, and farewells. Success consists of having a good relationship with all the passengers requiring that we give the best of ourselves.

The mystery to everyone is: We do not know at which station we ourselves will step down. So, we must live in the best way – Love, forgive, and offer the best of who we are. It is important to do this because when the time comes for us to step down and leave our seat empty; we should leave behind beautiful memories for those who will continue to travel on the train of life without us."   Author Unknown

Yes, life is like a journey on a train. However, one should keep in mind that during this journey you have the freedom to make choices. You can choose who you wish to associate with as well as the behavior you exhibit in those interactions. … What's more, as you reach out and explore this train on which you are traveling, you will discover a noteworthy collection of linked transports attached to your itinerant locomotive. It will be up to you to determine how much time, energy and effort you will utilize in each of these highly valued transports. … One bearing knowledge and wisdom, one offering skill building and training, one of fitness and leisure and the dining coach where you decide how you will nourish your body. The goals and habits you establish and follow in each of those cars will determine what kind of individual you will eventually become. Make these important life choices carefully and wisely … as they will be key factors in your ultimate peace, health, happiness, and prosperity!

"By believing passionately in something that does not yet exist, we create it."

Nikos Kazantzakis

"I'm starting with the man in the mirror,
I'm asking him to change his ways.
No message could have been any clearer,
if you wanna make the world a better place,
take a look at yourself and then make the change."

Michael Jackson

All ideas begin with a single thought.
All new beginnings arise when others fail.
A solid foundation is laid before you.
Exploring this philosophy was step one.
Having the courage to commit… is step two!

Bob Poor

Paco, Sano, Felico kaj Prospero

Part IV

YOUR NEW CHAPTER

Begin you New Chapter with **Truth** and **Courage**.

__Truth__ is your Armor,
Shield, and Sword!

__Courage__ is your resolve to
occupy that Armor, steady that
Shield, and ready that Sword!

Have Courage!   … <u>Now is your opportunity to reshape</u>
<u>yourself and emerge as the individual you wish to be!</u>

This concludes this guide.
Have you gained knowledge?
More importantly … what will
you do now?
Is this the end or a new beginning?
It is my hope that this is the genesis
and seedbed of your becoming a better
individual while enjoying Peace,
Health, Happiness and Prosperity!